W9-BSW-858

Please remember that this is a library book,
and that it belongs only temporarily to each
person who uses it. Be considerate. Do
not write in this, or any, library book.

Public Schools in Hard Times

Kindergarten children at the blackboard at Lake Dick (a Farm Security Administration Project). Jefferson County, Arkansas, 1938. Photo by Russell Lee.

Public Schools in Hard Times

The Great Depression and Recent Years

David Tyack

Robert Lowe

Elisabeth Hansot

Harvard University Press

Cambridge, Massachusetts, and London, England   1984

This book is printed on acid-free paper, and its binding materials
have been chosen for strength and durability.

Library of Congress Cataloging in Publication Data

Tyack, David B.
  Public schools in hard times.

  Includes bibliographical references and index.
    1. Education and state—United States—History—20th
century. 2. Public schools—United States—History—
20th century. 3. Depressions—1929—United States.
4. United States—Economic conditions—1971–   .
I. Lowe, Robert, 1947–   . II. Hansot, Elisabeth.
III. Title.
LC89.T93   1984   379.73   83-22679
ISBN 0-674-73800-4 (alk. paper)

For
Sue Lloyd
  Rosalind Lowe
    Jane Tompkins

and in memory of Harold Lowe

Acknowledgments

We are immensely grateful to the many people—librarians, secretaries, students, fellow historians, editors, friends, and family—who have helped this work along. Naming them all would make a long list, for one of the pleasures of our environment is lively intellectual exchange. But we would especially like to thank Ruth Bergman and Claudette Sprague for typing stages of the manuscript; Annette Bidart, Jill Blackmore, Mary Osborne, and William Tierney for their research assistance; Katarina Rice for her expert editing; Larry Cuban, Carl Kaestle, David Kennedy, Tom James, and Harold Silver for perceptive readings of the whole book in various incarnations; and Cynthia Ellwood, Maryellen James, Harvey Kantor, Milbrey McLaughlin, Jeffrey Mirel, Denis Phillips, and Andrew Spaull for advice on topics and chapters. We are also grateful to the National Institute of Education for its grant to Stanford's Institute for Research on Educational Finance and Governance, which supported our study, and to the Stanford Center for the Study of Youth Development and to Boys Town, which provided funds for research assistants. Needless to say, neither agencies nor individuals should bear responsibility for our errors, but we deeply appreciate their contributions. We also wish to thank the *Harvard Educational Review* for permission to reprint (in Chapter 5) parts of the essay "Hard Times, Then and Now: Public Schools in the 1930s and 1980s," which appeared in volume 54 (February 1984). Finally, we thank the *American School Board Journal* for its permission to reprint six cartoons originally published there; copyright is held by the National School Boards Association, all rights reserved.

Contents

Public Schools in Hard Times

Introduction

The Lamson Grammar School in the small town of Hamilton, Massachusetts, was a two-story yellow wooden structure that sat securely on its stone foundation. A black steel fire escape protruded from one side. The two entrances were recessed so that children could stomp off snow or mud on the porch before they entered from the big playground that surrounded the school. Inside there were six graded classrooms and a kindergarten. The big central hall resounded with children's voices at opening and closing hours and at recess times in the morning but otherwise was a dark and silent cavern.

The classrooms of 1935 looked much as they had thirty years earlier. The bolted-down desks with wooden tops and filigreed iron legs were equipped with inkwells and with storage space below for books and lunch and steel pen nibs. Big windows lined two walls and blackboards the others; portraits of George Washington and mezzotint pictures of Europe hung on the walls. Steam radiators banged on cold mornings. An upright piano stood in the corner (the worst punishment in first grade was to be banished behind the piano, where the naughty child had only a blank wall to contemplate). Sometimes the odor of freshly oiled wooden floors filled the building. On the last day of school the pungent smell of cleaned inkwells and scrubbed desks signaled freedom for the summer.

The teachers were women, mostly middle-aged, and trained at the Salem Normal School. They broke the day into clearly marked segments for reading, arithmetic, geography, history, spelling. From time to time a music teacher came to expose a captive audience of pupils to songs they heard nowhere else and mostly disliked. On Thursday mornings the sixth graders walked to the small high school nearby to take shop (boys) and domestic science (girls).

The sixth graders, the "giants" of the school, tormented their young teacher and acted superior to the kids below them. The boys were almost ready to doff their knickers and don long pants—the rite of passage to high school. They remembered the first-grade teacher, Miss Cutting, with affection, a kindly but stern woman who knew it was her duty to teach them to read and who kept strict discipline. They recalled their apprehension when they entered fourth grade, for its teacher was severe Miss Joseph, who was also the school principal, but they found that she was fair and lucid in her teaching.

All pupils, as they progressed through school, studied the same things at the same time from the same books. They recited from the second-grade reader; they put long-division problems on the board for correction; they memorized state capitals for tests; and they had spelling bees on the week's word lists. Each day they recited memorized Bible readings—"The Lord is my Shepherd, I shall not want . . . Valley of the Shadow of Death"—and pledged allegiance to the flag. The pedagogical and moral order, if not always the classroom discipline, was predictable and secure. Horace Mann would have approved.

The children in the Hamilton public schools in the 1930s were mostly lower middle class, living near the edge of respectability with their hand-me-down clothes, modest homes, and fathers' small wages. Some complained that on cold nights their families had no coal to heat the house. Some were regularly hungry. On the way to school they jumped over the ditches the WPA workers were digging for the new town sewer. Most had heard of President Roosevelt, although there were differences of opinion in that Yankee town about what he was doing. The younger children had known only the depression years. They individually went about their intense daily lives, reciting for Miss Joseph, skating on Miles River, weeding gardens, playing sandlot baseball or leapfrog, sitting beside a potbellied stove for warmth, listening to Jack Armstrong on the radio, playing hopscotch.[1]

The first four chapters of this book analyze public schools in the Great Depression of the 1930s. It is in part a story of diversity.

Hamilton was only one of 127,531 school districts in 1931. People sometimes talked about *the* American school system, but there was enormous variation between communities. The rural black children who went to Dine Hollow School in the Deep South sat on rough benches in a dilapidated building surrounded by weeds; they had no desks or books. The prosperous adolescents of Shaker Heights, Ohio, attended high school in a modern brick building on a landscaped tract of nineteen acres, complete with a library of twelve thousand books, a swimming pool, two gymnasiums, medical facilities staffed by two part-time doctors and a nurse, and an elaborate cafeteria. The depression meant quite different things in Hamilton, Dine Hollow, and Shaker Heights.[2]

While young Americans went to school in the early 1930s, its routines familiar, their parents sought to make sense of the greatest challenge the society had experienced since the Civil War. Following the Crash in 1929, the American people were caught in a great downward-sucking maelstrom of economic collapse. No one—not executives in New York corporate boardrooms, not miners in West Virginia coal towns, not auto workers in Detroit, not insurance salesmen in South Dakota—knew when the whirlpool would bottom out, nor did citizens in the late 1930s know if the economy would ever again resume its long-term growth. To some the dislocated society meant hunger, cold, and an endless search for work; to others it brought anxiety more than physical suffering. The depression posed a challenge to the everyday beliefs by which people gave meaning to their lives, for the crisis of the old order was partly material, partly ideological. Convictions that had once seemed self-evident no longer rang true. How could Americans still believe in the value of hard work and ambition when so many willing workers were fired and eager adults could not find a job? How could people trust the economic system when there was so much poverty and suffering amid potential abundance? One task of the historian is to try to recapture the daily experience, the perplexity, of diverse Americans living through those "years of the locust." We will try to look over their shoulders at their world.

But history also offers a long-term perspective, for survivors know how things turned out and can discern patterns only dimly apparent to contemporaries. Hence this book also analyzes the depression decade from a distance, raising questions about how public schooling in the 1930s appears in the longer trajectory of twentieth-century history. Many historians regard the depression years as a watershed in the private economy and Franklin D. Roosevelt's New Deal as a significant shift in government. The gross national product dropped by almost half between 1929 and 1933; the economy rebounded only partially and unevenly until World War II. During the depression the political parties underwent a major realignment and government undertook a new set of tasks: to provide relief to the needy, to stabilize and subsidize agriculture, to legitimize unions and collective bargaining, and to create a host of new agencies to regulate new domains and provide new services. The size and cost of the federal government burgeoned. New Dealers engaged in tugs-of-war with state and local governments to accomplish tasks high on the national agenda but ignored at the lower levels.

Did the Great Depression constitute an equivalent watershed in public education? What educational values did Americans uphold in hard times? How did educators respond to the fiscal crisis, and how did the politics of scarcity affect education during the 1930s? Were there major changes in the financing and governing of education? How did New Dealers regard public schools, and how did school people react to the distinctive New Deal style in education? Behind the schoolhouse door, what changed? Seen in long-term perspective, to what degree did the depression alter the trajectory of development of American public schools? These questions inform the first four chapters of this book.

The fifth chapter compares the depression experience with the impact on schools of the scarcity and pervasive uncertainty of recent years. The two periods—similar in some respects, unlike in more— were separated by an era of great expansion, of faith in the efficacy of schooling, and of reform. For most educators, as for most Americans, the Great Depression is a distant memory or a story told by elders and people whose business it is to probe the past. In the postwar years school people and interested citizens were absorbed by the problems of growth and reform in education. Leaders had to learn to manage expansion as children of the baby boom moved from one level to another of the educational system. Heirs of an optimistic belief in education, Americans trusted that improved public schools would assure social progress and individual advançement. Expansion and optimism did not mean complacency, however. Waves of reform swept over public education in the years after 1945. During the 1950s critics focused on international rivalry and the need to train the talented. During the 1960s and early 1970s activists sought to make public schools more equal.

Beginning in the 1970s, and gathering momentum in the early 1980s, those concerned with public schools confronted three shortages that altered the educational agenda: shortages of students, of money, and of public confidence. Largely taken by surprise by scarcity—for the trend of a generation had been unrelenting expansion—educators once again had to learn to retrench. Criticized by a public growing more skeptical year by year, school people complained that they were expected to do more with fewer resources and held increasingly accountable while their autonomy was eroded. Rapid shifts in the governing and financing of schools made planning for the future even riskier than usual.

Our examination of the recent past focuses on the three shortages of pupils, funds, and confidence, on how they interacted to compound problems, and on how scarcity altered the politics of education. We analyze how districts responded to fluctuating numbers of students and to a reversal of postwar demographic patterns. We investigate the origin and impact of tax revolts and retrenchment. We ask where the slide in public confidence came from and what it meant for the future of public education. And finally we return to the theme of equality of educational opportunity. Did scarcity threaten the tenuous gains made in equalizing public schools during the last generation? As the pendulum of public attention swung back toward concern for the talented, as a revived rhetoric of international competition again suffused public debate, would those on the bottom of society suffer neglect?

1 Maelstrom, 1929–1934

"It was the Depression because no white[s] and no blacks were working," recalled a black social worker and jazz musician. "The *whites* not working made it official." Statistics also made it official. From 1929 to 1933 the gross national product dropped from $103.1 billion to $55.6; personal income fell from $85.9 billion to $47.0; and estimated unemployment (no one really knew how many were out of work) soared from 3.2 percent of the civilian labor force to 24.9. From 1929 to 1932 the Dow Jones average of sixty-five stocks nose-dived from $125.43 to $26.82, while the profits of corporations after taxes fell from $8.6 billion to minus $2.7 billion. Income produced in agriculture declined by over one-half, manufacturing by almost two-thirds, and construction by about four-fifths.[1]

Americans had known depressions before and had come to expect some degree of boom and bust as a natural cycle. Many Americans on the bottom of society had never experienced the supposed prosperity of the 1920s. Some of them lived in the cut-over regions of the upper Great Lakes states, where the stumps of ancient forests lay close together like tombstones in a cemetery and where sawmills and trading towns were decaying. Black and white sharecroppers in the South existed on the thin edge of survival even before the Crash. So did many workers in textile mills, in the soft-coal mines, and in the immense factories in the field in the San Joaquin Valley. When interviewers in the 1930s talked with people who worked in meat-packing plants in Chicago or steam laundries in New York or stone-cutting shops in Barre, Vermont, the workers rarely mentioned the depression. As Ann Banks has observed, the dislocation of the thirties was just "one more hardship in lives made difficult by immigration, world war, and work in low-paying industries before the regulation of wages and hours."[2]

Still, the maelstrom of the Great Depression was different from any earlier hard times. Never before had so many Americans suffered so much, and even the lucky ones who had jobs and homes and food lived with fear: fear of losing a job, as a quarter of their fellows had done; fear of seeing a lifetime of savings vanish in a bank failure, as had happened to countless frugal families; fear that the whole economic system might collapse, for the traditional leaders did not seem to know what had gone wrong or what to do about it. There was a great cloud over everyday life. The prosperous worried about revolution; in 1930, for the first time, Lloyds of London began insuring wealthy Americans against "riot and civil commotion," and businessmen in their clubs talked anxiously about an uprising of the poor.[3]

The world seemed topsy-turvy. Orphans in secure institutions were lucky, for at least they had a roof over their heads and enough food to eat. One such child, a waitress in later life, talked with Studs Terkel about her memories of living in an orphanage in 1933. "We had plenty to eat," she recalled. As she and the other orphans walked to school, they would stop by the railroad tracks, find food in their lunch bags that they didn't want, and give it to unemployed men waiting there for them. "On Fridays, we used to give 'em our lunch, all of us. There might be 125 of us going to school, carrying the same paper bag, with mashed sardine sandwiches and mayonnaise on it." The men weren't threatening; they were just out of work and hungry. "They knew we were friends, and we knew for some reason that they were friends."[4]

In the early years of the depression, before the New Deal relief programs, President Herbert Hoover urged private charities and state and local agencies to relieve the distress of the unemployed. The proper role of the federal government, he thought, was to encourage such efforts, not to provide direct assistance. The head of the President's Organization on Unemployment Relief (POUR for short) was the president of the American Telephone and Telegraph Company. He thought it none of his business to discover the actual extent of joblessness, or how many people were hungry, or how much aid

Boys salvaging coal from slag heaps. Nanty Glo, Pennsylvania, 1937.
Photo by Ben Shahn.

actually went to the destitute. Hoover believed that it was permissible
for the national government to underwrite banks to assure their
recovery but that it would undermine individual and local responsibility if he were to help the unemployed. When a drought hit the
Southwest, he was willing to use federal money to help farmers buy
seed, fertilizer, and feed for their cattle, but not food for their families. Hoover based his policy on principle. Many Americans thought,
however, that he was oblivious to suffering. Ideology seemed to
conquer common sense and compassion.[5]

In the meantime, local private and public agencies struggled to
help. In Chickasaw, Oklahoma, restaurants dumped the scrapings
of garbage into five-gallon cans; the unemployed men of the town
earned a chance to eat the scraps by chopping wood. In Philadelphia,
in December 1931, 43,000 families received a relief allowance of
$3.93 per week. They were the lucky ones, for that month there

Coming home from school in a mining town, 1938. Photo by Jack Delano.

were 238,000 people out of work in the city. In Toledo the city allotted 2.14 cents per meal per person in its commissary. In Hot Springs, Arkansas, a black restaurant owner "carried black people on the tab during the Depression" and let down-and-outers sleep in his basement; he recouped some of his losses by overcharging white customers for watermelon and convincing them that he put a mystical batter on his fried chicken. Drifters looking for work lined up in Olympia, Washington, for weak broth and stale bread dished out after hellfire sermons in a mission, and then spent the night in rickety double-decker bunks in the cold room behind the church.[6]

A survey of 1,286 families in a fairly typical district of Detroit—an especially hard-hit city—in 1932 told a tale of pauperization. Only one-third were regularly employed, and three-fourths were looking for jobs. Median earnings had dropped two-thirds since 1929. Ten percent of the families with mortgaged homes had lost them; almost half of the rest were behind on their payments. Twenty-eight families had been evicted for not paying their rent. Close to half had lost their savings accounts. And so it went, a tale of slipping down into poverty: surrendering life insurance, taking children out of school (often because of lack of clothes), not having the cash to buy milk for the children, losing furniture bought on installment. Such people learned to put cardboard in the children's shoes, to buffer the cold wind by inserting newsprint under shirts, to make blouses from gunny sacks.[7]

Poor rural people far from the luxuries of restaurant garbage cans or soup kitchens found that the depression intensified the deprivation they had long known. Gaunt families sat down to dinners of corn pone and dandelion greens. "A piece of meat in the house would like to scare these children to death," said one mother. On cold winter days children might have to take turns going to school because the family had only one coat. Farmers papered their thin walls with newsprint to keep warm. If a tooth hurt, a common solution was to pull it out, for few and far between were the dentists and even scarcer the cash to pay them. In Maryland, in the mid-thirties, only a quarter of rural farm youth had visited the dentist in the previous year and almost a third had never seen a dentist. Poverty eroded the lives of the sharecroppers of the South.[8]

For farmers on the plains and in the Southwest who once had been

The wife and child of a submarginal farmer. Oswego County, New York, 1937. Photo by Arthur Rothstein.

independent, drought, dust storms, and grasshoppers intensified the man-made economic catastrophes of the 1930s. The mechanization of agriculture in vast farms pushed families off the land. Many thousands of them went west to find work, like the farmers described in John Steinbeck's *Grapes of Wrath*. Cesar Chavez recalled the day in 1934 when a giant tractor came to the small farm his father had inherited in the North Gila Valley in Arizona. The president of the bank that owned the land around the Chavez homestead foreclosed on the loan. The tractor moved in to demolish the corral where his father had kept his horses. Soon the land was lined with ditches. The Chavez family climbed into their Chevy and left their house and chickens and hogs for a life in California as nomad agriculture laborers, biding for a time under a bridge by a dry creek in San Jose, picking grapes in Delano, rebuffed as Mexicans by a waitress in Indio.[9]

Like Chavez, many of the migratory workers organized to help each other, but the odds against them were enormous. Over a third of all the biggest farms in the United States were in California, and both vigilantes and police were generally on the side of the big growers. In between jobs, some people lived off vegetables that had frozen in nearby fields and birds that their children had killed. If a car broke down, it was a crisis. The children rarely had more than a few weeks of continuous schooling.[10]

The life of the migratory farm workers, like that of the southern sharecroppers, was far from the ken of most Americans until writers and photographers and filmmakers highlighted it. Even more invisible was the suffering of many middle-class people during the depression. White-collar workers were less often unemployed than were factory workers, but they, too, found themselves hard-pressed. Their lives attracted little attention from writers of proletarian fiction or documentary artists, but their psychological scars were no less real. Periodic joblessness had been a common experience for many industrial workers and agricultural laborers before the depression but rarer for the middle class. So sweeping was the force of the maelstrom that it sucked into its vortex many white collar families—people who had been favored with a good education, had been imbued with the ideology of success, had saved money and bought houses, and kept up appearances. For many of them being unemployed was a new experience, a source of deep shame, and going on relief—the dole, as it was scornfully called by the fortunate—was traumatic. "I didn't want to go on relief," a former clothes salesman told Terkel. "Believe me, when I was forced to go to the office of the relief, the tears were running out of my eyes. I couldn't bear myself to take money from anybody for nothing." He thought of suicide, but then he remembered his children. Another father recalled that he put his hand five times on the county courthouse doorknob before he could force himself to open it to go inside to the relief office.[11]

Maintaining standards was hard work. A woman who was raised in "a lace curtain Irish family and went to a finishing school" found that her family had to live in a garage when her husband lost his job. The children took turns warming themselves by a coal stove and melted snow to wash their faces. But their mother insisted on setting the table right and on using napkin rings. "It was status with my mother," said her daughter. "She used to walk around and my father used to call her 'Queenie'." A failed businessman who found a job as a timekeeper with the WPA always wore his best clothes and kept well-groomed. In Oakland a husband stinted on food and clothing while spending a large sum on painting his house because "everybody could see that." Robert and Helen Lynd found in their study of Middletown that many families maintained with difficulty "the brave social front that local canons of respectability require a family to present to its neighbors." The suffering of the middle class was invisible partly because shame bade them hide it.[12]

The depression put on trial some of the most cherished beliefs— myths, some said—of Americans. It dimmed the dream of success that characterized Hoover's New Era and had been a middle-class mainstay for over a century. Citizens who had done all the right things—who had been ants, not grasshoppers—found their hopes and status evaporating. They had saved money only to find their bank collapsed. They had worked hard only to find themselves on the bread lines. They had trusted business leaders only to find them at first mindlessly optimistic and then as bewildered as ordinary people. One by one the sustaining folk beliefs were challenged. The warden of Sing Sing prison told a disillusioned American public that seven out of ten inmates had once been newsboys, thus undermining yet another familiar piece of folklore, the story of the upwardly mobile and virtuous newsboy.[13]

In "Melrose," a midwestern community of 19,000, one person especially symbolized misplaced trust. R. Williams McSwirtle was the town's leading banker and a devout Episcopalian who had lectured youth piously for thirty years on the topic "Banks and the Church." Marquis Childs wrote: "He was the personification of the small-town Middle Western banker, gray, respectable, shiny, with cold, fish-colored eyes concealed behind pince-nez, and a pompous smile. The very sight of this pious man was for a long time enough to reassure depositors." Yet in time citizens discovered that he had swindled some $300,000. With the failure of his bank fell the modest fortunes of the local people who had trusted him. Even the nationally prominent banker Frank A. Vanderlip, who opposed government relief to the jobless because it sapped their self-reliance, admitted that "human stupidity and cupidity were the taproots of this great financial disaster" of the bank failures.[14]

People were going hungry, even starving, while farmers were driving sheep off cliffs because they could not afford to ship them to market; leather factories were boarded up while Baltimore teachers collected used shoes so that children could come to school; people languished in hovels and tin shacks while construction workers stood in soup lines. In the midst of all this, governmental leaders before the New Deal seemed incapable of acting even to relieve the most elemental needs of the people. The governor of West Virginia told hungry miners that the Constitution forbade him to give them food.[15]

No one was sure where questioning of the social order would lead. Fearful of revolution, federal officials drove the veteran bonus marchers out of the nation's capital with troops and tanks. One survey found that one-quarter of unemployed working men agreed that "a revolution might be a very good thing for this country." Such people blamed the social order and not themselves for mass poverty and suffering. In a poll of 20,000 ministers, almost one-third favored socialism, while most wanted drastic changes in capitalism. Farmers in Iowa blockaded roads to keep products from reaching the market in an attempt to raise prices. There and in other parts of the nation farmers threatened sheriffs and judges trying to foreclose mortgages.

Standing in line at a camp for flood victims. Forrest City, Arkansas, 1937. Photo by Walker Evans.

They banded together at foreclosure auctions to offer dimes and quarters to purchase farm equipment, which they then promptly returned to the former owners. Men who were gathered around the stove in a small store in upstate Michigan "said if things got any worse and something didn't happen pretty soon, they'd go down Main Street and crash the windows and take what they needed . . . no man is going to let his wife and children starve to death."[16]

Observers at the time disagreed about whether the poor and un-employed were simply disoriented and humiliated or angry and ready to rebel. A poet talked in Chicago in 1932 with his literary idol, John Dos Passos, who believed that Roosevelt would fail and that labor unions would help people to construct a new social order. In Ensley, Alabama, the same poet visited a relief headquarters where a woman

Children living in a two-room slum apartment. Aliquippa, Pennsylvania, 1941. Photo by John Vachon.

was agitating to get milk for her baby (women there had been putting salt-pork gravy in bottles to feed their starving children). When she finally got a quart of milk from the top supervisor, he recalled, "she got back as far as she could and threw it up against the wall—Pow!— and smashed it. That was the kind of spirit, you see," he observed. Radicals tried to organize workers in the plants, the hungry in protest marches, the poor who had been evicted onto the streets in the cold winter days, the veterans on their bonus march, and the rebellious farmers.

For many artists and intellectuals, Marxism seemed to provide an accurate analysis of why the system was disintegrating, and it provided (in Malcolm Cowley's phrase) a "dream of the golden mountains"—an image of a future in which a new order would banish the illogic of poverty amid plenty and create a society in which social justice would prevail. But for all the economic dislocation and suffering, parties on the left were attracting few adherents. Between 1928 and 1932 the Socialist Party grew from about 7,000 to 15,000 members; in the latter year the Communist Party had only about 12,000. Shame, apathy, and hopelessness seemed as prevalent among the dispossessed as did militance.[17]

Looking backward, some radical leaders concluded that the left had never come close to organizing a revolution. A Trotskyite, rancorous toward the Communist Party, observed that "at bottom the unemployed worker was uninterested in communism. He was interested in one thing only: a job. The CP [Communist Party] could involve him in demonstrations, but it couldn't get him a job." A member of the Industrial Workers of the World recalled, "I ran into some ill-informed people who used the word revolution very carelessly—that things were so tough, we were going to have a revolution and so forth." But that was a pipe dream; the workers were not organized but browbeaten. "It isn't just a bunch of starving people that are going to make a revolution. It's gonna be a people that have been asserting themselves." The historian Christopher Lasch agreed with their assessment. What most Americans wanted, he said, was not socialism but "vigorous, authoritative leadership."[18]

Such leadership was not forthcoming in the early 1930s from most traditional businessmen, beyond pale pleas for balancing the budget. To an increasing number of citizens, capitalists were the source of their problems, not the leaders to guide them out of their woes. But people tended to personalize and moralize the issue: it was not the capitalist system that was at fault but bad capitalists—selfish gamblers, extravagant crooks in top hats. To the degree that mainstream leaders and thinkers questioned the capitalist system, they focused on the dangers of unrestricted competition and greed, features once glorified as free enterprise and individualism.[19]

"Planning" became a magic word, though its meaning was obscure and differed among those who invoked the concept. Declaring that "we have left the period of extreme individualism," a president of the United States Chamber of Commerce called for "an intelligently planned business structure" and collective action to stabilize prices and production together with plans to insure workers against job-lessness. Certain other business leaders, like Gerard Swope, president of General Electric, urged managing the economy through trade associations and a national economic council. Such cartels were hardly new in a society dominated by large corporations, but the notion that companies should share responsibility for unemployment insurance and maintaining jobs softened the image of corporate self-interest. Union leaders also endorsed the notion of industry-wide economic planning as a way to stabilize the economy. Institutional economists such as Gardiner C. Means, Rexford G. Tugwell, and Adolf A. Berle, Jr., joined the call for planning and urged policy-makers to recognize the fact that the concentration of power and profits in giant corporations had transformed the economy. The nub of the "planning" question was, of course, who was to do it and who was to benefit. On this issue proponents differed, as they did on the role of government, but they were agreed that the old market system had proved to be too unstable, that the economy needed to be managed by experts, and that some form of collectivism was preferable to the old individualism.[20]

Educators and the Crisis

In February 1932 Professor George Counts of Columbia's Teachers College gave a talk to the Progressive Education Association (PEA) that so challenged the audience—like a rousing sermon in a social gospel Methodist church—that the members sat to ponder it in awed silence rather than applauding. That night they gathered in small groups to discuss what he had said. The next day they canceled the scheduled speeches and hastily arranged panels to appraise his challenge and decide how to respond to it. Two days later Counts carried his ideas to the National Council of Education, the inner sanctum of the National Education Association (NEA), where he presented his theses with the conviction of an educational Luther. The reformation he proposed came to be known as social reconstructionism, a perspective on schools and the social order that shaped much of the debate on educational ideology during the depression.[21]

Dare the schools build a new social order? That was Counts's question to American educators. His answer was that they must take one side or the other in the contest over capitalism. The language of his speeches and the pamphlet with that question as its title sounded new and radical, but his sermon of social sin and damnation, his exhortation to change the world through education, and his vision of a millennial future were reminiscent of the nineteenth-century educational crusaders, who also had hoped to use the schools to remake the world according to values in which they had transcendent confidence. This message of "social reconstruction" was both intoxicating and reassuring: intoxicating because it seemed to make educators the builders of a new civilization, reassuring because the task was one in which science and professionalism had already shown the way to an abundant, cooperative commonwealth. Not that the task was easy. For George Counts as much as for Horace Mann, ease would have denied the virtue of struggle.[22]

Capitalism had shown itself to be not only "cruel and inhuman" but "also wasteful and inefficient," Counts told the progressive educators. The old doctrines of rugged individualism had proven to be economically disastrous and damaging to individual character. Only a new collectivism based on scientific planning could create abundance and justice, a culture in which true education of character, intellect, and aesthetic development could occur. Counts doubted that progressive educators—themselves from and mostly serving the middle class and devoted as "romantic sentimentalists" to an individualistic and child-centered education—could diagnose the causes of dislocation and gird themselves to teach students the evils of capitalism and the need for socialism. But teachers could not be neutral in the ideological struggle. Which side are you on? he asked educators. They could not avoid the choice, he said, for to fail to bring about a new social order was either to preserve capitalist injustice or to sit on the sidelines as the society moved toward violence and decay.[23]

Counts was challenging an educational establishment that had traditionally sought businessmen as allies, that had mostly been timid about issues of social justice, that was socially conservative in reflecting middle-class values in its official and hidden curriculum, and that had sought for decades to portray schools as a sacred domain "above politics." Was Count's call to action appropriate for professionals? How could he and his fellow "social frontier" thinkers have won an audience?

It is unlikely that his words would have struck sparks in 1930 or even 1931. The depression was slow to affect the political economy of public schools in many parts of the nation, particularly in urban systems and prosperous states, where most of the professional elite worked. The Baltimore superintendent of schools referred to 1931 as a pre-depression year. Anyone glancing through the articles in the *American School Board Journal*, or listening to the speeches at the NEA's Department of Superintendence (the meeting place of the mighty), or looking over the agenda of meetings of the prestigious Cleveland Conference during the first two years of the depression would hardly have known that the maelstrom had begun. Nationally aggregated statistics—which masked the severe impact of the downturn on poor districts—indeed told a tale of educational progress through 1931 and even into 1932. Table 1 illustrates this. Using standardized index numbers, with 100 in the year 1930 as the base, it shows that from 1929 through 1931 enrollments grew and along with them came a nearly proportionate increase in the number of staff. Salaries, total expenditures, and cost per child enrolled remained fairly stable. Only outlays for capital expenditures declined.

Table 1. Index numbers for certain public school statistics, 1929–1932 (1930 = 100)

| | Years ending June 30 | | | |
	1929	1930	1931	1932
Total enrollment	99	100	101	102
High school enrollment	94	100	105	111
Number of teachers, principals, and supervisors	99	100	101	102
Average salary of teachers, principals, and supervisors	98	100	101	96
Total expenditures	97	100	100	94
Expenditures for capital outlay	102	100	86	64
Cost per child enrolled	98	100	99	92

Source: NEA, "Current Conditions in the Nation's Schools," *Research Bulletin* 11 (November 1933): 97.

By 1932 expenditures were dropping but not precipitously, except in capital costs.[24]

The key decision-makers in most local schools at that time were district superintendents. Their local school boards were mostly composed of business and professional elites in cities and the more prosperous residents in the smaller districts. In the 1920s the dominant model of educational management had been one of "scientific efficiency." Ideally, the "educational executive" was to be an expert manager operating outside the arena of contending political factions and making decisions on the basis of specialized professional knowledge, always with an eye to achieving the greatest results at minimum cost. This "cult of efficiency" (as Raymond Callahan calls it) gave educational leaders a ready-made ideology for making decisions about retrenchment as well as a rational-technical process for planning budgets. It was also a system of management well tailored to appeal to the successful citizens who were their superiors on school boards.[25]

Through the first two years of the depression most local superintendents looked on the economic troubles as a temporary storm they could weather by battening down a few hatches. Since they realized that the public expected economies in government, they turned to their traditional allies, business and professional people, for advice about where to trim. In 1931, for example, the Department of Superintendence formed a committee of some of its members and "representative business or commercial interests" to study school costs. Its president that year told a reporter from the *New York Herald Tribune* that he was "of the opinion that no schools will close. We are here to study educational efficiency, and in the end that, of course, results in economy." The next year the chairman of the economy committee reported that "creative retrenchment" on sound business principles might actually improve schools through greater "compactness and efficiency." He called the attention of the members to the "extensive professional literature on economical school administration" and to the savings possible in capital investment and "improved business administration."[26]

In practice, of course, the notion that school budgeting or any kind of educational decision could be a technical and rational process "above politics" was an illusion. Budgets were the results of political contests both inside and outside the schools, and those budgetary struggles took place within a broader ideology of public schooling. At first, when schools seemed to be holding their own despite the downswing in the business cycle, educational administrators did not question the business-oriented philosophy that had well served their quest for power in the 1920s. But as the depression deepened, especially in late 1932 and 1933, and as the public mood grew ever more critical of businessmen, school leaders attacked their former allies. In part, their new-found hostility stemmed from a common belief that industrial and commercial leaders were spearheading a campaign to cut school taxes—an issue that we shall examine in chapter 2. But their attack on businessmen also resulted from a growing conviction that wicked men in high places had destroyed prosperity. School people saw themselves as the keepers of a dream that selfish capitalists had betrayed.

In a new litany that rang out at professional meetings and in the journals, educators spoke of the "stupidity and dishonesty—ignorance, selfishness and greed" of the business leaders who had brought the nation low. Superintendent Harold Campbell of the New York schools said that "many of the men we had looked upon as the leaders of what James Truslow Adams has called 'our business civilization' were found to be nothing more than gentlemen who bought things as cheaply as they could and sold them for as much as they could with little regard for the fairness of their dealings." "I am filled with resentment when I hear the criticisms of those who say that the American schools are failures," wrote Charles H. Judd, dean of the School of Education at the University of Chicago. "These are the smug exploiters who have been driving communities to the brink of ruin by their greed and self-seeking." Speaking in populist rhetoric, the *NEA Journal* in 1933 attacked "the Wall Street Power Trust oligarchy" and other sinister forces whose "agents reach into every community." It was quite a change of tune for an organization that had celebrated free enterprise in the 1920s. A veteran observer of the NEA commented, "All the moral spit-blowers are now being trained on the poor bankers." That was expedient, he said, because "it is as safe and about as courageous to attack them as it would be for a hero outside prison walls to hurl abuse at a life-timer."[27]

The rapid reversal of opinion of many educational leaders toward business and their apparently radical rhetoric struck some observers

Pedagog–
Pauper
1928

Pedagog–
Plutocrat
1933

PERSPECTIVE

Educators believed that the cataclysm of the early depression had enhanced their own stature while diminishing that of the businessman. Source: *Texas Outlook* 17 (July 1933): 4 (originally published in *Washington Education Journal*).

as skin-deep. Others, like the superintendent of schools in Gary, Indiana, worried that school managers were "turning red and using the schools to incite ultra-radical sentiment." They "have pledged themselves," he said, to propagandize and to force "the country over the precipice and into the abyss of communism." The truth, we believe, lies in between. Most educators were distressed by the suffering they saw and angered by cuts in school budgets, but few were radicalized.[28]

Teachers were "street-level bureaucrats" who, like social workers, saw daily the deep distress of the children of the poor. Detroit teachers collected shoes so that pupils could come to class; New York teachers learned that a fifth of the school children were malnourished and contributed funds for school lunches from their own diminishing salaries. In Chicago they saw Mexican and black students coming to school in rags from cold tenements to spend part of their days in a warm, well-lighted place. In San Jose, California, teachers volunteered five percent of their salaries to provide school children with clothing, blankets, medicine, and food. Close to everyday suffering, teachers needed to understand how the nation had been laid so low and wanted hope for the future. A few of them believed that relief efforts were only patchwork and that what needed to be renewed was the whole social order.[29]

Hence when George Counts and his colleagues called on them to build a new social order, some educators were ready to listen. They had learned to distrust capitalists if not capitalism. They liked Counts's tune (his evangelical call to redeem the nation) even if they were not so sure about his lyrics (his attack on elites and demand for collective action to bring about a collective political economy). His program for using public schools to advocate socialism, however, made many of them nervous—after all, conservative school boards controlled their jobs. To assert that there were classes in American society and that educators should take the side of the working class in the contest went well beyond platitudes about "planning" and "a new social order." It was one thing to condemn some selfish capitalists—even President Hoover had blamed speculators for the crash— but quite another to attack the capitalist system.

There is considerable evidence that mainstream leaders in the NEA and in state associations in the early 1930s were using "radical" rhetoric to express familiar ideas in a new garb. Discourse in the Department of Superintendence was amoeba-like, surrounding and absorbing whatever catchwords it encountered in the environment and assimilating them to older values. This had happened before, when the new argot of scientific efficiency became blended with the religious and social values educators had imbibed from their small-town pietist backgrounds. Even the social reconstructionists centered at Teachers College blended elements of the older social gospel with their call for a collective society. A North Carolina historian caught this religious flavor: "Just as the hot July and August days of other years seemed the most suitable season for getting religion in the old-time revivals, so have the pedagogical revivals of recent years been staged in the hot summer session days. Recent summer session preaching on the ills of the old social order differs but little from that which a century ago called sinners to the mourners' benches."[30]

There is little doubt, however, that the leading social reconstructionists sincerely believed that capitalism was in crisis, that rugged individualism was a corrupt and corrupting idea, that a planned society of greater equity and justice was possible, and that educators could play a leading role in constructing this new social order. The most influential leaders in the early and mid-1930s were a small band of professors at Teachers College, including Counts, William H. Kilpatrick, Harold Rugg, Jesse Newlon, John L. Childs, R. Bruce Raup, and others closely linked with them, like John Dewey. As C. A. Bowers has argued, this group was one modern expression of a long messianic tradition in American educational thought, a traditional faith in utopian reform through schooling. A large proportion of them had deeply religious roots and used religious language that could have been heard at social gospel meetings. Jesse Newlon, for example, argued that teachers were critical of an unjust social order because they are "chosen, or consecrated, or devoted . . . to the education of youth, to a collective service." To the degree that their reading had radicalized them, it was not so much Marx as it was American writers like Dewey and Beard—both imbued with a belief in American exceptionalism and progress—who inspired their belief in economic analysis and in evolutionary socialism.[31]

They differed among themselves in the explicitness of their class analysis and in their ideas of how to bring about societal change. Counts and Childs were more militant than Kilpatrick, for example, and another reconstructionist, Theodore Brameld, sought to link their thought with that of Marx. But their inspiration was more often the *New Republic* than the *New Masses*, and they were not so far left as many of the New York intellectuals and artists who wrote about the necessity of a Marxist revolution. For the most part the left-wing educators were more concerned with the antisocial effects of the profit motive on character—its miseducative quality—than with the dynamics of capital accumulation. Like religious abolitionists wanting to dissociate themselves from the evil of slavery, they wished to free the schools from subservience to the ideology of capitalism.[32]

The social reconstructionist group at Teachers College had begun to form its ideas on the relation between education and social change well before the depression. Several key members had formed a discussion group in 1927. Dewey had visited Russia that year, Counts and Kilpatrick in 1929. Much of the reconstructionists' faith in planning stemmed from liberal thought of the progressive era of the early twentieth century, with its stress on democracy but also on social control and social efficiency. Counts himself had done much during the 1920s to document empirically the inequalities in secondary schooling and elite dominance of school boards. It was the depression that convinced them and their followers that collectivism was necessary and that the old order was doomed. What was at stake was how that change was to come about—by violence that endangered democracy as capitalists fought a bitter last stand, or by a peaceful evolution pioneered by an educational vanguard allied with the people and clarifying its needs and interests.[33]

The reconstructionists—or frontier thinkers, as they called themselves—believed that experts could perceive where the society should be moving and should inspire teachers and administrators with a sense of direction. They were confident about the potential power of the "1,105,921 allies" in the schools, the total number of teachers in the nation. They believed that scientific technology could produce abundance and that rational social planning could assure that this abundance was properly distributed. They shared a technocratic vision with many other left-liberals of the era, but their optimism about the future was also predicated on an assumption that enhanced their own prestige and power: that better education was the key to that progress. To know the good was to be ready to do the good. Underlying their faith in social engineering through education was a certain elitism, even toward other educators. Their trust in expertise sat uneasily with their commitment to democracy. As we shall explore in the next chapter, they saw themselves as a part of a progressive vanguard in struggle with conservative forces in the political economy of public schooling. Counts and the other social reconstructionists received a hearing for a time from educators who were bewildered by economic collapse and angry at school cutbacks demanded by business groups.[34]

The great mass of educators, however, were probably more influenced by circumstances in their own communities than by the speeches and writings of the "frontier thinkers." The actual impact of retrenchment fell with quite different force in the multitude of districts that constituted American public education.

The Uneven Impact of Retrenchment, 1929–1934

Shortly before the Crash, President Hoover appointed a group of leading educators to advise him on educational policy. In October 1931 it made its self-congratulatory report, full of suggestions about how to make government more efficient. It scarcely referred to the depression. Local control was still the glory of public education. "To a European accustomed to the operation of education through a single, authoritative ministry in a central government, it seems nothing less than a miracle that more than 145,000 local districts [an overestimate] operating in 48 states could give us schools so much alike by voluntary agreement. In responsiveness to popular sovereignty, in adaptability to varying need and aspiration, and in richness of experimentation conducive to flexibility and to progress, our management of public school is without a peer." These "folk-made" schools were the key to equality of opportunity: "Our schools are, in spite of all their imperfections, relatively free from class stratification. The kind of education offered is based on the individual, the local, and the national need, and not upon the assumption that membership in a social or economic class or group limits personal opportunity for education." An ambitious and able student, asserted the report, can pursue the same upward climb as his "economically more privileged neighbor."[35]

Seven years later another advisory committee presented its report to President Roosevelt. It rejected many of the key beliefs of the Hoover group. It declared local finance of public schools to be an obstacle to improvement of education. And it held that public schools, far from being a ladder to the stars, "may be a force to create class, race, and sectional distinctions . . . and instrument for creating those very inequalities they were designed to prevent." If the oncoming generations are "drawn in disproportionately large numbers from those areas in which economic conditions are poorest, if the population reserves of the Nation continue to be recruited from economically underprivileged groups, and if the inability of the depressed economic areas and groups to provide proper education for their children is not corrected by aid from areas and groups more prosperous, the effect on American civilization and on representative political institutions may be disastrous."[36]

Did the different assessments stem from different world views, or had conditions changed sharply between 1931 and 1938? If the earlier committee had studied the 1930 census or studies by scholars like George Counts of the class and racial bias of schools, they would have seen that public education was highly unequal in its resources and impact well before the depression. But its more conservative members, unlike those on the later committee, tended to see society from a perspective that stressed the competition of individuals rather than from an outlook that emphasized structural barriers to opportunity. By 1938 nearly a decade of painful reminders of inequality had aroused the social conscience of the liberal second committee.[37]

Despite optimistic claims to the contrary, even before the maelstrom American public education was not a single system with 145,000 local branches but rather a spectrum from affluence to shocking scarcity. Certain parts of the educational system, like some sectors of the economy (farming, coal mining, textiles) were already in the throes of depression well before the crash. It was on such districts that retrenchment fell the hardest. These were the schools that had the lowest paid and most poorly trained teachers, the shortest terms, the worst buildings, the least equipment, and the highest rates of early school-leaving and of nonattendance. Needing health and other social services the most, they had the least.[38]

The depression drove home to sensitive observers some basic defects in the system of public schooling in America. One defect was inequity in school finance and educational opportunity in rural schools. About one-half of all children attended school in rural communities. These schools emerged from a period of history when the population had been scattered, transportation had been difficult, and wealth in most parts of the nation had consisted of ownership of land. Fiscal support for common schools had come mostly from local property taxes. But with the rise of cities and industry, the concentration of great wealth in forms other than material property, and the development of elaborate structures of schooling in prosperous communities, the gaps between rural and urban schools widened. Educational opportunity increasingly became a function of the pupil's place of residence. As farmers went broke and real estate values declined during the 1930s, the property tax proved insufficient to support many country schools even at a near-starvation level. The depression exacerbated the gross inequalities of rural public schooling in the United States.[39]

Part of the educational inequalities between rural and urban communities stemmed from different birth rates. In 1930 rural areas had 686 children under five years per 1,000 white women, compared with 384 in cities; the figures for blacks were 799 and 360, respectively. Hence cities had far fewer children to educate in proportion to adults in the productive age cohort. The regional variations in the number of children of school age per 1,000 adults aged twenty to sixty-four were enormous, ranging from 603 in the Southeast to 336 in the Far West.[40]

That was only the beginning of the problem of educational equity. By and large, states with the highest birth rates also had the greatest poverty and the lowest per-pupil educational expenditures. Lumped at the bottom in school expenditures but at the top in the birth rate were Texas, Louisiana, Virginia, Tennessee, Georgia, Kentucky, North Carolina, South Carolina, Alabama, Mississippi, and Arkansas. In 1930, when high school attendance was soaring to the 60–70 percent mark in the North, only 34 percent of youth aged fourteen to seventeen were enrolled in secondary schools in the Southeast. Not only educational opportunities but also health and cultural services tended to be lowest in communities with a high ratio of children to adults.[41]

In 1930 one-quarter of all school children lived in rural counties later identified as "serious relief problem areas." These vast stretches of the nation were not just demographically different and impoverished communities—"pockets of poverty"—but were in many ways different social worlds from northern industrial areas. Nationwide, expenditures for rural schools in the 1930s were about half those in

Crowded conditions in a schoolroom. Breathitt County, Kentucky, 1940. Photo by Marion Post Wolcott.

urban systems, and the number of pupils served in each was about equal. These hard-hit areas—the Appalachian-Ozark sector, the cut-over lumber region of the upper Great Lakes states, the arid parts of the Great Plains, and the eastern and western cotton belts—contained about one-half of the farm tenants, four-fifths of the share-croppers, and one-half of the rural families on relief in 1934.[42]

Added to these disabilities of the white rural underclass was the curse of racism for blacks living in the shadow of the plantation. Rejecting the optimism of their white colleagues on President Hoover's committee, the black members of the commission called young blacks under the southern caste system "by far the most heavily

Interior of a black school. Heard County, Georgia, 1941. Photo by Jack Delano.

Front door of an old black school house. Greene County, Georgia, 1939. Photo by Marion Post Wolcott.

disadvantaged group of children in the entire field of education." One-half of black children in the South were not even in school, they reported; three-quarters of those enrolled were below the fifth grade; black teachers earned an average of $524; and the average yearly per-pupil cost for blacks was less than $15, compared with a national average of more than $80. Forty percent of these black schools did not even have desks. "In hundreds of rural schools," asserted the state agent for Negro education in Mississippi, "there are just four blank unpainted walls, a few rickety benches, an old stove propped up on brickbats, and two or three boards nailed together and painted black for a blackboard. In many cases, this constitutes the sum total of the furniture and teaching equipment."[43]

Before the crash, the poor rural states were paying school taxes that were proportionately much higher than the rich states. When the depression struck, farm prices hit bottom, banks and landlords foreclosed mortgages (750,000 in the 1930s), and people struggled just to stay alive. The public schools were in a desperate state. In many depressed rural communities trustees cut teachers' salaries, stopped buying supplies, and simply closed the school when the money ran out, regardless of the official school term. Arkansas had a school year of less than sixty days in 300 schools. Some southern communities revived the practice of "boarding round" the teacher in lieu of salary, keeping school open by offering bed and board to the local teacher. In Iowa, where local property taxes funded 95 percent of school costs, the legislature mandated a flat salary of only $40 a month for all teachers, while Oklahoma called for a ten-year adoption of textbooks.[44]

Many rural communities had no alternative to closing schools when property tax collections slumped or stopped. By April 1, 1934, an estimated 20,000 had closed, affecting over one million students. In 1933–34 ten states reported having schools with terms shorter than three months, while twenty-one states had schools with terms shorter than six months. The worst-hit states were mostly in the South and the Great Plains, but parts of Michigan, Ohio, and Montana were also in serious straits. Almost 300,000 rural teachers earned less than $650 a year (the minimum wage of factory workers under the NRA code); 85,000 earned less than $450.[45]

Table 2 illustrates the uneven impact of retrenchment by state for both rural and urban schools. The figures are to be taken with a grain of salt: they are partly estimated. It is also important to recall that the table presents ratios and not absolute numbers. In calculating the meaning of a 30 percent drop in funding it is important to know the starting point. Cutting 30 percent of $40 per pupil is very different from cutting 30 percent of $100. In 1930 Arkansas spent $33.56 per pupil per year compared with New York's $137.55; the national average was $76.70. But certain points are salient: there were enormous differences between states in the scope of retrenchment; for the most part the heaviest slashes came in the poorest states; and overall the rural and urban schools suffered about the same proportionate cuts, even though within states there was a good deal of variability in the urban-rural patterns of finance.

Aggregation into a category called "city schools" obscures immense differences between local systems. That category includes wealthy suburbs like Grosse Pointe as well as devastated Detroit. Some cities entered the depression burdened by enormous debts for new building programs or by civic corruption of monumental proportions (as in Chicago). Some cities funneled large sums into relief programs for the unemployed, while others were parsimonious. Although Baltimore had a larger population than Boston, it spent only about half as much on its public schools. Table 3 illustrates these differences by pairing New York and Los Angeles, Boston and Baltimore, and Somerville and Evansville.

Despite these differences among cities, it is possible to make some general comparisons of urban and rural systems. Retrenchment came more slowly and struck less severely at classroom instruction in most urban areas than in rural communities. Country schools, especially in the economically depressed regions we have discussed, never had much slack in their budgets. The decision-makers in rural education—local trustees, county and state superintendents, state legislators—generally had little choice about where to cut. In slicing salaries, length of school term, or textbooks and supplies, they were trimming bare necessities. Those who made budget reductions in cities—mostly superintendents and school boards—had more leeway. Urban schools of moderate to large size were complex, costly institutions. School terms were generally longer than in the country; teachers' salaries were considerably higher; class sizes could be more

Table 2. Changes in school conditions by states, 1930–1934

States	Rural schools: percent of change, 1930–1934			City schools: percent of change, 1931–1934			Higher education: percent of change, 1930–1934, in expenditures by state universities
	Term	Staff	Total expenditures	Staff	Current expenditures	Capital outlay	
Continental U.S.	− 4	− 3	−23	− 4.6	−19.5	−80.1	−17.7
Alabama	−36.0	+ 6	−47	− 6.5	−32.4	−93.9	−27
Arizona	0.0	−15	−31	−16.3	−42.8	−62.6	—
Arkansas	− 2.7	−14	−39	−15.6	−41.8	−20.5	—
California	− 0.6	− 1	−21	− 4.6	−15.1	−80.6	−28
Colorado	− 4.0	− 4	−27	−11.6	−38.2	−97.8	−36
Connecticut	+ 0.5	− 2	+ 3	− 3.5	−19.5	—	− 6
Delaware	0.0	+ 6	+15	—	—	—	—
Florida	−18.0	+ 3	−27	− 1.3	−35.9	−84.3	− 1
Georgia	−20.0	0	−23	− 0.7	−18.4	—	+23
Idaho	− 1.0	−10	−30	− 6.5	−33.7	−66.1	− 7
Illinois	− 6.0	− 2	−28	− 7.9	−32.2	−68.0	−21
Indiana	− 1.0	+ 1	−26	− 8.7	−31.1	−79.8	− 2
Iowa	+ 0.5	− 4	−17	− 7.4	−29.0	−54.1	—
Kansas	− 0.6	− 4	−29	− 5.6	−28.8	−84.0	−39
Kentucky	− 5.0	+ 6	−30	− 3.6	−16.0	−50.2	−26
Louisiana	−24.0	+ 3	−18	+ 0.6	—	—	+59
Maine	− 2.0	− 2	−19	− 1.8	−15.2	—	− 7
Maryland	0.0	− 1	−19	—	—	—	− 8
Massachusetts	− 0.6	− 2	−11	− 2.7	− 4.9	−98.8	—

Michigan	− 19.0	− 6	− 13.0	− 37.9	− 91.1	+ 1
Minnesota	0.0	− 1	− 3.1	− 18.1	− 94.3	− 9
Mississippi	− 4.0	− 4	− 5.7	− 23.5	—	− 81
Missouri	− 4.0	− 1	+ 0.9	− 25.6	− 93.2	− 22
Montana	− 2.0	− 7	− 7.8	− 9.7	− 85.6	− 23
Nebraska	0.0	− 2	− 6.5	− 14.0	− 97.2	− 31
Nevada	− 5.0	+ 6	—	—	—	− 18
New Hampshire	0.0	− 3	− 3.2	− 11.9	+ 9.7	− 11
New Jersey	− 0.5	+ 2	− 0.8	− 24.4	− 54.7	—
New Mexico	− 5.0	− 3	− 6.3	− 35.4	—	− 18
New York	0.0	+ 2	− 2.3	− 13.1	− 97.0	—
North Carolina	+ 5.0	− 3	− 2.2	− 31.4	—	− 1
North Dakota	− 5.0	− 7	− 7.7	− 24.4	− 86.3	—
Ohio	− 9.0	− 5	− 11.9	− 20.1	− 45.4	− 11
Oklahoma	− 10.0	− 5	− 8.5	− 24.9	− 76.6	− 21
Oregon	− 4.0	− 1	− 14.7	− 36.1	− 51.6	− 56
Pennsylvania	0.0	0	− 2.0	− 14.8	− 71.2	− 30
Rhode Island	0.0	+ 2	+ 1.3	− 12.7	− 88.9	− 12
South Carolina	− 4.0	− 9	− 5.2	− 39.4	—	− 43
South Dakota	− 2.0	− 21	− 10.1	− 25.2	− 89.1	− 24
Tennessee	− 2.0	+ 1	− 3.4	− 17.0	+ 1.9	− 40
Texas	+ 2.0	0	− 10.5	− 28.4	− 88.4	—
Utah	0.0	− 6	− 2.4	− 23.5	− 99.6	− 23
Vermont	+ 0.6	− 5	− 7.1	− 18.8	—	—
Virginia	− 5.0	− 3	+ 2.2	− 21.9	− 90.6	+ 21
Washington	+ 3.0	− 6	− 5.8	− 29.5	+ 47.6	− 42
West Virginia	− 26.0	− 3	− 13.3	—	—	—
Wisconsin	− 0.6	− 1	− 1.3	− 15.6	− 74.5	—
Wyoming	− 4.0	− 8	− 13.2	− 22.2	− 98.2	− 17

Source: NEA, "Current Conditions in the Nation's Schools," *Research Bulletin* 11 (November 1933): 111.

Table 3. Expenditures (in millions) in paired cities, 1933

City	Population in thousands	Unemployment relief	Debt service and repaying current loans	Capital outlay	Total general fund expenditures	School expenditures
New York	6,930	72.8	352.9	17.3	496.5	140.3
Los Angeles	1,238	0	13.9	NA	30.2	NA
Boston	781	14.7	59.1	1.9	123.6	14.9
Baltimore	805	0	28.2	0	45.0	7.8
Somerville	104	.7	7.1	1	10.2	1.4
Evansville	102	0	.1	0	1.1	1.3

Source: Adapted from Clarence E. Ridley and Orin F. Nolting, *The Municipal Yearbook: An Authoritative Resume of Activities and Statistical Data of American Cities* (Chicago: International City Managers' Association, 1934), pp. 212–213.

easily increased; social services could be trimmed; ancillary parts of the curriculum could be cut; whole programs, like summer schools or evening schools, might be eliminated; and programs of building or maintenance could be postponed or abandoned.

During the first year or two of the depression, as we have said, urban educators did not feel much fiscal pinch in most communities. A U.S. Office of Education study found that its sample of urban schools actually had a slightly larger budget in 1931–32 than in 1930–31. The next year, however, cuts went deeper, varying from 3 percent in the North Atlantic states to 16 percent in the South Central cities. Budgets were planned a year in advance and typically reflected optimism about the economy's prospects. Most school districts were fiscally and governmentally independent and were authorized to levy taxes up to a fixed rate adequate to their needs. By and large, citizens found a way to pay their property taxes in 1930 and 1931, and deflation meant that those dollars bought more. Teachers' salaries in cities did not generally decline until after the 1931–32 school year, and superintendents' pay actually increased that year from $4,000 to $4,200.[46]

By 1932 the handwriting was on the wall, however. Urban schools, like other sectors of the economy, could not escape retrenchment. Property owners could not pay their taxes, tax leagues were forcing revaluations of real estate and demanding cuts in public spending. In the large cities assessments of real property fell 17.8 percent between 1929 and 1933. A number of cities also found themselves burdened with large indebtedness because of bonds floated to erect new buildings in the late 1920s and money they borrowed for current expenses. The interest that school districts paid on their debts rose from $93 million in 1930 to $137 million in 1934 (more than double the capital outlays that year). The two largest cities, New York and Chicago, were close to bankruptcy and spent vast funds servicing their debts. For a time public spending in Chicago was controlled by a consortium of bankers and businessmen with veto power over budgets. Other cities, more prudent in good times, had to draw down their cash reserves. A financial expert commented wryly on one such contrast: "A New York controller faces a $200 million deficit with the statement that there is no cause for alarm, while across the continent in Los Angeles city officials view with alarm the possibility that the cash surplus may be somewhat reduced by the end of the year."[47]

Trained to manage growth, urban educators had little taste for cutting budgets. It was especially hard to do so when high schools were expanding fast, for they were more expensive than elementary schools to run. From 1929 to 1934 the number of secondary students grew from 3,911,000 to 5,669,000, and retention rates improved markedly: the number of high school graduates per 100 youths of age seventeen jumped from 26.2 to 39.2. One way to save money was to increase class sizes, especially in secondary schools. Nationally, the elementary pupil-teacher ratio remained fairly constant at about 33:1 from 1930 to 1934, but class sizes in high schools grew from 20.6 in 1930 to 24.9 in 1934. Again, the national figures mask big differences between districts; some cities increased class size markedly to as many as 40 pupils or more. Another economy measure was "social promotion," or passing children from grade to grade rather than holding them back until they had met certain academic standards. This was often coupled with plans to group children by ability—as measured by I.Q. tests—and differentiating the curriculum. Such homogeneous grouping was touted as both progressive and cheaper. "The recent tendencies to eliminate pupil failure entirely in the elementary school, to individualize instruction, and to regard each grade as merely a level of experience," said one educator, "have all assisted in the reduction of costs arising from repeaters." And faced with declining elementary enrollments because of a dropping birth rate, some districts closed small elementary schools. "In normal times, parents likely would object," a committee on school economy remarked, but if there were room in a larger school, "the smaller one doubtless could be closed now as an economy measure with little public objection." Some educators argued that such measures—larger classes, social promotion, ability grouping, and school consolidation—actually improved schooling by making instruction more efficient.[48]

Advice manuals on how to save money on the business side of education proliferated—a growth industry in hard times. They drew on the philosophy of scientific management and developed budget making in mandarin detail. A good superintendent, said one, should lay out a "*work* plan, which is a definite statement of the educational policies and program," a *"spending* plan, which is a translation of the accepted policies into proposed expenditures," and a *"financing* plan, which proposes means for meeting the costs of the educational program." Such manuals told how to save costs on construction and maintenance, to place funds in a sound bank, to set salary scales adequate to retain the best teachers, and to purchase supplies economically. They sought to create managerial virtue from fiscal necessity.[49]

Sooner or later, most hard-pressed urban districts had to cut teachers' salaries, for such pay constituted about three-quarters of the budget. From 1929–30 to 1933–34, average teachers' salaries dropped from $1,420 to $1,227, a decrease of 13.6 percent. That seems a hefty drop, but it does not account for the enhanced value of the dollar because of deflation or the comparative income of other workers. Their income dropped far less than that of ministers or engineers, for example. In fact, teachers were better off in comparison with most other workers in 1933–34 than they have ever been since. The ratio of teachers' pay to the average per-capita income increased from 2.02 in 1929–30 to 3.27 in 1933–34. But teachers, like other Americans, often feared that they might lose their jobs and wondered where the spiral of retrenchment could lead. Between 1930 and 1934 large numbers of principals and superintendents did lose their positions. In twenty-six states the number of supervisory specialists in fields like art, music, and physical education declined by over one-third, while in eighteen states almost half the elementary principals were dismissed or demoted to head teacher or teaching principal.[50]

Cutting professional salaries was painful and could hardly be justified as improving schooling or demonstrating managerial prowess. Equally painful to administrators who had spent their careers elaborating urban school systems was the growing campaign by lay groups and school boards to eliminate "fads and frills." Budget cutters' knives were hitting programs that were never more needed than in the 1930s, argued Professor George Strayer of Teachers College, perhaps the most influential leader of the time in school administration. Health services, physical education, night schools and adult education, summer schools, kindergartens, the arts, vocational schooling, new media, and textbooks were not frills, he said, and striking at these was not a true economy. But as table 4 shows, it was precisely such new programs that were reduced or eliminated.[51]

Many educators regarded the cutting of such social services and new curricula as sheer retrogression, a return to the pattern of schooling common a quarter-century earlier. But these programs seemed to other educators and citizens peripheral to the central core of schooling—the self-contained elementary classroom and academic fields in the high school—and hence less vital to preserve. Could not other agencies take over social services?[52]

The problem with such reasoning was that other local public agencies—especially those most needed by the poor—also suffered severe cutbacks in the early depression. Two exceptions were fire and police departments, which local elites maintained nearly at predepression levels because they considered that protection necessary for their property and their safety. But services aimed at the poor suffered heavy losses before the New Deal came to their support. Local appropriations for parks and recreation dropped by nearly 50 percent from 1929 through 1933 while public demand for free recreation

Table 4. Reductions in certain types of school training in city school systems from 1931 to 1933

Schools or classes relating to:	Number of cities reporting	Percent of cities reducing or eliminating this work
Physically handicapped children	193	9.9
Homemaking	654	12.8
Industrial arts	630	13.0
Physical education	696	15.6
Mentally handicapped children	321	15.6
Art	632	16.2
Music	722	19.2
Kindergartens	404	19.8
Playgrounds and recreation	502	20.3
Continuation work	181	32.1
Americanization	247	34.5
Summer schools	240	41.3
Night schools and adult classes	266	42.5

Source: NEA, "Current Conditions in the Nation's Schools," *Research Bulletin* 11 (November 1933): 109.

soared. In public health the depression also increased the demand for assistance to the indigent sick, for diet supplements for school children, for prenatal and sick-baby clinics, dental care, and for nursing and hospitalization for people unable to afford medical care. But funds dropped; cities with populations over 100,000 had spent an average of $1.00 per capita on public health before the crash, but by 1934 the average was just $.58. Similarly, public libraries felt a severe fiscal pinch just when more and more people were crowding the reading rooms and borrowing books. A survey of seventy-seven libraries in large cities found that between 1929 and 1933 there was an increase of 23 percent in books circulated, a rise of 19 percent in registered borrowers, and a drop of 23 percent in revenues. One hard-pressed librarian, Julia Wright Merrill, wrote that the unemployed turned to free libraries for "serious reading . . . study of economic, social and governmental questions; of ways to earn money at home; of preparation for a new kind of job. Branch libraries became new social centers . . . What libraries meant in maintaining morale, perhaps even sanity, to many out of work can never be adequately told."[53]

During the maelstrom of the early depression, fiscal support of schools, parks, public health, and libraries dropped while public demand for social services increased. Perhaps even more frightening than the actual extent of retrenchment for school people was uncertainty about what the future would bring. Educators felt beleaguered by tax cutters and abandoned by former allies. The apparent detour of the upward course of universal schooling challenged school people to mobilize themselves and the American people. They saw the time as one of emergency, an hour for concerted action.

2 Educators and the Politics of Money

Henry Filer grew angry. As president of the Florida Education Association, he had pleaded with state legislators in 1933 to provide money to keep the schools open and to give teachers a living wage. The lawmakers had sympathized but argued that the people demanded cuts in taxes. So where did they slice? Only on the automobile license, whose fees went to the public schools. Back in Dade County (Miami) Filer found the commissioners adding $250,000 to the highway budget while asking the schools to absorb a 10 percent cut. "After that happened," he recalled, "I decided it was time for the school people to fight."[1]

Filer called county teachers together to discuss what had happened. They formed the Florida League for Better Schools "to elect senators and representatives and other state officials who would support a radical program for the public free school system," staying clear of local and county politics. As it spread to other counties the teachers were careful to elect noneducators—members of the American Legion, Kiwanis, Rotary, or PTA—as chapter presidents. That was not enough to still the public outcry against teachers in politics. Newspapers publicized the new phenomenon. Politicians felt threatened. "I was fighting the governor of the state, the press of the state, the state road department, and all of the politicians of the state," Filer declared. The opposition boomeranged: the teachers won the publicity they needed. When they paid their poll tax, they went in a body of five hundred and became front-page news. Filer agreed that the teachers had become *political* "in a broad sense" but claimed that "as the word was commonly used it was not true, because we were fighting for the greatest of all American institutions."[2]

Filer assembled leaders in education and other civic groups to plan a tax program—a fourth of the gasoline tax—that would ensure $600 for every teacher in the state. Then educators canvassed all state candidates to ask if they would support that or an equivalent program. They tried to get the response in writing, so that if the legislator balked they could pull a letter from their files in Tallahassee. All but two state candidates agreed to increase school appropriations by $7.5 million, and the two who dissented were defeated. Five school teachers were elected. Even the governor became converted three days before the election. They won their battle. Do not fear to speak out, Filer told his colleagues at the NEA: publicity and opposition bring power.[3]

In Chicago there had been a long tradition of political action among the teachers who had been especially militant in Margaret Haley's Chicago Teacher's Federation. The distress and anger produced by corruption, work without pay, and the refusal of bankers to honor teachers' pay warrants mobilized them again in the 1930s. The catalyst for protest was a high school gym teacher named John M. Fewkes, a fiery organizer popular with both students and teachers. In April 1933, Fewkes led twenty thousand parents and children in a march to the mayor's office to protest the destruction of the school system and the suffering of the teachers. When that brought no results, he assembled five thousand teachers at the Loop with carefully guarded orders to march into five of the large banks that had refused to redeem their pay. Inside, the teachers splashed ink on the walls, jammed the tellers' windows, and tipped over desks. At City National Bank the target was Charles C. Dawes, chairman of the board, who had just received a large federal loan. Fewkes demanded pay, but Dawes's response to the thousand teachers was "To hell with troublemakers." Again Fewkes came back, this time with three thousand male teachers armed with schoolbooks. They invaded another bank, broke its windows and partitions, and fought the police. The conventional image of acquiescent teachers was shattered along with the glass. The *Chicago Tribune* editorialized primly: "The spec-

Chicago teachers demonstrating in the streets in 1934. Reproduced from the *Chicago Daily News* in the *Journal of the Illinois State Historical Society* 64 (Winter 1971): 378.

tacle of school teachers taking part in a rough-and-tumble street melee is not conducive to respect for education.''[4]

Illinois teachers did not have much respect, in turn, for the business interests of which the *Tribune* was exemplar and spokesman. Ordinarily American Education Week had been a bland occasion to celebrate the progress of the American economy and educational system, but in 1934 in Illinois it promised to be something quite different. That year the secretary of the Illinois State Teachers Association, in collaboration with a Chicago teacher, proposed a set of resolutions aimed at the committee of financiers who were gutting the educational program of Chicago by refusing to lend money unless the school board made deep cuts. Beginning in a stinging litany of "whereas" clauses, the resolutions condemned the "predatory economic habits and practices tolerated in a materialistic age"; the cabal of rich "entrenched interests" bent on destroying the schools that seemed "immune to prosecution for their criminal activities" and bent on prostituting "the sources of public information into propaganda"; the creation of a fascist conspiracy of "taking charge for the people of the people's affairs" and the resulting decay of the schools and precipitous decline in teachers' morale. Instead, they resolved, the people should "take charge of their own affairs, which is their privilege and duty in a democracy" and restore the health of the public schools, rejecting the predators who brought on the "economic cataclysm" in the first place.[5]

The militance of the Chicago teachers found parallels elsewhere. In Kellogg, Idaho, for example, unionized teachers formed an alliance with copper miners to secure more taxes for the schools in a political campaign resisted by the mine owners and bankers. When the local school board fired three leaders of the teachers' union, the teachers won primary campaigns for the offices of county superintendent of schools, probate judge, and state legislator. The united miners and teachers then pushed on to solid victory in the local and county elections.[6]

It was not just militant teachers in places like Chicago, Kellogg, and Detroit who talked and acted tough in the early 1930s. A number of educational administrators joined the ranks of those who believed that organized elites were seeking to slash school expenditures well beyond temporary and inevitable economies, thereby undermining the whole enterprise of public education. Glenn Frank, president of the University of Wisconsin, was a leader among those who took the offensive against the "wreckers." What were their purposes? he asked. The first aim was "the determination of a discredited economic leadership to shift the blame for the depression to the shoulders of government" by accusing the public sector of waste and mismanagement. The second was to starve public services so that the well-to-do would

DESTROYING THE CORNERSTONE
This cartoon expressed the anger many Americans felt toward indiscriminate cost-cutting in public education. Source: *Texas Outlook* 17 (June 1933): 4 (originally published in *New York American*).

not have to pay higher income and inheritance taxes, however "drastic the drop in revenue from property taxes may become." And the third was to curtail the role of government so that private entrepreneurs might enjoy "an unfettered freedom to reenact the ventures in irresponsibility that landed the nation in economic disaster and may land many of the idols of yesterday in jail or exile." The superintendent of Harrisburg, Illinois, agreed with this analysis. The real extravagances and graft were those of the business elite, he argued, who had bilked the public and their stockholders while earning vast salaries and building great temples of commerce. But now these same men were forming self-appointed committees of bankers, real estate magnates, and railroad and utility executives in major cities. Such committees were "an extralegal dictatorship over the schools and the city in the interest of public economy." "We are expected to become penitent for our petty sins of extravagance," he wrote, "under the criticism of the men who are responsible for this saturnalia of ruin."[7]

One reason for the escalating anger and political action was that educators regarded the public schools not simply as another branch of the public sector but as a sacred institution, one justified by decades of millennial rhetoric that saw "in the equalized school, the only hope of the mass of our people for that civic security, that economic salvation, and that opportunity for living that are the very life of our democratic civilization." The outcry against "bureaucracy" could not be aimed at the public school, Edward Elliott told his colleagues in the NEA, for "every rightly conducted public educational institution has an inherent right to be exempted from the invidious classification as a bureaucratic part of government." To Elliott, a leader in scientific management and elaboration of school systems, nothing so necessary as schools could be "bureaucratic." If one accepted that premise, any campaign to slash school budgets was unpatriotic and anarchical. An editorial in *Texas Outlook*, the magazine of the Texas State Teachers Association, declared that "those businessmen who advocate taxpayers' strikes, who are using every opportunity to create distrust of governmental agencies are *exceedingly stupid*. They are destroying the very thing that they must depend upon for protection of their lives and property. It may be they are not so stupid as their actions seem to indicate. In which case treason is the only word that is adequate."[8]

In the early 1930s, when attacks on tax-cutting businessmen were common, when some teachers were taking militant action, and when educators like Filer were openly entering state politics, observers of the scene might have concluded that fundamental changes were under way in the political economy of education. Surely that was the hope of the social reconstructionists, who believed that a saving remnant of aroused school people might lead Americans to a new social order. But such a conclusion would have been an exaggeration of what was actually happening. The reconstructionists challenged the existing order by a powerful alternative vision of America, but their strategy seemed naive to many radicals, their goal seemed dangerous to many conservatives, and their grasp of educational realities seemed tenuous to many fellow school people. Socialism was the road not taken.

Aggressive language toward selfish capitalists was new in the conservative meetings of the NEA, but it hardly constituted a rejection of capitalism. Teachers could be mobilized to protest payless paydays and tax-dodging financiers and desperate conditions, as in Chicago or Detroit, but as a whole teachers acquiesced in reduced salaries and in control by superintendents and school boards. And even liberal spokesmen influenced by the reconstructionists, like the superintendent Frederick H. Bair, looked backward to a millennial faith in education quite as much as forward to a new order of social justice. Educators, he wrote, "must admit that we need most of all to be born again into the best of American tradition. Education for effective democracy . . . is more than a job; it is more than a profession; it is a crusade."[9]

As crusaders, school leaders sought to reinvigorate consensus on education as a common good by the familiar means of publicity and exhortation. They mobilized themselves to win greater fiscal support in an arena in which they had traditionally been a powerful interest group, the state legislatures. They worked to win over citizens in local communities to their cause. In all this activity they typically saw themselves as St. George going forth to meet the dragon of retrenchment and despair. Intent on preserving their self-proclaimed purity of motives, they continued to trust in professionalism and expertise and to see schooling as a domain above politics. To comprehend why, even in the hardest of times, there were few basic changes in the governance and finance of education, one needs to examine the peculiar but durable political economy of schooling that educators inherited and ultimately buttressed during the depression decade.

The Political Economy of Public Education

For more than a century before the depression, the unique governance and finance of public schools in the United States puzzled foreign observers. In structure the political economy of public education was highly decentralized in local districts even though constitutionally the states were responsible for their systems of schooling. This local control was embedded in a persistent folklore—echoed by professionals—that held that such decentralization kept schools close to the people who created "folk-made schools" and promoted beneficial experimentation and variety. At the same time that public schools were heralded as a quintessentially democratic institution, they were also supposed to be "above politics." By and large the major political parties did not differ in their educational policies. Educators claimed to be politically virginal and aspired to be professionally autonomous.[10]

Despite the enormous heterogeneity of districts, foreign visitors were surprised to find considerable uniformity of educational ideology and similarity of professional aspiration and pedagogical programs nationwide. Clearly, by the 1930s there were strong pressures toward homogenization exerted downward on the local districts by national and state private professional associations and by public agencies.[11]

Although most educators subscribed in principle to the folklore of local control, they were in fact ambivalent about local citizens' capacity to run their schools without expert guidance from professionals. In cities, leading educators had joined with civic elites in the early twentieth century to remove the schools from "politics" by adopting a corporate model of school governance that placed most decisions in the hands of trained superintendents. Most school people also favored the consolidation of rural schools into larger units that would buffer educators from the direct control of parents and patrons. Experts in educational administration favored state laws that made school districts independent units of local government, each with their own boards separate from all other agencies and capable of raising school taxes within limits authorized by the state. In the 1930s Ellwood P. Cubberley, for example, argued for the retention of such independent districts by claiming that if schools were subordinated to local governments they would lose out in the political battles over retrenchment. Local politicians, he said, would slash the "nonpolitical" school departments while favoring their cronies elsewhere because schools were "carried on largely by public-spirited women, whom it is usually impossible to organize and vote." Education must be buffered from partisanship, for it was a sacred trust involving "the proper training of the next generation of citizens."[12]

Although local school districts were the arena for day-by-day decision-making in public education, such school systems were legally only component parts of unified state systems. For this reason, state governments had more direct fiscal and regulatory responsibilities over public education than over other more distinctly local services such as police, parks, fire, and library departments. When hard-pressed during the depression, therefore, school people turned to state legislatures for financial aid to relieve the drain on local property taxes (the major source of school funds). In so doing they had to organize politically and often found themselves allied in the 1930s with real estate interests and other groups not traditionally known as friends of public education. Educators' campaigns for greater state aid paid off; the proportion of school budgets supported by the state nearly doubled during the 1930s.[13]

Through their state and national educational associations, in tandem with state departments of education, school people also lobbied for new state regulations that limited the autonomy of local districts and increased state control over schooling. They pressed, for example, for teacher tenure laws, higher certification requirements, consolidation of rural schools, standardized curriculum and school facilities, and funds for school transportation (busing was then regarded as a solution and not a problem). Educators did not always win what they wanted from legislatures, and they were not the only lobbies seeking school laws, but they were the most persistent and successful political interest group dealing with public education. As we shall suggest, however, they were often ambivalent about their own political activities at the state level.[14]

Although educators tended to favor an activist educational role for the states, they were as a rule hostile to control by the federal government. Indeed, they pointed to excessive regulations in federal vocational education programs as a prime example of what they did *not* want. What they did want was federal money without strings, citing the sacred principle of local control as the wisdom embossed on the temple wall.[15]

Even though educators did not want the national government to control the schools, they worked to create a nationally-minded and

HANDS OFF!

This cartoon revealed the ideal shared by educators and school boards
that schools should be free of dictation from city governments. Source:
American School Board Journal 84 (March 1932): 25.

THANKS! BUT ONLY ON CONDITION THAT FEDERAL SUPPORT
IS NOT FOLLOWED BY FEDERAL CONTROL!

For educators local control was holy writ (though the chaste maiden
representing the schools appears ready to accept federal money without
federal control). Source: *American School Board Journal* 93 (December
1936): 13.

unified educational profession. The main agency for this nongovernmental pressure toward consensus and united action was the NEA, at whose annual meetings delegates from states and local districts gathered to confer on educational policy and practice. But the NEA, reflecting the mixed political economy of education, was a federated body composed of state and local associations whose particular characteristics and interests often diverged. Thus there was pressure to avoid controversy that might rend consensus—for example, on racial segregation or strongly redistributive plans for fair school finance. Rural and urban districts might have quite different notions of what constituted equitable state fiscal plans, while rich states and poor states might disagree on formulas for federal aid to public education.[16]

In the NEA and other associations, educators joined together in private groups to set a national course for public policy in education. In such groups, as in associations in other professions and businesses, "hidden hierarchies" of leaders emerged. Unrecognized in law as part of the apparatus of government, but representing private power in the public domain, such groups had considerable influence on public agendas as well as on the members of their occupation. In public education such pace-setters and arbiters of the normal and desirable were experts and administrators from universities, foundations, key state and city superintendencies, and other pinnacles of the educational establishment. These leaders gained influence over a nationwide agenda in education and possessed power to nominate others to important posts. We shall call them administrative progressives, for their interest focused on the restructuring of power and programs in public schools. To say that their power was private is not to imply conspiracy. Their program for modernizing education was openly announced and well publicized, and their success depended on persuading others by the authority conferred by their expertise and institutional position.[17]

The school-survey movement offers one illustration of the mode of operation of the administrative progressives. The school survey consisted of a report by experts from outside the district—customarily from universities, foundations, and federal and state bureaucracies—appraising the work of local schools and advising them on needed changes in facilities, curriculum, and administrative organization. Such surveyors provided school boards and local superintendents with the modern templates of approved practice. This process of change—cosmopolitan and expert in origin but voluntary, as opposed to obligatory federal control—preserved the isolated and antique virtue of the temple upon a hill, the local district.[18]

Through such private but potent means as the survey, the authoritative commission, the preparation and placement of trained superintendents, and the dictates of "scientific" research, the administrative progressives exerted considerable national influence over the development of public schooling. Almost all of them supported the principle of local control, but only in the sanitized version of the corporate model of school governance, above the din of city politics and free from the provincialism of rural communities. Business and professional elites had been their most reliable allies in the first three decades of the twentieth century, and despite a temporary disenchantment that some educators felt toward a business-led tax revolt during the early 1930s, most of the administrative progressives continued during the depression to work with national and local elites.[19]

Education was itself a business that operated in a national market even though local districts were the "firms" that did most of the purchasing. Large national companies produced textbooks, school furniture, heating and ventilating systems, testing instruments, and supplies. Manufacturers advertised their products in national magazines and hired sales people to merchandise their wares. Private businesses that produced textbooks and I.Q. tests did much to shape what actually happened to millions of students in the course of their schooling. Such organizations were, however, subject to minimal public control.[20]

The schools operated within a larger political economy in which business remained the predominant force, despite the changes wrought by the maelstrom and the New Deal. National industries, national media, national markets for products and ideas crisscrossed regions and penetrated from cities to the countryside. As in education, federated business associations spread ideas to members in the states and local communities and sought to shape national governmental policies. In comparison with other pressure groups in government— even after the New Deal gave new clout to labor and agriculture—

MESSENGERS OF PROGRESS!

In this complicated illustration the Roman woman representing public education, in her temple far above the din of factories and everyday life, reads a report by experts on how to improve the schools. The "school surveyors" buzz about the heights with their plans for enlightened educational change. Source: *American School Board Journal* 88 (March 1934): 13.

business exerted the greatest influence at all levels of government. Few political leaders proposed any alternative to the economic crisis other than restoring the health of capitalism.[21]

For all their anger at tax-cutting financiers, educators depended upon the recovery of the national economy for school taxes. They wanted favorable publicity from the business-owned media. They faced businessmen as their superiors on local school boards. Study after study has shown that the members of school boards came mostly from the upper reaches of the social structure of their communities, especially in towns and cities. The mere fact that so many school board members were businessmen, however, does not indicate that they had identical agendas or that their decisions were based on self-conscious class interest. Even elite politics of education had a pluralistic cast. In Detroit some of the upper-class board members fought hard to retain threatened educational programs, while in Chicago bankers slashed deeply. The Elmtown, Illinois, board members wanted to be sure "that teachers conform, in the classroom and in their personal lives, to the most conservative economic, political, religious, and moral doctrines prevailing in the community," while in Altoona, Pennsylvania, tenth graders read Ibsen's *Enemy of the People*. Some businessmen wanted to expand vocational education, while others thought it a waste of money. And in many, perhaps most, districts where there were elite boards, the members probably took little direct interest or action in the everyday running of the schools but rather left that to the professionals.[22]

The "zone of tolerance" for diverse opinion and practice in public education differed widely depending on the community, the attitudes of board members, and the skill of superintendents and staffs in protecting their autonomy. In the 1930s the range of permissible socioeconomic dissent probably widened in the schools in comparison with the 1920s. But the major influence of business in the political economy of education, at both the national and the local levels, meant that it could set the outer limits of acceptable controversy. And as we shall suggest, educators were quite aware of those limits, reminded by national state attacks on "reds" and local proscriptions of ideological deviance.[23]

The political economy of public education in the 1930s, then, was a complex interaction: of local governance and finance, of growing assertions of state power, and of national influence of various kinds exerted largely through powerful private organizations. It was partially a time of conflict, both within the educational system—between liberals and conservatives, teachers and school boards—and in the larger community, over the funding of education and over the ideological ferment the depression created. But for the most part, it was a period when educators pulled together rather than splintered apart and when a broad public consensus on the importance of schooling among different groups sustained the educational program. The fields of force were hard to track, however, so much did they intersect with one another and so much did they depart from the folklore of "folk-made schools" that had dominated educational ideology for a century.

The Road Not Taken: Creating a New Social Order

An advertisement appeared in the pages of the magazine of the Texas State Teachers Association in 1933: "Select the tour that attracts you most in the vast and variegated land projecting its gigantic social and industrial achievements from polar seas to tropic sands. Follow your own bent in visiting the stupendous building, intense social activities, factories and giant farms, research institutions and amazing art theaters, model villages and mighty cities." What was this country, this inspiring road to the future? The Soviet Union.[24]

"Cumulative evidence supports the conclusion that, in the United States as in other countries, the age of individualism and *laissez faire* is closing and that a new age of collectivism is emerging." A new manifesto of radicals? Not quite—it was a central tenet of a new framework for public school social studies issued by a commission appointed by the American Historical Association and widely discussed by educators.[25]

Exploring new ideological terrain, some educators speculated in the middle years of the depression about a boldly transformed social order. They were willing to listen to different voices and entertain prospects of change that had been unthinkable in the profession only a few years before. Once regarded as a radical who questioned the disinterestedness of the founding fathers, Charles Beard became a favorite speaker before the Department of Superintendence and warned managers of education that deeper than the outward distress was "a crisis in American thought" resulting from a disjunction between economic ideology and actual economic conditions. In 1933 the U.S. Office of Education invited Beard to provide high school libraries with a book list to "acquaint teachers and pupils with facts, known and unknown, about this new world we are entering."[26]

From the time of Horace Mann onward, educators have typically had a vision of what Dewey called "a deliberately preferred social order" and of education's role in bringing that order into being. The suffering and dislocation brought on by the depression—privation in the midst of plenty—called into question the wisdom and virtue of economic leaders. With the decline of business prestige came a questioning of the ideology of economic individualism. But even more potent in arousing educators against business than their role in bringing on the crash was what some perceived as an organized campaign of business elites to discredit the public schools and to deny them funds. That was not simply ineptitude but actual treason against the American ideals which public schools so patently represented.[27]

Educators publicized the actions of tax-cutting coalitions of economic leaders in the National Economy League and the United States Chamber of Commerce and its state and local branches. On December 19, 1932, the manager of the finance committee of the U.S. Chamber of Commerce sent to members a letter requesting their consideration of a range of possible retrenchments in school budgets, including the elimination of evening classes and kindergartens, the shortening of the school day, an increase in the size of classes, and the imposition of tuition for high school attendance. The letter provoked angry responses. The *Idaho Journal of Education* spotted a cabal of big businessmen "firing from a bush and . . . operating behind a smoke screen." It asserted that in Idaho, Chamber leaders were working to remove public schools to the private sector and advocating the slashing of teachers' salaries in elementary schools. In Nebraska, bankers distributed pamphlets proposing that school salaries be cut in half. By such actions, the Idaho magazine editorialized, "the very foundations upon which our republic rests are being undermined."[28]

It was under such conditions of anger and desperation that the social frontier educators like Counts won a hearing in 1932. His challenge to take the side of evolutionary socialism, however, frightened many school people even while they found his rhetoric appealing. The consensual ideology that had prevailed from Horace Mann's time obscured the perception that educational leaders had as a rule buttressed the existing division of power and wealth, though softening its more obvious inequities. The social reconstructionists underscored this unselfconscious support of capitalism when they discussed socialist "indoctrination." The nervousness of school people increased when the radicals suggested how a national leadership cadre of frontier educators would actually operate.[29]

It was essential, the reconstructionists argued, that the direction of education be centralized to correspond with the concentration of economic power at the national level. To create such "new institutions which are in harmony with the necessities of the age," the best solution lay in "the development of a great national profession of teachers which through organization would proceed to think and act in terms of the country as a whole, but through its local divisions would be ready and willing to adjust broad principles to the needs and differences of regions and communities." An obstacle in the path of reforming the schools was the dominance of local boards by members of the business and professional classes. It was essential to replace those elites with "persons drawn directly from those elements whose position in society rests not on property but on some form of labor or service," for otherwise teachers could not "deal honestly with the economic problem."[30]

Even under a conservative board, the liberal superintendent could work "to make the school a genuinely constructive force," but he had best avoid "the glare of publicity, at least with reference to the matters in which he is most deeply interested, not because he would conceal anything from the public, but because he prefers to give the manipulators of stereotypes little opportunity to draw red herrings across his path." Such a man "knows that laissez-faire individualism is played out and that a planned economy of some kind is inevitable . . . While seldom committed to a definite program for economic and social reconstruction, his sympathies are with labor, with the farmers, and with the liberal political groups that are fighting the battle of the people against privilege."[31]

Just how the national leadership might be organized was by no means clear. "To exercise educational leadership," declared the *Social Frontier*, "can only mean to define the issues of contemporary life and to initiate persistently and consistently clear-cut movements, in the school and out, calculated to achieve the goals of a good life." That definition must stem from "a realistic understanding of the forces underlying contemporary society" and a proper weighting of "the rights of property versus the rights of man." On these grounds the NEA's Department of Superintendence failed the test of leadership, thought the reconstructionists, for its vapid resolutions rarely penetrated "beneath the surface of social phenomena" and its concept of "planning" was timid. It never occurred to the department that educators should abandon the ideal of neutrality in social policy, which in practice simply supported "our inherited system." Instead of seeing the world whole, the typical administrator was preoccupied with his progression up the hierarchy, with the administrative details of running the system, and with "the many local political and social connections to be made if prestige was to be maintained." Only a "transvaluation of the present administrative mentality could redeem the superintendent, and then his main function would be to encourage the "organized rank-and-file toward professional solidarity and meaningful collective allegiances."[32]

But what of the teacher who was to transform society? "It is admitted without argument that American teachers as a group are timid and docile," wrote a reconstructionist in an unusually harsh assessment. "Their mental horizon does not reach significantly beyond the three R's. Their professional equipment is limited to 'special methods.' Seldom is the distance between what a profession thinks it is doing and what it actually is doing so great as in the case of the teachers." While they should be shaping society, teachers mainly "retail hackneyed facts and fix a few simple skills in the tool subjects"; they know nothing about the arts; "politically and socially they are illiterates"; and "their mental picture of the world is a patchwork of newspaper stereotypes, movie sentimentality, and popular wisdom." They fear a fall from their tenuous middle-class status and "do not recognize that they are workers." How could such people create a new social order? Teachers "are potentialy powerful because they are numerous, because they are strategically placed to re-fashion the mentality of the nation, and because education occupies an important place in the traditionally sanctioned democratic way of life." And they can emulate "those [avant-garde] teachers who recognize the irrationality and essential inhumanity of existing social arrangements and who are committed in principle to a society free of economic and human waste."[33]

In this description of the actual "rank-and-file" of teachers and administrators, this reconstructionist critic was addressing an in-group that might be expected to share not only his reconstructionist ideology but also his elitist stance. The "frontier thinkers" were a small cadre; in 1936 there were only 3,751 subscribers to the *Social Frontier*. When they spoke not to the coterie but to the masses of teachers, they generally adopted a more hortatory mode. Indeed, exhortation and high rhetoric were the strong suit of the reconstructionists, as with the majority of educational reformers before and after them. They appealed to conscience, to hope, to professional pride. They were certain at a time when many others were confused and vacillating. They gave educators a reason to feel important, a utopian cause. They also gave life to a compelling vision of social justice.[34]

To perceptive observers on the left, however, the more hortatory reconstructionists often seemed naive in their analysis of power and too optimistic about reforming society through education. The British socialist Harold Laski was one of these critics. He was sympathetic to the ideals of the social frontier educators and believed that they had raised fundamental questions. But in analyzing the 1934 report of the Commission on Social Studies, which was influenced by a reconstructionist point of view, Laski found certain "vital presuppositions" that he believed were unexamined and dubious.[35]

The members of the Commission on Social Studies seemed to believe, he wrote, "that there is an interest of a unified America over and above the interests of the economic classes of which it is composed." Was there any reason to believe that through education the members of the separate classes could be led to abandon their classes in favor of this larger unity? Could an educational system designed to preserve the inequities of capitalism really be changed, with the consent of capitalists, to bring about a society that would undermine individual ownership of the means of production? If that dream of change actually came about, peacefully and through education, it would be the first time in human history that the powerful had so easily capitulated.[36]

Why should the ruling class so easily abandon its power? asked Laski. Why would businessmen so "horrified by the very moderate program of social reform sponsored by President Roosevelt" have such a "change of heart" as to allow collectivism to be achieved through education? How successful would educators be in keeping businessmen and the Daughters of the American Revolution from the schools? Could they protect the tenure of a teacher in a Pennsylvania mining town while she told "the whole truth about the existing social order" and get more tax money for schools in the process? "Anyone who thinks for a moment of how this program would appeal to Mr. Hearst, to the National Civic Federation, to the Chancellor of Pittsburgh University, to the Associated Chambers of Commerce, to the public utility organizations, to the 'patriotic' societies, to the ten thousand Main Streets of America, will, I think, be inclined to skepticism about its prospects."[37]

The fact is, Laski wrote, that "men think differently who live differently." How could the reconstructionists ever overcome through persuasion "that one class, which possesses today all the power and privilege that go with the ownership of the means of production" and win its cooperation "in effecting its own erosion"? Any educational system reflects the political economy of which it is a part. Businessmen may say that they want better schools and will respect "academic freedom," but their position in the social system—the way they live, the interests they defend—dictates quite different ways of thinking about what good schools, good textbooks, and academic freedom must mean. So strong is "the religion of ownership" that if the ruling class should read the report, its impact would "lead less to conviction that conversion was desirable than to the angry perception that the liberal teacher is an even more dangerous heretic than they have hitherto been accustomed to believe."[38]

Conservative Counterattack

Laski was accurate about the backlash of conservatives toward the sort of liberal collectivism the social frontier group represented.

Newspaper editors reacted strongly against the report of the social studies commission. The prime foe of educational "radicalism," William Randolph Hearst, filled his national chain of newspapers with cartoons and editorials warning of the red menace in schools and colleges. Rugg wrote that "Hearst reporters admitted, in interviewing Professors Kilpatrick and Counts of Teachers College, that they were red baiters and that 'Hearst is engaged at present in conducting a Red Scare.' " One of Hearst's targets was Beard, a member of the commission and an author of high school textbooks that had sold millions of copies. In a rump session of educators the day before the NEA met in 1935, Beard made a rousing attack on Hearst to a group that gave him a standing ovation. "There is not a cesspool of vice and crime that Hearst has not raked and exploited for money-making purposes," he charged. "No person with intellectual honesty or moral integrity will touch him with a ten-foot pole for any purpose or to gain any end." The American Federation of Teachers resolved to boycott Hearst publications.[39]

Hearst had his defenders, however. Matthew Woll, the right-wing union leader and then acting president of the prestigious National Civic Federation, wrote to the chairman of the congressional committee investigating "un-American activities" to say that Hearst had raised important doubts about how far "academic freedom" should be taken. We should not take "too seriously," he wrote, "the reported statement of Professor George S. Counts . . . to the effect that 'if William Randolph Hearst succeeds in his efforts, he will reduce American universities and schools to the ignominious condition of German schools and universities under Hitler.' "[40]

Educators faced intimidation not just from people like Hearst, who tried to stir up reactionary public opinion, but also from state legislatures that passed loyalty-oath laws to rid the schools of subversives and that passed legislation requiring patriotic instruction and rituals. Of twenty-one states that by 1936 had enacted special oaths of allegiance, fourteen had passed their laws since the onset of the depression. Educators in Massachusetts who protested such a bill, reported the *New Republic*, "were heckled and jeered at by the legislators" who used Elizabeth Dilling's book *The Red Network* to try to trap scholars, McCarthy style, into admitting membership in subversive organizations. One public school teacher "told how four teachers in Taunton had feared to comment in the classroom even on a routine local strike."[41]

In 1935 the Congress attached a "red rider" to the appropriations bill for the District of Columbia, forcing the teachers to sign a statement that they were not teaching communism. Representative Blanton of Texas mailed a questionnaire to all teachers in the capital asking them: "Do you believe in God? Do you believe in any of the doctrines of communism? Do you approve of Dr. George S. Counts' writings? Do you approve of Dr. Charles A. Beard's writings? Have you been to Russia?" Two years later Congress repealed the rider, but in the meantime teachers had learned that their autonomy was shaky.[42]

Patriotic groups led attacks on presumed radicalism in the schools. The Daughters of the American Revolution had long been on the watch for new-style revolutionaries. In 1928 they had even listed the NEA among groups "sympathetic with communist ideals"—an odd judgment to make about an association that had denounced the menace of radicalism and glorified business during the 1920s. The American Legion spearheaded the drive for loyalty oaths for teachers, published an article about treason in the textbooks, and distributed a newsletter to state superintendents of instruction about radical youth groups.[43]

As Laski predicted, big business was hardly eager to applaud while left-liberal educators instructed the young about the evils of acquisitive individualism and the virtues of collectivism. Indeed, business elites employed some of the same organizations to attack frontier ideas that they had used or created to assault the New Deal. Discredited and confused in the early 1930s, they soon recovered their sense of common cause and took the offensive. One tactic, employed in the 1920s and revived in the second half of the 1930s, was to use advertising to sell capitalism both within and outside the public schools. Businessmen had no guilty conscience, as did educators, about the dangers of indoctrination. The National Association of Manufacturers (NAM) pursued a vigorous public relations campaign, posting 45,000 billboards with messages like "What Is Good for Industry Is Good for You," sending out free radio propaganda, and arguing that free enterprise should be sold "just as continuously as the people are told that Ivory Soap floats or that children cry for Castoria."[44]

A positive approach was not enough; businessmen also joined the Legion and other patriotic associations in attacking radicalism in textbooks. Groups like the U.S. Chamber of Commerce, the Advertising Federation of America, and the New York State Economic Council pounced on the left-liberals. The NAM commissioned a survey of social studies books to detect "creeping collectivism" and sought to instill "pro-American doctrines" instead. When the results of the textbook survey hit the front page of the *New York Times*— as summarized by the director of the study, a banking professor at Columbia—many educators were outraged at accusations of incompetence and subversion of capitalism.[45]

The furor over the textbooks of Harold Rugg illustrates the methods and values of the business critics. More than any other reconstructionist, Rugg had managed to get into the school curriculum by the most surefire strategy of all: writing popular textbooks that were used in 4,200 school systems. Rugg told a colleague that in the 1930s, because of the general interest of teachers and citizens in broad economic and social questions, he was able to treat controversial issues that would not have been discussable during the 1920s in the schools. But his hostility to the profit motive, his awareness of chronic inequalities, and his faith in social planning were anathema to conservatives. One of these, Merwin K. Hart, president of the New York State Economic Council and a friend of and spokesman for right-wing groups, accused the Rugg books of "promoting unrest, of fomenting class struggle, of proposing unworkable government planning, and of retailing inaccurate views of the Constitution." Other antagonists included B. C. Forbes, a Hearst columnist and owner of *Forbes Magazine*; Alfred T. Falk, head of "research and education" for the Advertising Federation of America; and other "professional publicists for business enterprises." The foes used many tactics of attack, from suggesting book burnings in local communities, to writing editorials in national magazines, to warning newspaper editors of the anti-advertising bias of Rugg's books. Rugg himself observed that the attacks on his books were part of a recurring pattern in the history of education: campaigns by conservative publicists, aided by patriotic groups and certain newspapers and magazines, that flourished when progressives in government and in education were vocal and well-organized and thus conspicuous targets for the liberal-baiters.[46]

The heightened awareness of social issues aroused by the social frontier group, the vehemence of the attacks on liberals by Hearst and other right-wing people, the sense of insecurity and dislocation caused by the depression—these created both anxiety and a new interest in defending academic freedom in educational associations like the NEA and the AFT and prodded them to adopt strong statements in favor of free expression. In many communities the liberal teachers and administrators, buoyed by a new sense of support from like-minded educators elsewhere and a new alertness to issues they had often taken for granted or failed to perceive, became aware for the first time that there was such a thing as "academic freedom."[47]

Despite this new attention to academic freedom, school people were still fired if they offended local elites. After describing the fate of a skilled principal who had been dismissed in Winston-Salem because he had written a novel, *Just Plain Larnin'*, in which he told how a tobacco company ruled an imaginary community, the editors of the *Social Frontier* added: "Teachers of sound character and high ability may be dropped without trial or charges, if their views displease a tiny minority who possess wealth and control. No individual merit, no level of past success, will save them. Resolutions will not reinstate them."[48]

It is difficult to assess how far the reconstructionist ideology of public education penetrated the educational establishment, much less how much it influenced the educational grass roots. Some thought they knew. William Wirt, superintendent of schools in Gary, Indiana, was reported in the *New York Sun* as saying that school managers were "turning red and using the schools to incite ultra-radical sentiment." They "have pledged themselves," he said, to propagandize and to force "the country over the precipice and into the abyss of communism." But others thought it foolish to think that one could change the mentality of so conservative an occupation as school superintendents.[49]

A skeptical educational leader once asked a reconstructionist this question: "If the superintendent of schools appeals over the head of the vested interests to the great American people, how long will he remain a superintendent of schools?" There is much doubt that more than a handful of superintendents would even have wanted to do so. Leaders in education were asked their opinion on this statement: "The national professional organization should enter vigorously and directly into the field of political, social, and economic discussion and reform." Only 5.8 percent agreed (as compared with a slightly higher percentage of teachers—11.6). Instead, 82 percent believed that organized educators should avoid "partisanship" and merely call attention to "the educational aspects and implications of existing socio-economic conditions." That was the traditional and safer route to follow.[50]

The Outlook of Local Superintendents

If one looks at the social background and social values of everyday educational leaders, instead of the view from Teachers College's Morningside Heights, the conservative outlook of local superintendents is understandable. The majority of them probably had little knowledge of reconstructionism, and most of those who did would have agreed, in looking at their local districts, with the superintendent in Allentown, Pennsylvania, who declared, "Those of us who have not taken leave of our senses know that the schools and schoolmasters are not generally going to be permitted *to take the lead* in changing the social order, nor in conducting experiments likely to lead to a radical redefinition of the aims of that character." The average superintendent was likely to nod in agreement when a former NEA president said in 1935 that the key to civic salvation was creating "standards of morality through universal Christian and religious education" in the public schools. To most educators this made more sense than a plea for collectivism. Many of them probably sympathized with the superintendent from Coleraine, Minnesota, who said that the Teachers College folk at the NEA conventions should "be put in the rear seats and muzzled."[51]

In 1934 Frederick Bair published a study of the origins and outlooks of 850 local superintendents from all parts of the country. He found that 98.5 percent were native-born and 90 percent Anglo-Saxon in background. Over half of them grew up on farms, and 85 percent in rural areas. Over 90 percent attended church—almost entirely Protestant—and almost 50 percent were active in Sunday

School work. Religion deeply colored their view of the world, wrote Bair; inspired by the age-old vision of "Thy Kingdom come on earth" and ready "to invest his life for a social order more to his liking, the Superintendent may indeed have derived in his very blood from Puritan—even Pilgrim—ancestors a tenacity equal to his job." They came from educationally and culturally humble origins, for the most part. Their median age was forty-three, and they had typically worked for their entire lives in the schools. There were more than twice as many Republicans as Democrats; only two were Socialists. They were avid joiners; the average superintendent was a member of eight organizations (such as the NEA, the Rotary, the Masons, the Chamber of Commerce, and the YMCA). They were thus connected by close ties to the business and professional people who typically were on their school boards, to the churches, and to fellow educators both inside their system and to superintendents elsewhere; these were their reference groups.[52]

Such leaders were not likely to challenge the status quo. Over half said that they experienced no pressures from any segments of their communities, and those who did reported that it was most often religious, temperance, and commercial groups that caused trouble. The superintendents blended in well with their patrons. They said they believed that schools should deal with social problems, but when their own views on instruction were further probed, it became apparent that their open-mindedness had its limits. Here are the percentages of superintendents who agreed with some sample statements:

"Histories written for elementary or high school use should omit any facts likely to arouse in the minds of the students questions or doubt concerning the justice of our social order and government." *84 percent*

"Every boy and girl in American schools should be taught to give unquestioning and unlimited respect and support to the American flag." *80 percent*

"In teaching the vital problems of citizenship, teachers should so impress on the students the approved opinion in these matters that life's later experiences can never unsettle or modify the opinions given." *26 percent*

In the depths of the depression more superintendents were willing than before or since, probably, to approve some of the more liberal items on Bair's questionnaire, but four-fifths disagreed with the re-constructionist view that "our educational forces should be directed toward a more thoroughly socialistic order of society."[53]

The everyday life of administrators and teachers did not much reflect the aspirations of educational revolutionaries. The point of view of local school boards and administrators came through more clearly in the pages of the *American School Board Journal* in the 1930s than in the columns of the *Social Frontier*. The former stressed issues such as improving the moral character of youth, separating schools from politics, educational efficiency and cost-cutting, budgeting, public relations, and the planning and maintenance of facilities. Teachers, very much under the eye and thumb of local influentials, were curbed both in their expression of opinion and in their private lives. Local elites and national figures like J. Edgar Hoover turned to public education to tame youth and to keep alive conservative social and political values in a period of trial.[54]

In the early 1930s educators experienced a combination of fear, anger, and puzzlement that made them willing for a time to consider what was for them a radical explanation of why things were out of joint. Some of the exponents of this "frontier thinking" were established and eloquent spokesmen like Newlon and Counts, who used evangelical appeals that fit well with the millennial tradition that had infused earlier reforms. They argued not for stablizing an existing social order but for restructuring the political economy based on an analysis that saw the defects of capitalism not as anomalous and remedial faults but as intrinsic to a decaying and immoral social order. But as the society seemed to stabilize and as public education recovered from the worst blows of retrenchment, the new ideas began to seem dangerous and were tamed into forms more consonant with the traditional roles and values of educators. Administrators were urged to be more "democratic" in their dealings with subordinates. The call to look with clear eyes at the whole pattern of inequality and power relationships in the society became diluted into considering "the problems of democracy" in an eclectic and disjointed fashion. And the demand that educators present a united front for social change became transmuted into a search for a consensus through which the profession could unite and achieve more limited goals.[55]

EDUCATION: THE NATION'S SAFEGUARD FOR THE FUTURE

These cartoons give the flavor of the approved educational ideology of
boards and superintendents: the serene female figure of education ex-
presses the dedication of disinterested teachers; the suited figures of
superintendent and board member represent the ideals of businesslike

GET OUT!

efficiency and incorruptibility; and the sinister figure at the right reveals the ever-present dangers of politics and graft. Sources: (left) *American School Board Journal* 85 (September 1932): 19; (right) *American School Board Journal* 92 (February 1936): 17.

Publicity and the Building of Consensus

"We have been meek long enough," concluded John K. Norton, a professor at Teachers College and activist chairman of the Joint Commission on the Emergency in Education (JCEE). The NEA appointed the JCEE in 1933 to take the offensive against the accelerating pace of retrenchment through publicity and political action. School leaders began to realize that they were out of touch with public opinion and politically unorganized. A member of the Minneapolis Taxpayers Association underscored the vulnerability of professional educators in an article on school costs in 1932: "One thing is certain, unless public understanding is increased, education will not continue to receive the generous support it has enjoyed in the past." Citizens often feel, he wrote, "that organized education has cold shouldered [them] out of their field on the theory that we are blundering amateurs."[56]

The tasks of the JCEE were tricky. One was to create a united front against retrenchment among the diverse constituencies that comprised the employees of the educational system; this was in keeping with the NEA's goal to create a united educational profession from the men and women who worked as administrators, specialists, and teachers. A second task was to use publicity and other methods to inform, persuade, and involve the public in support of free schools. While this fit a 1920s model of school public relations and a traditional rhetoric of local lay control, public relations had typically been a top-down affair of providing favorable publicity, and lay control had been as often feared as sought. Finally, the task of mobilizing educators for political action—to secure, for example, greater state financing for schools—was fiscally vital but endangered the apolitical image of teachers as disinterested advocates for children and the general welfare.[57]

Before two months had passed, Norton and his colleagues had begun to organize a professional united front, building on efforts already under way in the states to rouse public support for schools. People at the grass roots of the educational system were clearly aware of the need for rapid and united action. In Texas, for example, a state educational committee created 750 local committees in 1932. These committees sponsored over 500 educational addresses to community organizations, published 345 articles in newspapers, produced thirty-five radio programs, and distributed many thousands of copies of publicity releases on the needs of the schools—all in the space of four months. Dallas high school teachers distributed 55,000 pamphlets and spoke to local clubs and civic groups, while the grade school teachers worked with the PTA to press a legislative campaign. In 1933 Norton said the Joint Commission "will profit from the effective work that is already being done by [local districts and state associations], will seek to pool their experience, and to develop plans for united action" through a series of regional conferences. There they could share information about where retrenchment was taking place, how to plan for necessary cuts, and how to persuade the public to maintain the integrity of free education. His tone was militant toward the "shortsighted and selfish interests" that wanted to slash budgets but confident that school people would pull together, despite infighting in their ranks.[58]

By 1934 Norton could report that the Joint Commission had made further progress. It had collected and publicized reports on the gravity of cutbacks, held eight regional meetings to plan strategy, sponsored twenty-five nationwide radio broadcasts by prominent citizens, investigated and publicized the names of the friends and critics of the schools, and cooperated with other groups in seeking federal emergency aid for education and a revised state tax structure. In 1935 he said that the committee was moving beyond such emergency measures to recognize that the earthquake of the depression had revealed basic faultlines in American education, a highly unequal pattern of school finance, a multiplicity of small and inefficient districts, and a lack of vision of a better, planned society. To bring about the basic changes needed, he argued, would require the support of an informed and aroused citizenry and long-term professional planning. "The myth of a self-regulating economic system has exploded in our faces," he claimed. "We are frantically groping for those controls which will bring the untamed machine to heel and make it the servant rather than the master of mankind." A new sense of purpose was vital to the reconstruction of society as of education.[59]

The conferences, journals, and yearbooks of the educational administrators resounded with calls for better public relations in education and for more involvement of lay citizens in policy. Some regarded the task as one for the specialized salesman, the PR man. The superintendent of schools in Pasadena commented that when the depression hit, educators panicked because many citizens regarded the public schools not as "the foundation upon which our governmental structure rested" but simply as "another government service competing with highways, municipalities, police and fire departments, relief, and social security for a living share of the social income." Across the country, he said, "the immediate response of the friends of public education was to turn to the public relations agent, the professional public opinion builder, the fashion setter in a desperate and dramatic appeal to rebuild the faith of the American people in public education and to restore the support of public education. The spectacle of these antics would be ridiculous were they not so tragic." The American people were tired of snake-oil salesmen and hype. What was essential was to have a planned professional direction, he argued; then that could be communicated through public relations.[60]

The most common approach to gaining support for schools was not to "sell" them, as bond levies had been touted during the 1920s, but to build natural constituencies in local communities. Teachers were urged to visit parents' homes and to stimulate active PTAs, administrators to speak to local civic and service clubs, schools to hold public activities that would demonstrate the work accomplished. This approach required a change of attitude on the part of educators. The Rockford, Illinois, superintendent told his peers: "The conduct of schoolmen is often inexcusably stupid . . . instead of encouraging parents to visit our schools, we frequently allow them to gain the impression that their presence is not wanted." Above all, it was important to interpret what the schools were doing within the context of a social philosophy of public education. In the previous decade there had been too much haphazard incrementalism without regard for the unifying purposes of the schools. "The present quite general criticism and distrust of the public schools are largely due to the public's misunderstanding of the goals of free public education."[61]

The depression years were a time when educators attempted to broaden the public forum in which issues of schooling were debated and to include lay people in that task. John Norton ridiculed the previous tactics of whipping up enthusiasm "to 'put across' a plan 'with a bang' " by emulating business. He recommended "continuously interpreting the schools fully, calmly, and frankly" in a process that "enlists the active participation of laymen of all types as well as teachers, pupils, and administrators." One technique for this public airing of views on the schools that was recommended by Norton and the JCEE, in collaboration with the professional honorary fraternity Phi Delta Kappa, was to hold conferences in local communities in which educators and citizens had a chance to discuss widely voiced criticisms of public education.

The JCEE and Phi Delta Kappa distributed in 1933 a mimeographed booklet called "Evaluating the School Program" as a guide for such conferences, in which were listed the most common criticisms of the schools, arguments about the costs of education, and brief justifications of the parts of the school program that were most under attack. "Although it is difficult to envisage further progress toward the realization of the essential idealism of democracy except from the point of view of an ever-growing and developing program of public education, we should realize," wrote Norton, "that this critical period of economic and social readjustment subjects even our most cherished tenets to review."[62]

From an analysis of sixty-four articles in lay magazines and twelve professional books, the pamphlet presented thirteen frequent criticisms of the schools, many of them contradictory; the top five criticisms were "soft" pedagogy, lack of contact with life, overemphasis on vocations, severe discipline and overwork, and neglect of character. But above all the tone and temper of the document was one of justification of the present system and opposition to the recommendations for cuts and economies proposed by the U.S. Chamber of Commerce and the International City Managers' Association, save for the changes already part of the conventional wisdom of educators, such as consolidation of rural schools. And it made clear that "although different points of view are invited and a certain amount of debate is permissible, the primary purpose of the conference was agreement rather than conflict."[63]

Although some of Norton's language was tart toward "the selfish interests" (a code phrase for business proponents of tax cutting), the JCEE itself comprised mainstream educators: besides Norton, three city superintendents, a dean of education, a state superintendent, and the president of the NEA department classroom teachers. It was hardly an antibusiness group, nor was there strong evidence that business in general opposed public education or indeed public services in general. In 1932 an editorial in *Business Week* argued that public services should be maintained since they were "demanded by citizens and . . . can be performed easier and more economically as a community venture financed by taxation." Education cost 22.2 percent of the city budget, the editorial pointed out, and "regardless of possible extravagances in school operation, few would suggest that they, privately and for less money, could provide for their own children all the advantages of a modern city school system." "Extravagances," and not the worth of public services as a whole, were generally at stake in criticisms by business interests, although the hyperbolic rhetoric of some educators might have suggested otherwise, so accustomed were they to seeing any attack on themselves as a heretical undermining of a sacred institution. In fact, business had good reason in the tumultuous years of the depression to support an institution that contributed as much as public education did to social stability and to the hope for betterment through individual self-improvement rather than through a reconstruction of the social order.[64]

One index of business opinion on education during the depression years can be found in editorial commentary in newspapers. Educators fared well—surely far better than in their treatment by the media in recent years. Charles R. Foster examined twenty-five newspapers in different parts of the country in the years from 1930 to 1935 and found editorial comments on the value of public education overwhelmingly favorable; of 1,168 references to the social purposes of the schools, only 2.8 percent were negative. The arguments for the common school—political, economic, moral, humanitarian—might have been written by educators themselves. This is not to say that editors were uncritical of the schools. Foster found that 44.5 percent of their total references to all aspects of education were favorable, 32.4 percent neutral, and 23.2 percent negative. Writers had much to criticize in fads and frills, high taxes, and corrupt school boards, not to mention losing football teams and inept coaches. But newspapers reflected a highly positive view of the importance of public schools and their teachers and administrators, as indicated in table 5.[65]

Editors were bothered by the high cost of schools and frequently criticized what they regarded as an overblown set of courses and services and bureaucratic elaborations. Nonetheless, they were scarcely less flowery than the educational publicists themselves in praising teachers:

The *Emporia Gazette*—"Who ever heard of a teacher giving less in service, in sacrifice, in personal interest in the youngsters under her care, because of reduced salary?"

The *Memphis Commercial Appeal*—"The reproach has been truthfully cast upon our civilization that it pays least to its most faithful and potent guardians, its teachers."

The *New York Times*, on teachers—"No group in the community has been more interested in the cause of the child's education and none has made more sacrifices on its behalf."[66]

The editorial tune about "unsung heroes of the depression" quickly changed if teachers became militant or politically organized, however. While docile schoolmarms received rhetorical bouquets, editors called feisty teachers the "payroll brigade," a "self-serving" lobby,

Table 5. Favorable and unfavorable ratings of selected topics among the ten subjects most frequently mentioned by editors

	Percentage favorable	Percentage unfavorable
Public responsibility for supporting education	89.7	1.7
Ability of teachers	67.7	14.1
Teachers' salaries	66.7	5.7
Superintendents and administrators	62.0	24.5
Boards of education	27.8	41.5
Cost of education	7.5	77.9

Source: Charles R. Foster, *Editorial Treatment of Education in the American Press*, Harvard Bulletin in Education, No. 21 (Cambridge, Mass.: Harvard University Press, 1938), p. 39.

and "taxeaters." "Lobbying and propaganda have no place in the public school system," warned the *Pittsburgh Press*.[67]

The Joint Commission on the Emergency in Education helped to give school people a sense of efficacy in the midst of the downward-spinning economy and may have contributed to the generally positive regard that newspaper editors—and indeed Americans in general—had for the public schools. But the need to justify public education continued, and in 1935 the NEA and the Department of Superintendence created a new body, the Educational Policies Commission (EPC), as a prestigious national forum. At a time when economic and governmental agencies were becoming more centralized, the EPC sought to develop a common sense of purpose in a decentralized educational profession and to communicate that ideology to influential lay people.[68]

In more prosperous times, said an EPC spokesman, Americans typically had maintained "a more comfortable matter-of-fact attitude toward the schools, their financial support, their control, their management, and their fixed place among the indispensable services of government. Schools were a matter of course, like the air we breathe." No longer was that the case. Early hope that the depression would soon end and all would return to normal had proved too optimistic. The depression continued, and the federal government was creating national educational programs of its own for youth, preschool children, and adults, with little planning or involvement from educational leaders. Teachers continued to experience economic insecurity, rural children still lacked even basic educational opportunities, and youth faced unemployment. In the midst of such challenges the EPC was determined not to write yet another report to sit on library shelves. Its goal was rather to enlist "lay groups of unquestioned influence and power . . . in support of a program of public education."[69]

The EPC planned a series of reports on the purposes of education, the role of the schools in securing democracy, the economic contributions and needs of the public schools, and the structure and governance of public education. It hoped to go beyond the usual threadbare arguments about public education as a generator of wealth, a foe of crime, and a guarantee of civic virtue. The EPC publicized the work of groups like the American Council on Education, the American

Youth Commission (both also supported by the General Education Board), and President Roosevelt's Advisory Commission on Education. By 1938 it was ready to give mass publicity to its own work, distributing tens of thousands of copies of its publications, securing editorials in the press and articles in professional and lay magazines, being the focus of an entire conference of the American Association of School Administrators to discuss its policy recommendations, and sponsoring a conference of "organized labor, agriculture, business, racial, religious, and civic groups" to enlist their support.[70]

From one point of view the EPC was a continuation of the earlier efforts of the national educational elite to consolidate its power, to define the normal and the desirable, and to set the policy agenda. One EPC member, Frederick Hunter, expressed this elitist conception when he said that EPC definition of democracy was that of Mazzini: "the progress of all through all under the leadership of the wisest and best." They had no wish to discard the mantle of scientific expertise, but they merged this source of legitimation with a renewed concern for the role of education as a means of sustaining democracy. They sounded again the older evangelical tone of Horace Mann. Hunter spoke this way: "In no selfish way do we look upon education as a great cause; of course you and I are investing our lives in it, but after all, the highest and finest idealism that can motivate life is to invest with reasonable return in so great a purpose as the triumph of democracy through education. Let us forget small issues, personalities, local factionalism; let us forget petty selfishness at this tragic time, this time of great crisis."[71]

In the late 1930s, the EPC attempted to create a consensus within the profession about the purposes of education and to persuade the public of the need for a vigorous system of public schools. It was an insider's view of a proper social contract, one which deplored lay "political" meddling with educational matters and which reflected much of the way of thinking of the earlier "educational trust." But the commission did address real issues—fascism and retrenchment and unemployment were not mirages—and probably did much both to create a sense of common cause among educators and to convince citizens that public education was vital to the public interest.[72]

Political Action at the State Level

Attacking budget slashers as selfish and un-American, publicizing
the good work done by schools, and involving the public in discussion
about the common good in education—these were consistent with
the ideology of public educators, if not always with their practice.
What about direct political action—for example, in securing better
state or federal fiscal support of schools? Here one finds considerable
ambivalence among the educators of the 1930s. They did not regard
themselves as "lobbyists" or "politicians." An NEA official in 1930
expressed what was then an orthodox view of educators' proper role
in state school legislation. Professionals had useful expertise to offer
legislators and were adept in long-term planning for the public good.
But they were not to sully themselves by politicking: "Generally
speaking, experience seems to show that it is unwise to enter into
any form of alliance, concession, or bargain to secure the passage
of school legislation. 'Be sure you are right, then go ahead' is a good
motto for a program of school legislation. When the school people
begin to bargain, they weaken their fundamental position." Even
though school people had shaped school legislation more than any
other state interest group, the attitude of many educators toward
lawmakers was one of disdain and fear of contamination: "No one
having the slightest acquaintance with the ignorance, selfishness,
greed, partnership, logrolling, and hamstringing to be found in the
average legislature," said one educator, "can have any great respect
for all provisions of law simply because they happened to be passed
by the legislature."[73]
    When educators entered state politics, they typically portrayed
themselves as St. George, wrapped in the sacred insignia of their
cause, sallying forth to take on the dragon of selfishness. That may
have been in fact politically astute. In actual combat, however, they
often allied with groups they had previously condemned as shortsighted. The National Association of Real Estate Boards, composed
of local members who wanted lower local property taxes, proved to
be a useful partner in securing more state funding through sales and
other non-property taxes. Likewise, educators often portrayed farmers as opposed to educational progress—especially for their opposition to eliminating one-room schools—but in places like Illinois

and California, educators found farmers useful members of a coalition to shift the costs of education more to the state level.[74]

A spokesman for Phi Delta Kappa explained why the organization had abandoned "the traditional policy of innocuous impotence." In prosperous times the notion that schools were above politics might have worked (partly because the very ideal of leadership by disinterested experts was itself a politically clever ploy), but in hard times more aggressive tactics seemed necessary. Politics were dirty only because clean people did not engage in it; and who were cleaner, better informed, or more honorable in intentions than educators? Accordingly, the Council of Phi Delta Kappa adopted policies favoring political activism by the brotherhood. It applauded the work of its members in Oregon in defeating a constitutional amendment limiting taxation, in California in raising the state grants to schools, in Texas in opposing a one-third cut in the state budget, and in Utah and Alabama in electing schoolmen to the legislatures. An editorial in *Texas Outlook* also scorned the idea that teachers should stay out of politics. "We used to hear the same thing in reference to women. We hear the same thing with regard to preachers. In fact, you are likely to hear the same remark about any class, profession, or individual—when some complaining demagog or private interest has reason to fear the effects of the proclaiming of some militant truth."[75]

School people campaigned for federal aid to public education—unsuccessfully, as we shall describe in the next chapter. They won many battles against retrenchment in local districts. But they won their most signal successes in state legislatures, where they and their allies pressed for local property tax relief and for added state taxes and revenues for schools. Between 1929–30 and 1939–40 the states increased their contribution of total school expenditures from 16.9 percent to 30.3, almost doubling the ratio. In 1934 alone twenty-seven states considered school finance reform, ranging from relieving the burden of bonded indebtedness to reapportioning state funds to raising new income and sales taxes. Educators pushed hard for laws that would earmark new revenues for schools so that they would not have to compete with other agencies for scarce resources (in 1935, for example, eleven states earmarked part or all of the personal income taxes they collected for the use of public education). In 1930 only seven states provided 30 percent or more of total school funds;

by 1934 eighteen did so, including North Carolina, which paid essentially all costs for eight months of schooling by 1933. All told, thirty-two states increased their proportional contribution of public school budgets between 1929–30 and 1933–34, while sixteen decreased their ratio. Some states used the additional revenues to bring about somewhat greater fiscal equity between rich and poor districts, but the primary purpose of state aid was to provide local tax relief.[76]

Politicized educators also sought and obtained greater job security by passing state tenure laws. And in practically every state, school people raised entry requirements into the profession by pushing for new certification laws. The combined effect of such legislation was to raise the value of the jobs held by educators. Educators also pressed legislatures to grant greater discretion to school administrators over budgets and the hiring of teachers.[77]

A study by Irving Hendrick of school finance reform in California illustrates how educators and some unlikely allies worked together to secure more dollars for local districts. California schools were far more fortunate than most others in the nation. California's per-pupil expenditures were at or near the top of all states, while its cities maintained their tax collections better than most of those elsewhere. San Francisco passed a large bond levy in 1933 for building new schools, while Los Angeles stayed far more solvent than most big cities. In the golden state, however, there was suffering of the kind described by John Steinbeck, and there was sufficient radicalization that a socialist, Upton Sinclair, won the Democratic nomination for governor in 1934 and campaigned with the slogan "END POVERTY IN CALIFORNIA!" The governor in 1933 was James Rolph, Jr., who was determined to cut the state budget at the expense of the schools by dropping an annual state grant per student from $30 (a figure set in 1920) to $24, to remove budget control from local school boards, and to curtail a number of school programs. Legislators were introducing bills to repeal tenure for teachers, to abandon adult education and kindergartens, and to slash budgets. Such proposals, wrote the *Los Angeles Examiner*, were "put forward by pinchpenny politicians who want to save on education, not for the avowed purpose of balancing state budgets, but to have more money to squander on their friends and supporters."[78]

A lopsided tax structure compounded school finance problems.

Schools and other local and county services were funded primarily from local sources—85 percent from the property tax—while powerful corporate lobbies composed mostly of utility companies fought to keep down state expenditures even though their tax rates were well below those of homeowners. Between 1911–12 and 1930–31 the proportion of school funds coming from the state had declined from 24 percent to 15 percent. Pressed to draw funds from local taxpayers, educators saw their own incomes drop 20 percent from 1930–31 to 1932–33 while all other units of government in the state lost only 3.5 percent.[79]

By 1932 the enemies of educators were obvious: the governor, tax-cutting legislators, and the lobbies for retrenchment symbolized by the California Taxpayers Association, a group heavily subsidized by utility companies that used its high-minded rhetoric as a cloak for their desire to evade taxes. A researcher of the California Teachers Association put the call to battle this way: "Educators, like the public generally, have always been prone to endure much, and to accept attack without active resistance. This attitude of non-resistance may be laudable where only their own interests are at stake. When, however, as at present, the rising generation of California citizens are threatened with a curtailment of their rights and opportunities, the time has arrived for open warfare in behalf of the accepted principles of American political and social democracy."[80]

Educators in California mobilized to fight the battle on two fronts— local and state. In local districts they pursued the strategy of better public relations. The president of the California Teachers Association warned against "the tendency of some school people to arrogate unto themselves complete ownership of all things educational," a habit that was "partly responsible for the present unrest and distrust in education and educators." To restore confidence required "help from everywhere, from our co-workers, from parents, from taxpayers, and from leading laymen." The best approach, he said, was to assemble people and say to them: "These are your schools. These are your children. Here are the facts. Here are my recommendations. What suggestions and criticisms have you to make for the best interests of the education of our children?" Schools did enjoy considerable support in local districts. In 1933–34, 133 communities voted to determine whether to exceed the state-mandated minimum level of increased budget of 5 percent; in all but one district the people favored higher levels.[81]

On the state level the California Teachers Association (CTA) acted in a more direct political fashion by forming coalitions and trying to exert direct pressure on legislators. It was necessary, they believed, to change "antiquated tax laws" in the interest of greater equity between districts and more state aid as relief to the pressed property owners. It was also important to work as a veto group to defeat legislation adverse to educators, and here the CTA was successful in defeating bills to destroy tenure, to compromise the fiscal independence of school districts, and to retrench in school services. They were sufficiently potent as a veto group that the *Los Angeles Times* editorialized that timid legislators were caving in to the "taxeater" lobby of the teachers.[82]

In 1932 the CTA was ready to make its first major push for tax reform in alliance with the Real Estate Association, the County Supervisors Association, the Tax Equalization League, and other groups. Though some of the other groups were less than enthusiastic about helping the schools fiscally, they did want to cut property taxes and needed the large membership of the CTA and its links to local electorates for getting signatures for an initiative measure and for rousing the voters. The CTA managed to persuade its fellow lobbyists to press for laws that would more than double the state appropriation per child, impose a sales tax, and require counties to levy enough taxes to meet the budgets set by local school districts. The package proved too costly for the voters to accept, especially since the governor warned of a higher total tax bill.[83]

The tax initiative that finally won voter approval was designed not by the CTA but by an official of the Farm Bureau Federation. The measure shifted the school tax burden of $30 for each elementary pupil and $60 for each high school student from counties to the state; it also limited tax increases for schools to 5 percent of the previous year's total in individual districts (a measure far less crippling in a time of deflation or slow rise in prices than of inflation). This initiative passed in 1933, buoyed by the claim that it would provide tax relief to homeowners and farmers while it also "saved the schools." That year the legislature also passed new taxes to raise school revenue. The result of the new funding was a dramatic increase in the percentage of total district costs borne by the state, from 26 percent in 1932–33 to 55 percent in 1933–34. The new sources of funding increased school funds by 11 percent in the next two years, while teachers' salaries rose and were less subject to local fluctuations because a large portion of state funds were earmarked for that purpose. The CTA had good reason to believe that it had won the war even though it had lost some skirmishes. By 1936 the state superintendent of schools, who had asked educators to "meet the challenge of the new day" in the early 1930s, could announce that confidence had been restored in teachers: "Unselfish, devoted servants of youth and adults, they are fired with a missionary zealousness making them the grandest army fighting for righteousness in our commonwealth." Likewise for the administrators: "Their leadership is acknowledged; their eminence recognized." And so the political story ended—for a time—to the tune of "Onward Christian Soldiers."[84]

A Tale of Two Cities

As in the different state capitals, so in local communities the politics of dollars in public education varied enormously. As we have shown, the impact of the depression was highly unequal depending on local economic structure and wealth. But differences of response also reflected the political cultures of different communities and the kind of leadership provided by local school boards and superintendents. In some places where there was a strong consensus in favor of education, citizens sought to hold the schools immune insofar as possible from the effects of depression, while in others the politics of scarcity brought bitter conflict and gutted school systems. Chicago and Detroit illustrate the importance of such local political cultures in mitigating or exacerbating the impact of retrenchment.

Alike in many other ways, Chicago and Detroit had very different educational histories in the depths of the great depression. The maelstrom hit both cities with devastating force, driving hundreds of thousands into unemployment and pushing the city governments close to bankruptcy as they strove to relieve suffering, maintain public services, pay off civic debts incurred before the crash, and collect taxes from impoverished or obstinate property owners. In both cities, committees composed of financiers and elite businessmen gained great power in shaping public budgets because their approval was a prerequisite for the bank loans needed to keep city services operating. In effect, Detroit and Chicago were in receivership to these representatives of big business, who retained veto power over public expenditures and who were primarily interested in cutting taxes to the bone in order to bring budgets more closely in balance. The president of Chicago's Joint Conference of Teachers and Principals put this extraordinary private power over the public wealth this way: "Since the American people have permitted private banks to become practically the sole custodians of credit for public as well as private purposes, veto power over the extension of that credit becomes as effective a weapon of dictatorship as would the control of any military force." The business elites of the 1930s often sought to eliminate, for reasons of economy, some of the very programs that earlier elites had worked to introduce into American public schools. But the actual politics of money in Detroit and Chicago schools in the early 1930s turned out quite differently, despite these similarities of context.[85]

To educators across the nation, Chicago was a byword for political corruption and insensitivity, "financial fascism," and suffering among teachers and pupils. The financial problems of the Chicago schools started well before the crash. Throughout most of the 1920s the school system had been badly managed fiscally and was a notorious source of graft and patronage for crooked politicians. Well before the depression it had adopted the practice of borrowing money to cover the next year's expenses. By 1928 it had already spent eleven years of taxes in the previous ten years. Large corporations and landholders had been dodging taxes or had obtained ridiculously low property assessments. Wealthy property-holders organized a tax strike. As early as December 1929, teachers got their first taste of payless days. By May 1932 the city owed teachers $20 million, or $1,400 apiece. Losing their savings when banks failed, cashing in their insurance policies, giving up their homes for cash equity to feed their families, teachers were nearing the breaking point. Coming daily into contact with the children of the slums, where unemployment, hunger, and desperation were destroying families, they were witness to disaster and struggled as best they could to find clothing and food for their pupils.[86]

Fred W. Sargent was president of the Chicago and Northwestern Railroad and chairman of the Citizen's Committee on Public Expenditures, which served as an arbiter of public spending. His priorities in public services were clear: "First on the list of essentials comes police, fire, and health protection in the order named." He demanded that educational expenditures be slashed by 33 percent below the tax rates authorized by the legislature while other city costs would be cut by only 11 percent. The committee was determined to cut the educational program back to the three *R*s, observed one teacher, and "to starve the teaching force into submission to their programme and to cripple the city's educational system."[87]

Most of the members of the school board during the early depression had been holdovers from the corrupt administration of Mayor William Hale Thompson. While preserving the salaries of their cronies—the school "engineers" (or custodians) and other sources of patronage and graft in the business department—the appointed board members trimmed instructional programs and teachers' salaries. But it was left to a later board, appointed by Mayor Edward J. Kelly, to make the deepest cuts in the "fads and frills" that were anathema to the financiers. Kelly was a machine politician acceptable to Sargent and a protégé of the owner of the *Chicago Tribune*, a major advocate for budget-cutting in education. On July 12, 1933, the members of that board voted to fire 1,400 teachers (10 percent of the total number), cut kindergartens by half, abolish the junior high school system, slash physical education programs, require elementary principals to supervise two schools, discontinue the junior college, abolish continuation schools and the bureau of special education, stop buying textbooks, and drop or curtail several other services. A teacher observed: "Superintendent Bogan had not been consulted in any way on this tearing up of the entire instructional system, planned by coal dealers and other small businessmen with little education themselves, and only a few days of service on the Board of Education . . . Superintendent Bogan sat with his grey head in his hands and said nothing. He did everything he could to prevent such a disaster." The coal dealers saw to it that the coal companies were paid, but the teachers continued to subsidize the system with payless weeks and months. A board member gave his comment on the cuts: "I ain't got no axe to grind . . . the young people of today are getting so much education that they don't know what to do when they get out of school."[88]

Appalled citizens reacted swiftly. Teachers, PTA members, and women's clubs formed a "Save Our Schools Committee" to protest, and in two weeks collected 350,000 signatures on a petition to the board that deplored such cuts made without consultation or public hearings. At a mass meeting of more than 25,000 people at the Stadium, representatives of the Chicago Federation of Labor, the University of Chicago, and the PTA spoke against "unfair reduction of taxes for big taxpayers and political control of school jobs." Teachers volunteered to work without pay until the deficits were cleared if the board would restore the cuts and if it would permit an independent firm to audit its books.[89]

But the protest failed. Protected by the political machine, supported by the business elite, and knowing that the large proportion of the citizens who sent their children to parochial schools would not feel the cuts so harshly, the board "maintained a sphinx-like silence toward all questions or objections," wrote Mary Herrick, an observer and historian of the debacle. President Robert Hutchins of the University of Chicago said in an editorial that the board's behavior was based "either on a complete misunderstanding of the purpose of public education, a selfish determination that its purpose shall not be fulfilled, or an ignorant belief that a system which has been wrecked can still function. The economic and social condition of Chicago will be worse for twenty-five years because of what the Board of Education has done."[90]

In Detroit, by contrast, no teachers were fired, their salaries mostly kept pace with the deflated cost of living, and the educational program was preserved largely intact, even though the city was ravaged by the depression. A study by Jeffrey Mirel of the politics of retrenchment there provides important clues about why Detroit differed from Chicago.

Detroit staggered under the impact of the depression. An estimated half of its workers were unemployed or only working part-time, and its rates of tax delinquency (over one-third in 1932–33) were the worst in the nation. As revenues slid, the city government under Mayor Frank Murphy, a liberal, faced a growing burden of public relief for the unemployed added to the costs of maintaining other public services like education. When Detroit tried to borrow money to keep going and to avoid bankruptcy, it found it needed the approval of a Committee on City Finance headed by the banker Ralph Stone. Like Sargent's committee in Chicago, this was a group of private citizens from the major businesses of the community. Despite the fact that it had no official standing in law, it had immense power derived from its ability to veto needed loans. As Mirel writes, "Throughout Murphy's administration the Mayor publicly denounced the growing control of 'economic royalists' and 'financial dictators,' but the Stone committee, in fact, had a stranglehold on the public purse." Unlike the situation in Chicago, where the machine politicians were mostly willing to toe the line proposed by the Sargent committee, liberal public officials in Detroit had a running war with the financiers.[91]

The seven school board members of the early 1930s were, like the Stone committee, drawn mostly from the city's prosperous social elite. Four were listed in the social register. Since the "good government" charter revision of 1917, the board of education had closely conformed to the corporate model of urban school governance and had modernized the school system in accordance with the program of the administrative progressives. On issues basic to the continuation of capitalism they remained conservative; they denied left-wing groups permission to hold rallies in school buildings, for example, and continued Detroit's rigid tracking system for "abstract-minded" and "motor-minded" students. But they, like Murphy, frequently fought the Stone committee and sought to preserve teachers' salaries and to maintain the new elements of the school program—the supposed fads and frills—added during the 1920s.[92]

Superintendent Frank Cody, appointed in 1918, lasted in the job an astonishing twenty-three years. He was an astute politician and publicist who worked effectively with his staff and the elite board. He urged others to work openly as defenders of the system while he operated behind the scenes with his customary wit and political savvy to influence newspaper people and community influentials. His strategy, his staff said, was to retreat here and there in retrenchment, "husbanding his forces, regretfully increasing pupil-teacher ratios, junking the new building program, lopping off a course here and there. But his plan was balanced, it had its limitations; and when he had reached his winter line of defense, he halted." In the midst of the pressures for budget cuts he prepared 260,000 leaflets that claimed that the average homeowner got his money's worth for the $1.76 per month he paid for the schools. Well-connected in state educational and political circles, he helped to spearhead the drive for increased state funding. He kept an open door to militant members of the American Federation of Teachers and recognized that pressure from teachers was part of the political field of forces that could mitigate retrenchment.[93]

Under pressure from Stone, and recognizing that the city deficits were becoming intolerable, the school board and Cody did cut teachers' salaries during the worst days of the depression. After the bank failures, staff went without pay for short periods or received discounted scrip—a fate painful to Cody, who had called payday "the most beautiful word in the English language." Despite complaints from financiers and the conservative Detroit *Free Press*, this opposition to retrenchment was popular with the voters and with the labor press. The teachers organized themselves politically and worked actively to elect favorable school board members. They also lobbied—as did Cody—for more state aid. A committee on school salaries appointed by Mayor Murphy pointed out that the teachers were poorly paid in comparison with those in other large cities and recommended only small cuts. In an election on April 6, 1931, citizens reelected two board members who had supported teachers' raises and soundly defeated a candidate who had called for more retrenchment.[94]

The most heated political conflict in the early 1930s in Detroit arose over "fads and frills" in the school curriculum: art, music, physical education and athletics, and manual training and home economics. With the exception of one maverick board member, the school committee supported these additions to the curriculum while business conservatives railed against them, as in Chicago. School board members who defended the modern curriculum won elections over critics. A wide spectrum of civic groups also gave their support for the expanded scope of the school, ranging from socialist newspapers (who saw the retrenchment battle as an instance of class conflict), to liberal politicians, to trade unionists, to elite women's clubs and the American Legion. By the end of 1933 the defenders of the modern subjects had largely won the battle.[95]

Class loyalties and interests explain only part of the alignments in Detroit's educational politics of retrenchment. The school board came mostly from class backgrounds similar to those of the budget-slashing financiers. But as competing elites the financiers and the school board differed sharply on whether the school budgets were bloated or necessary. The board members committed themselves to preserving the school system they had helped to build in the 1920s. In 1933 six of the seven were serving their second six-year terms. "Long years of service to an institution," comments Mirel, "can create a loyalty which transcends other powerful social influences." People often did not interpret their class interests in the same way in education. Socialists had a different set of social goals from those of the school board, but they also strongly fought retrenchment. Trade union people differed on "fads and frills." School politics in Detroit showed that people of different classes and ideologies could work together to maintain the school system, and that people of the same class could contend with one another.[96]

The tale of the two cities, like the other complexities of the politics we have examined in this chapter, suggests the powerful impact of state and local political cultures and economic structures on educational decision-making in the era of retrenchment. These pluralistic patterns of interests and power, these competing elites, produced quite different results in different places. But people could argue fiercely about the particulars in part because they did not dissent on fundamentals. Critics said they were not attacking public schools but only certain costly accretions or self-aggrandizing educators. Even in Chicago the school board members took great pains to show how patriotically they had kept the school doors open. And despite challenges to capitalism by a small band of social reconstructionists, who wanted a new social order, public school politics took place well within a zone of tolerance comfortable to those who profited most from the old order.

3 A New Deal in Education?

The children in a nursery school in Philadelphia invented a new game—eviction. They collected all the doll furniture in one corner, then moved it to another. "We ain't got no money for the rent, so we's moved into a new house," one of them said to the teacher. "Then we got the constable on us, so we's movin' again." In the daycare center the preschoolers from families on relief found a refuge from cold tenements and bare dinner tables. They built block castles or dressed dolls in a warm, well-lighted room. They ate hot lunches. They received medical care. But they carried the memories of what they saw and heard on the outside with them into that haven.[1]

The men rolled into camp in army trucks, hot and dusty from clearing fire trails or building stone culverts. They showered, gulped down dinner, and decided how they were going to spend the long summer evening. About half went to the classes the camp's educational adviser had arranged. The army captain in charge of the camp taught a course called "Decisive Battles of the World"; a foreman showed enrollees how to repair auto engines; a corpsman coached men who wanted to build radios; some went to class to learn business English. Dozens learned to read. For many of the corpsmen it was the first time they had been in a school since the elementary grades.[2]

In the rural South young men and women who lived in isolated shacks—many of them in hovels without doors and with cotton plants and weeds marching up to the foundations—began to gather in training classes and in resident centers. Few of them had had more than the first years of elementary schooling. In one sewing class in the Kentucky mountains, a sewing supervisor asked the sixteen girls in her group what were the major events of the past year. "My grandmother died," said one. "It sleeted," said another. "The flood," mentioned a third. No one knew who was the governor of the state, though one thought it might be Abraham Lincoln. In Arkansas 445 boys and girls, mostly from tenant and sharecropper families, lived together in houses called resident centers, where they learned new techniques for raising livestock, dairying, halting erosion, and growing vegetables. Boys worked at welding, auto repair, operating power plants, and forestry. Girls learned to remodel homes, make table linens and curtains from flour sacks, plan and cook meals for their group, and provide first aid and home care of the sick. Some of the youths had never had a full meal in their lives, and most gained ten to twenty pounds during the first six weeks.[3]

These examples illustrate the New Deal style in education. Not public education, for such programs were not part of the mainstream of the public school system. Not common schooling aimed at all segments of the population, for they were specifically designed for the poor and staffed largely by people on relief. Not based on the canons of professionalism and designed by certified experts, but premised on the notion that all kinds of people can teach and that learning can take place in all kinds of settings. But these New Deal ventures in educating the poor—like the New Deal programs to enhance and disseminate both popular and high culture by employing artists and scholars—did constitute a new vision of the education of the public.

Leaders in the public schools at first hoped that Franklin D. Roosevelt and his New Deal would assist them through federal aid and honor them and their mission. In this they were disappointed. Hope for a sympathetic ear turned to ambivalence toward the federal government and then hostility to the alternative educational institutions the New Deal had created alongside the public schools.

Historians disagree about the extent to which the New Deal was evolutionary or revolutionary in its policies and programs for relief, social welfare, economic recovery, and relations between labor and capital. Nevertheless, few would deny that in the 1930s the political parties were realigned and the size and cost of the federal government

Young women making pies at Lakeview (a Farm Security Administration Project). Phillips County, Alabama, 1938. Photo by Russell Lee.

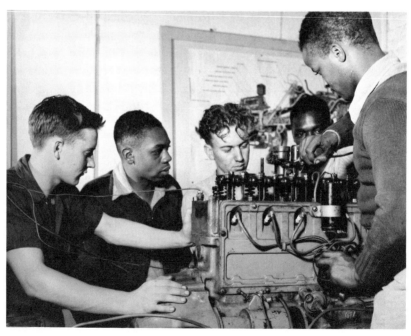

CCC men learning engine repair. Unidentified photo, CCC files, National Archives.

were transformed. The paid civilian employees of the federal government rose sharply from 603,587 in 1933 to 1,042,420 in 1940; budget outlays jumped in those years from $4.7 billion to $9.6 billion. In 1930 local public expenditures exceeded federal, but by the mid-1930s the central government far outspent local agencies. The nature of aggregated federal-state-local social welfare expenditures changed also. In 1930 education took by far the largest chunk of such welfare budgets, but in the early 1930s public aid (relief) and then veterans' benefits exceeded education's share of the total. Not only new patterns of expenditure but also new agencies altered the power of the central government in an era of transition to a welfare state.[4]

These changes in the scope and functions of the central government, however, altered the political economy of public education only a little. The New Deal may have been a watershed in politics and in the centralization of government, but it was clearly not one in the governance and finance of public schools. Public schools gained slightly in federal funds, but the total barely exceeded 1 percent of total expenditure until 1940, when it reached 1.59 percent—still far short of what educators wanted.[5]

Why was it, then, that the confident expectations of educators for federal aid were so baffled? Why did the New Deal attempt its educational experiments—many of them imaginative and effective— outside or at the margins of the public schools, choosing to create new institutions rather than institutionalizing innovation within the school system? What were the long-term consequences of seeking to build alternative bureaucracies—short-lived, as it turned out— instead of trying to assist and reform an old and established agency? In this chapter we explore some answers.

A Moral Equivalent of War

In the early days of the New Deal some educators spoke of it as practically the Second Coming. The magic of Franklin D. Roosevelt's rhetoric seemed to express their deepest hopes. "What some choose to call the national recovery program or the 'New Deal' is in reality an effort to accomplish by legislation and government action the very things that education in the past should have accomplished," said the New York City school superintendent in 1934. Another NEA

WHY THE DISCRIMINATION?
This cartoon illustrates the resentment educators felt at being left behind while the New Deal marched other groups to the "Recovery Show." Source: *Phi Delta Kappan* 17 (February 1935): 127 (originally published in a pamphlet by the National Committee for Federal Aid to Education).

leader declared in October 1933: "If we are to succeed, we must find a moral equivalent to war to hold us together. Perhaps that moral equivalent lies in the new recovery act." In Texas that fall the state educational magazine proudly displayed the eagle of the National Recovery Administration (NRA), while the Pep Squad of Breck-enridge High School formed itself on the football field into a giant NRA. The superintendent of schools in California urged teachers to explain the NRA to students. Other leaders, from professors to the governor of Hawaii, urged up-to-date social studies instructors to teach the new consensus on social planning. So ardent were such friends in the schools that the NRA warned against using schools for propaganda purposes.[6]

"No group of people in America is more in sympathy with the social ideals and objectives of the New Deal than are teachers," asserted the executive secretary of the NEA. An observer at the

Department of Superintendence in 1933 wrote that educators were militantly determined to create "a world good enough for their pupils to live in and productive enough to support our people and their schools. They insist on being the co-fashioner as well as the servant of the new deal." They hoped—indeed, assumed—that the federal government would assist them in financing and reforming public education. An NEA committee declared that "the necessity of greatly increased federal cooperation in education is evident to all who accept the New Deal . . . The New Deal has now accepted that unity of national interest which school workers have long maintained exists with reference to public education." On occasion Roosevelt himself was quite capable of echoing the sentiment that public education uniquely reflected the common good. "The teachers of America," he told the NEA, "are the ultimate guardians of the human capital of America." Both educators and Roosevelt shared a taste for a rhetoric of hope, set to a background of millennial music. Had not the President included education as a fundamental human need when he intoned in his inaugural address that "the only thing we have to fear is fear itself"?[7]

But the resemblance was only abstract and rhetorical. The honeymoon between educators and the New Deal did not last long, at least for most leaders in public education. By February 1934 the *NEA Journal* was complaining about the New Deal's neglect of public schools. By 1935 the mood was even angrier. A writer for the U.S. Office of Education reported to the New Deal director of press relations that the leaders of the NEA were furious about how they and the commissioner of education had been neglected in policy-making: Roosevelt's "declared aims to help the common people are the aims [educators] have pursued for years. But when it comes to carrying out some of these social improvements the leadership of these groups has been flouted. Their proposals have received a chilly reception. *Writing as an objective reporter* I can say that person after person in education, feels that the President has gone out of his way to kick their professions in the shins. The only group that gets a break is the *social service group*." Leaders of the NEA began to attack the Civilian Conservation Corps (CCC), the National Youth Administration (NYA), and the administration of education programs under the Works Progress Administration (WPA). First the NEA leaders asked that the educational functions of these New Deal agencies be transferred to the Office of Education and run by public educators, and then they called for the abolition of the agencies through an EPC report and by lobbying in the Congress.[8]

Educators were mostly agreed on what they wanted from the federal government: financial assistance without control. "Leave the teaching to us" might have been the motto of the guild called the NEA. An official of the Civilian Conservation Corps (CCC) thought that public educators seemed "opposed to anyone but school people teaching anybody anything." In fact educational leaders were committed to protecting their turf, seeing all instruction as the province of licensed professionals. Credentials could be—and were—justified as a guarantee of expertise and quality in instruction. But such professionalism could also be interpreted in economic terms as a protective tariff for jobs endangered by the depression. Investment in training and time on the job were the only kind of "capital" that many teachers possessed, and certification and tenure gave some security in an uncertain time. New Dealers seemed ready to hire nonprofessionals to do professional work, perhaps because of "political" motivation. In the 1930s educators felt safer in leaving control of schooling in the domain of state and local governments.[9]

Although school people feared federal domination, they wanted federal money. A decade before the depression had imperiled local and state finances, leading educators had developed a case for federal aid to public schools. In 1918 the NEA had appointed a Commission on the Emergency in Education with George Strayer as chairman. The "emergency" had arisen when the wartime draft had shown that millions of young men were poorly educated, many of them illiterate and in bad health. Strayer's committee pointed out that the sources of these deficiencies were miserable rural schools, especially in the South and other poor regions, badly trained teachers, and inequitable financing of schools. It called for the distribution of $100 million by the federal government to remedy these conditions. Little came of the campaign, but a large number of states did seek to equalize somewhat the disparities of opportunity in schools by providing "foundation grants," or flat-sum allocations to school districts on a per-pupil formula. President Hoover's blue-ribbon National Advisory Committee on Education—which well represented the views of the educational establishment—also discussed federal aid to public schools in its report in 1931. That commission was highly disenchanted with federal programs that sought to install and direct specific programs (like vocational education mandated by the Smith-Hughes Act of 1917 and controlled by a federal board) and it extolled local and state control as the American way. But it did open the door to possible federal grants to states for purposes they should determine, if and when studies should show them to be necessary. The only restriction, the commission said, should be a report to Washington on how the money was spent.[10]

The rapid forced retrenchment in the early 1930s and many studies of fiscal inequities convinced educators that federal aid was indeed a necessity. Paul Mort was one of the leaders in school finance reform and head of the National Survey of School Finance supported by the General Education Board. He wrote in 1935 that "all signs point to the need of a thoroughgoing program of federal participation in the financing of education. Nearly half a million classrooms are operating with financial support below what can reasonably be taken as an American standard of public education." State tax reform was proceeding fast and was helping to lessen intrastate inequalities. Great inequalities between states, however, made some form of federal relief essential. The migration of people from poor rural areas to cities, from the South to the North, made the quality of schooling a national question. And because of the highly unequal distribution of wealth between rich states and poor ones, destitute states like Mississippi would not have come up to a decent level of support even if they had devoted *all* their taxation to public schools.[11]

The argument of Mort and the other school finance reformers seemed sound and in keeping with the desire of New Dealers to reach the most needy. Roosevelt and his officials repeatedly said that insofar as the federal government should be involved in financing education, it should be to raise "the level at the bottom." But the actual programs the NEA and other prominent groups sponsored in their bills before Congress and in their publications left much to be desired if the central goal were to equalize educational funding and to reach primarily the poor. There was no guarantee that when the federal government put the money on the stump, the states would use it mainly to improve the education of the poor. Indeed, in the South the white power structure had systematically cheated black education and continued to do so throughout the 1930s, as black leaders testified in Congress. And for political reasons having to do with the constituencies and structure of the NEA, it was highly unlikely that the group would support legislation that gave nothing to prosperous states while funneling money to the impoverished. The NEA was, in essence, a coalition of state associations. The state units reflected the values and distribution of power within the states. Southern NEA affiliates, for example, remained segregated until the 1960s. To gain unity on federal aid such a coalition as the NEA needed to give something to each of its component parts, since benefits for poor Arkansas meant nothing concretely to comparatively rich Nevada.[12]

The so-called foundation plans used in state finance illustrate the principle at the state level. Although formulas for state aid varied, typically the foundation plans gave uniform state aid to districts per pupil (sometimes the amount varied depending on whether the students were elementary or secondary). Such a measure did, of course, have an equalizing effect and was intended to place a floor (or foundation) under local finance of schools. If one district had an average per-pupil cost of $100 and another $35, and both were given $15, the "foundation" helped the poorer district more than the richer. The absolute gap remained intolerable, however, if one wanted to sever the connection between place of residence and equality of educational opportunity. The same problem arose with most of the plans for federal aid to the states.

Mort was a liberal who wrote eloquently about the need to help the needy districts. The plan he devised under the National Survey of School Finance in 1935 illustrates, however, how inadequately federal aid would have addressed the underlying problem. He found that at the tenth percentile of district costs per pupil the range went in 1930–31 from $12.66 in Arkansas to $78.15 in New York. He proposed that the federal government should implement a $15 foundation plan that, according to a complicated formula, would give states a range from $6 for Delaware (the richest state in school resources) to $11.84 for South Carolina (the poorest). This was better than a flat grant to each state, but not much. While he advocated further federal funding to equalize schools up to a $60 per-pupil level, he apparently believed that the lower sum was all that was politically feasible and all that the poorer states could initially use with efficiency. And his other form of federal support—aid in the construction of consolidated rural schools—was one that applied to all states (though more to some than to others).[13]

From 1933 to 1943 the NEA and its allies continued to press for general federal aid, making an especially concerted effort in 1934, 1937, and 1939. The NEA's tactics were complicated. School people frequently attacked New Deal figures for being too "political." Their own ideology dictated a low-profile approach to lobbying and a high-minded idealism in their frequent testimony and writings on federal aid. Publicly, they had what might be called a tooth-fairy view of politics—that self-evident virtue is what would attract funding. Behind the scenes, they were willing to deal.[14]

The NEA turned to Senator Patrick Harrison of Mississippi as their chief sponsor of bills and their main spokesman. Harrison was a segregationist who had opposed federal antilynching legislation and fought the enfranchisement of blacks. The NEA found him a staunch ally, however, and praised him after his death as "a splendid American and a true friend of education." Although he was in other respects a foe of centralization of power in the federal government, Harrison had repeatedly sought money from Washington to keep Mississippi schools open. The poorest of the states, it was seventh in the percentage of state income spent on the schools. Harrison saw in federal aid an opportunity to upgrade schools in Mississippi without breaking the state budget. His approach was similar to that of the NEA: money on the stump. The bill he sponsored in 1936 would have awarded $100 million to the states, divided according to the number of children from five to twenty in each state; states were to be free to spend the funds as they wished. The bill was redistributive to a degree: the funds would have come disproportionately from the richer states, and the poorer ones with large numbers of children would have been able to raise their per-pupil expenditures. But the flat rate per school-age child avoided the basic issue of equity for the poorest students while it seemed to reflect the bureaucratic norm of uniformity. This also matched the political interests of the NEA as a coalition of state associations.[15]

Educators thought in 1938 that their time had finally come when a commission appointed by Roosevelt to investigate federal-state-local relations strongly advocated federal aid. This presidential advisory committee on education, headed by Floyd Reeves of the University of Chicago, was a far more liberal group than the mainstream educational leaders of the 1931 presidential report. Educators on the committee were in a minority, surrounded by people from labor, industry, agriculture, and government. Supplemented by special reports on conditions in the schools and the work of New Deal agencies, the committee made an eloquent case for equalizing the funding of schools through federal grants. It proposed a more activist role for the national government in making sure that funds would go where they were intended—to the needy—and endorsed the idea that schooling could be used to promote social reform. It called for equal distribution of funds to blacks and whites, accepting the inevitability of segregation but demanding equity. It recommended that federal funds be given to private schools for textbooks, transportation, scholarships, and health services. On the crucial issue of how to allocate funds to provide equalization, the committee said that it was "reluctantly forced to the conclusion . . . that the statute providing for the proposed grants should avoid the specification in exact detail of any formula for the allocation of the funds to the states" and should only specify procedures and policies. In its other recommendations for federal aid—for improving teacher education, consolidating and building rural schools, and upgrading state departments of education—the benefits would have gone equally to all states.[16]

The Reeves report, as it became known, was considerably to the left of what most members of Congress—and many educators—wanted. Senator Harrison and the NEA assumed that because the president's own group had made the recommendations, the administration might help get a bill passed. They were mistaken. Even when the bill was reworded to remove any implication that the federal government could control education and to give the states control over the allocation of funds, an increasingly conservative and budget-minded Congress was not interested. The bill's coup de grace came when Floyd Reeves said in congressional testimony that Roosevelt was opposed to it.[17]

Federal-aid-to-education bills got nowhere on the Hill, in large part because of the opposition of Roosevelt. The president's men in Congress managed quietly to bottle the bills up in committee. Harrison repeatedly complained about being sandbagged by Alben Barkley and others who managed the discussion of bills. Congressmen listened politely to favorable committee testimony from educators. As the historian Gilbert E. Smith notes, however, the conservative leadership of the NEA—which represented a heavily Protestant, middle-class, and racially segregated confederation—was walking a tightrope. It needed the help of liberals in Congress, of Catholics, and of blacks in order to gain federal appropriations, yet its ideology of state and local control matched that of conservative Congressmen. And at home the superintendents feared alienating elite boards of education. At one point in 1937 some observers thought that a bill might pass if it reached the floor. But many Congressmen, like FDR, had doubts about federal aid. What would it do to the cherished principle of local control of schools? Some worried that parochial schools would get aid—or would not. A number of southerners were concerned that the federal government would force the South to allot the funds equally to black schools, while the National Association for the Advancement of Colored People worried that the federal government would not. Race, religion, and fears about radical centralized government—the three *R*s—undermined whatever slim support existed on the Hill for federal aid.[18]

Roosevelt and the Educational Establishment

Consistency has never been regarded as one of President Roosevelt's strong suits, but his policies toward public education form a coherent, if not entirely harmonious, pattern. Despite his reputation among conservatives as a spendthrift, he worried about deficits a great deal and sought to control spending. He was concerned, he wrote his wife, that federal aid to education could easily balloon the debt. He believed that public schools in general were in pretty good fiscal shape—as indeed they were, compared with many other sectors. He spoke of the need for "good business management and the doing away with the extravagance and frills" in public education. He thought teachers were fairly well paid.[19]

Helping schools by placing money on the stump was simply not a high enough priority for FDR to warrant spending the political chips necessary to get a federal aid bill through Congress. Eleanor Roosevelt believed that with "too many other pressing needs" her husband was unwilling to "expose himself on this kind of issue." Controversies over federal aid endangered his coalition of urban liberals—many of them Catholic and opposed to a bill that did not help parochial schools—and southern conservatives, many of whom feared disrupting the racist system in their states.[20]

Repeatedly, Roosevelt asserted that he believed in state and local control of schools. As governor of New York he had believed in that principle, and there is little evidence that he ever changed his conviction that the traditional governance and finance of public education should be maintained. In many respects he was quite conservative in his attitude toward basic institutions and indisposed to try to change them in fundamental ways. This was true of public education.[21]

But FDR's conservative impulse to leave institutions intact was tempered by his humanitarian desire to help the needy. One pragmatic way to preserve the structure of public education while assisting those on the bottom of society was to create alternative educational agencies to help the "underprivileged," and this is precisely what the New Dealers did through the NYA, the WPA, the CCC, and other new ventures. From Roosevelt's point of view, that approach had a number of advantages. It targeted funds and services directly to people who needed jobs and who could benefit from the new educational services. It cost far less than general federal aid, much of which would have gone to school systems that did not need the money, and agencies designed to meet supposedly temporary problems of relief could be cut back more easily than federal aid regarded as a continuing entitlement. And it was apparent to New Dealers that the Democratic Party would get the credit for such programs. In short, such ad hoc organizations gave the president more control over budgets and programs and recipients while he and his party reaped more political advantages than they would through costly general aid.[22]

In fact, Roosevelt, Harry Hopkins, Aubrey Williams, and Harold Ickes did funnel money into the public schools, although they did so through the mechanism of relief and public works rather than through direct support under the control of public educators. When FDR and his colleagues saw a pressing need—as in opening rural schools closed when taxes ran out—they found funds for teachers' salaries. Hopkins's Federal Emergency Relief Administration (FERA, the forerunner of the WPA) paid over $14 million to teachers in poor states like Alabama, Arkansas, Georgia, Louisiana, Mississippi, North Carolina, Oklahoma, Tennessee, Texas, and West Virginia. In Arkansas alone, the emergency funds kept open over 4,000 rural schools serving over 150,000 pupils. Nationwide, the figures of federal aid to teachers varied from month to month, but on the average probably over one million pupils were enabled to go to school because of FERA subsidies.[23]

Hopkins and FDR were determined, however, not to encourage states to substitute emergency federal money for their own funds, for they wanted the limited relief dollars to go to the most needy people. Hopkins used his influence to lever more adequate state support for schools. In Arkansas, for example, where a conservative governor had been starving the schools and had vowed to abolish state support for high schools, Hopkins cut off all federal emergency funds for relief until the legislature passed new revenue bills.[24]

Besides paying teachers' salaries in hard-pressed states, various New Deal agencies also aided local districts in consolidating and refinancing their debts and in constructing and repairing schools. From 1933 to 1939, the federal government aided 70 percent of all new school construction. By August 1, 1934, the public works authority had already allotted over $95 million of grants and loans for building and improving schools. Relief workers in the NYA and the WPA painted and restored tens of thousands of schools, bound school books, made or refinished furniture, and created jobs for teachers' aides, cafeteria workers in school lunch programs, and other workers in the schools.[25]

The total contribution of the New Deal to public education is hard to assess, in part because many of these funds were tucked away in relief budgets. Thus salaries for rural teachers in stricken states came from the FERA, support for the NYA came from WPA coffers rather than from a specific Congressional appropriation, and dollars to refinance school indebtedness came from the "Levee, Drainage, and Irrigation Division" of the Reconstruction Finance Corporation. Perhaps this approach of smuggling money to school projects arose from the president's doubts about asking for direct appropriations for schools. In 1935 Roosevelt told a group of state school superintendents that he had "stretched the law tremendously" in employing school teachers and in assisting students through the NYA to attend high school and college. He told them that he saw these strategies as "entering wedges" in teaching the Congress—"another place we have to start education," he said to the educators off the record—about the needs of the schools.[26]

However roundabout his strategies, Roosevelt's purposes were fairly clear. He wanted to use education to help people at the bottom of the social system. While he gave some assistance to regular schools for regular programs—as in paying rural teachers or building new schools—he and his staff were primarily interested in expanding and reforming that system to make it more responsive to what were called, in the language of the time, the "underprivileged," hoping that in time the innovations would be incorporated into the regular system. The New Dealers had a broad concept of education and groups to be educated, including nursery schools for the poor; varied programs of education for adults; learning by doing in CCC and NYA camps for youth; education through art, theater, and music programs; and educational components of programs like the Tennessee Valley Authority (TVA) and the Resettlement Administration for poor workers and farmers. An educator strongly opposed to the New Deal educational program nonetheless caught its significance. They were the result, he said, of "long generations of disappointing experience on the part of socially minded lay leaders with the traditional school." He observed that the past experience and present attitudes of school leaders gave social reformers "every reason to believe that if educators were called upon to do the job the program would be largely even if unintentionally sabotaged."[27]

Although they shared some of Roosevelt's desire to equalize education, members of the educational establishment took a different view of proper reform. They wanted from the federal government the freedom to administer all formal schooling, general financial aid without strings, and deference as fellow crusaders for public betterment. Educators failed to win any of these.

Roosevelt's lack of attention toward educators was a hard pill to swallow, for in the early phase of the New Deal many educators sensed that he was a kindred spirit. Most of the evidence suggests that Roosevelt did not have a high regard for what he called "the school crowd." He had little in common with the evangelical and prohibitionist Washington staff of the NEA, assembled under the Nebraska-bred James W. Crabtree. He saw them neither as a powerful potential constituency nor as people whose counsel he desired. When he wanted advice about education he turned to university elites (men like Professor Eduard Lindeman of the New School for Social Research and Presidents James Bryant Conant of Harvard, Frank Graham of North Carolina, and Robert Hutchins of Chicago); to people of a social-work background on his staff, such as Harry Hopkins of the WPA and Aubrey Williams of the NYA, and the secretary of labor, Frances Perkins; and to his wife and her friends.[28]

In the early years of the New Deal, the president's lack of response to educators seemed to them inexcusable, though some of the neglect may have been the result of poor staffing in the White House. An open letter in *School and Society* to Roosevelt in 1933 from 220 educational leaders called for the president to help in the crisis; it brought no answer from FDR. A letter from the chairman of the NEA Legislative Commission asking for his moral support brought a letter from the president's secretary saying that the boss was too busy to deal with their concerns. The executive secretary of the Progressive Education Association wrote a letter to the president asking him to clarify his position on educational issues and received an equally perfunctory reply from the president's secretary. The biggest blow to the educators' pride came at the convention of the NEA in 1934, which was held in Washington in part because leaders hoped that Roosevelt would address them. But when Mr. Chips came to Washington, the president was on vacation and had not even left a cheering message. "It is all too clear that we have little recognition as a power," complained one delegate. "We determined to come to Washington in the heat, thinking it probable that the President would like to address us. We have sweated and sweltered but not one single personal or official word has come from him." When a speaker voiced resentment over the slight from Roosevelt, loud applause broke out. Later Roosevelt expressed regret to Crabtree, but the damage had been done.[29]

Roosevelt's low opinion of educators apparently extended to his own United States Office of Education, whose budgets and staff he cut during the 1930s. The office had more money in 1932 under President Hoover ($280,000) than during the New Deal through 1939. In 1935 the staff dwindled to eighty-three from a high of one hundred in 1933–34, and only rose slowly to ninety-two in 1939.[30]

Even more galling to educators than this fiscal parsimony was the way Roosevelt consistently bypassed his own commissioner of education, John Studebaker, in formulating policy in the new educational programs undertaken by the New Deal. The historian George P. Rawick writes that "there is little doubt that Roosevelt disliked Studebaker. In all the inter-office memos referring to Studebaker, the President would include a sarcastic attack. Studebaker's way of doing business simply did not fit in with FDR's pace." Roosevelt's decision to place the NYA under the WPA instead of the Office of Education bothered Studebaker, for he had drawn up a plan for guidance and adjustment centers, mostly under the control of local school officials, which was ignored in favor of a plan for the NYA devised by non-educators like Hopkins, Perkins, and a group of advisers gathered by Eleanor Roosevelt. Drew Pearson and Robert S. Allen claimed in their column "The Washington Merry Go-Round" that the president was piqued because Studebaker had maligned the CCC in a memo to Roosevelt—a slur on his favorite reform.[31]

The split between Studebaker and the New Dealers ran deeper than a single incident. Relief programs like the NYA represented the philosophy of social reformers who were concerned about alleviating widespread misery and unemployment and who wished to get help as quickly as possible to those who needed it. While pursuing such redistributive efforts, these social reformers also shared a larger vision of social justice and chafed at the turf-protection of organized groups that opposed them, whether it was the American Federation of Labor worrying about wage scales and training in crafts or the protests of the NEA about infringement of their domain by noncertified people on relief. New Dealers like Williams, director of the NYA, were convinced that few teachers would have the courage to teach the truth about the injustices of American society, that educators regarded many people as uneducable, and that the present system of schooling did not equip either youth or adults to cope with the massive dislocation of society. "These smug individuals," wrote a relief administrator about educational leaders, "who seem to think that any system of education that teaches children and gives instruction to a small percentage of our young people in college, is an adequate system of education for a democracy such as ours, have not taken the first peep at the problems that confront America today." The New Dealers who were developing a new style of education were primarily concerned with the poor and with the working class. By contrast, educators who had long trumpeted the notion that schools should be class-blind blamed the New Dealers for creating programs designed primarily for those on the bottom of society. People like Williams knew that the schools were in fact neither class-blind nor color-blind, and they believed it a virtue that the educational programs of the NYA, the CCC, and the WPA deliberately favored families on relief.[32]

Not all educators disliked the CCC and NYA and other educational ventures of the New Deal. Charles Judd of the University of Chicago, for example, helped to design the programs and defended them against attack. Some continued to be charmed by FDR's human warmth and compassion and hoped that he would one day come to their support. Many local teachers and administrators could see first-hand the beneficial results of NYA programs in keeping secondary students in school, the value of hot lunch programs, and the WPA's help in improving educational facilities and services. An editor of a progressive educational journal declared in 1935 that "speaking among ourselves, it seems a bit disingenuous and ironic for educational leaders to scold about the boondoggling and fancy schooling carried on in the past under FERA and the Civil Works Administration (CWA) when they must know that the public school would in very few cases be equipped with philosophy or temperament or staff to do better—indeed, they must hesitate to assert that the school would have done as well."[33]

But it was tempting to criticize. A professor from the University of Utah summarized thirteen sins of the NYA as they were revealed in the educational press of 1935:

it is run by educationally inexperienced administrators
it ignored the proper channel, the Office of Education

it centralized control in a federal agency
it duplicated other agencies, state and federal
it wasted money by this duplication
its financing is so puny it is a "mere political gesture"
it may turn into "another propaganda machine for the New Deal"
it may become permanent
it gives grants to private schools
it promotes boondoggling
it puts schools into politics
it is unconstitutional
it "stresses the economic need of the teacher," not competence.[34]

Otherwise the critics liked it.

Willard E. Givens, executive secretary of the NEA, expressed what was becoming a common complaint in the educational establishment when he wrote in 1935 that the New Deal was "a Raw Deal for Public Schools." Givens protested that in federal programs students were learning to throw the lariat, play harmonicas, and boondoggle. People in Washington were forever inventing new programs to place alongside the public schools and were bypassing "the authorities which the people have themselves legally chosen to direct the schools." They were undermining quality by hiring uncertified teachers. Worst of all, they were hiring "politically appointed" staff whose loyalty was to the New Deal rather than to the profession. Givens warned that teachers could no longer be assumed to be the natural constituency of Roosevelt: "They will lend their support only to those who befriend" the school system. If that sounded political, then so be it. But as Roosevelt demonstrated the next year, when he swept all but Maine and Vermont in an election that gave him the biggest popular plurality in history, the New Deal was the only game in town. FDR did not need the support of educators, but they wanted his.[35]

However skillfully educators had played politics at the state level while seeming not to do so, they were outmaneuvered at the federal level by the adept Roosevelt. There was one exception, however: the vocational educators, whose fame and fortune had long been tied to federal subsidies. They had cultivated friends on Capitol Hill. In 1938 the president reluctantly signed an appropriation bill that allocated $10 million more than he had requested for vocational education. Why had the Congress done this? It was the fruit of the backroom work of "an effective lobby of vocational teachers, supervisors and administrative officers in the field of vocational education, who are interested in the emoluments paid in part from federal funds." At least these were people you could bargain with, as Williams found. Members of the American Vocational Association complained to him that the NYA was invading job training. You may do the job better, Williams replied, but "if we can get the money for relief work with you, we can both benefit by together providing both training and paid work for youth."[36]

Obviously, there were profound differences in educational policy between the New Dealers and most educational leaders. Roosevelt was openly and effectively political, educators covertly so. The grassroots leaders—the local superintendents—were tied to conservative community power structures. After a brief period of hope that they could share in the largesse of the New Deal and weave their own visions of social improvement with those of FDR, they became disenchanted with the president. The cosmopolitan radicals in the social reconstructionist group mostly regarded Roosevelt as too conservative in his ideology and too parsimonious in his programs. They blamed him for preferring to prop up a waning capitalist system than to inaugurate a new social order. NEA leaders, tied to a power base of state professional associations, sought uniform federal aid without strings, a goal that seemed too costly to FDR and one that did not address effectively the basic problem of inequities in finance between states and regions. Each group was responding to different constituencies, different policy goals.[37]

The reformist New Dealers who ran most of the educational programs were seeking to represent constituencies usually neglected by local and state governments and by most members of Congress. Their constituencies were the poor, those who faced discrimination, the dispossessed. These were also groups to which educators responded only fitfully. Seeking to represent such groups amid the opposition of those who spoke for established power was often no easy matter, as a reformer in the Agriculture Department, C. B. Baldwin, found when he testified before Congress about the federal migrant labor camps established to make the lives of agricultural workers less desperate. A Congressman from California roared at him: "You don't represent the people of my district! I represent them!" Knowing that the big growers of the San Joaquin Valley resented the camps because migrants might use them as a base for union organizing, Baldwin replied: "I have a national constituency. And a very important part of that are the migrant workers . . . I'm gonna build this camp." What was often neglected by critics of federal programs in education and advocates of local control was that in the supposedly universal system of public schooling in the United States there were many forgotten people, and to these the New Deal programs were primarily addressed.[38]

The New Deal Style in Education

Floyd Reeves, director of the American Youth Commission, believed that "the impetus given to education by the emergency program [of the New Deal] constitutes one of the the most significant developments in the history of the United States." This was a strong statement, one justified by the achievements of new agencies like the emergency educational program of the FERA and the WPA, the CCC, and the NYA. These agencies served new clienteles, developed new subjects and methods, and provided important services to the needy. Many New Dealers wanted to popularize culture and political discussion through new channels. Programs differed from one another, and one at least—the CCC—was more conservative in conception and operation than the others.[39]

The initial impetus for the new programs of education arose from the need to put millions of people back to work, to engage in producing goods and services rather than simply lining up for a dole. In this task of providing work relief Hopkins and his lieutenants worked with astonishing speed. A West Point engineer who observed Hopkins's methods firsthand commented that Hopkins engaged "for employment in two months nearly as many persons as were enlisted and called to the colors during our year and a half of World War I mobilization, and to disburse to them, weekly, a higher average rate of wage than Army or Navy pay." Working through state WPA directors and the local agencies (including schools), he was determined to get money in the hands of those who most needed it, not

A model school in a model community planned by the U.S. Resettlement Administration. Greenbelt, Maryland, 1938. Photo by Arthur Rothstein.

"feeding the horse in order to feed the sparrows" but trying to make relief funds go as far as possible by avoiding simply subsidizing existing agencies. As a result, most of the emergency educational relief programs supplemented rather than supplanted regular systems of educational service; they were temporary programs rather than elaborations of existing bureaucracies. That became both their greatest strength, for it permitted flexibility and experimentation in reaching the most underprivileged, and their greatest weakness, for with the death of New Deal relief programs many of the most promising innovations failed to become incorporated into the established educational system.[40]

Hopkins and Williams and their colleagues had a vision of education that went beyond immediate relief or the employment of white-collar workers. As Melvin R. Maskin has demonstrated, they shared an optimistic assessment of the educability of the common people, believing that blacks, for example, had a full capacity to learn that had been clouded by impoverished and racist environments. It has been estimated that New Deal education programs taught 1.3 million illiterate adults to read and write, half a million of them black. The emergency education programs sought to build on and strengthen institutions in poor neighborhoods—black churches, ghetto schools, settlement houses, community cultural centers—and typically employed persons on relief who were similar in background to those whom they taught. WPA teachers in such programs developed new educational methods and materials adapted to the cultures of their students. They had a strong commitment to schooling as a means of social change and an avenue of equality of opportunity.[41]

But classroom instruction was only part of the New Deal style in education. The New Deal educational innovators had a deep faith in the democratization of culture and of learning through a variety of educative agencies. They sponsored performing artists in the theater and music to bring those arts closer to the people. They hired artists to paint murals and pictures for public buildings and writers to create state guidebooks and other useful literature. They supported workers' education, public forums, and educational radio to promote discussion of socioeconomic issues. In work projects ranging from the massive TVA to a handful of NYA youth building a small suspension bridge over an Appalachian stream, New Deal innovators stressed how people can learn from working cooperatively.[42]

The directors of a variety of New Deal cultural programs thought of their work in educational terms. Roy E. Stryker, head of the gifted group of photographers in the historical section of the Farm Security Administration, for example, wrote this about their work: "Was it education? Very much so . . . If I had to sum it up, I'd say, yes, it was more education than anything else. We succeeded in doing exactly what Rex Tugwell said we should do: *We introduced Americans to America.*" Benjamin Botkin was the chief of the folklore section in the Federal Writers' Project. He called that work "the greatest educational as well as social experiment of our time," one that gave writers "a social and cultural consciousness too often lacking in ivory-tower writing." Such exuberance, not to say exaggeration, came in part from a common feeling among such cultural workers, as Stryker phrased it, "that things were being mended, that great wrongs were being corrected, that there were no problems so big that they wouldn't yield to the application of good sense and hard work."[43]

Drawing on the didactic tradition that went back to the Populists and Progressives, some New Dealers saw politics itself as an instrument of mass education. Quite as much as Teddy, who used the presidency as a "bully pulpit," Franklin Roosevelt used oratory and his fireside radio chats to instruct and exhort. "I want to be a *preaching President*—like my cousin," he commented. "The New Deal itself became a great schoolhouse," wrote Arthur Schlesinger, Jr., "compelling Americans to a greater knowledge of their country and its problems." Appealing directly to the people by radio—and trying to counter a largely hostile press—FDR saw the presidency as "the most important clearing house for exchange of information and ideas, of facts and ideals, affecting the general welfare." And in 1935 he claimed that his "biggest success" was "making people think during these past two years."[44]

In its early phases, when social planners were still influential in the organization, the TVA exemplified this multifaceted approach to education. Besides building dams, making and selling electricity, promoting flood control and conservation, promoting local industries, and creating navigable waterways, the TVA also had an education section in its Social and Economic Division. Floyd Reeves, then director of that division, described its educational program in 1935. One part of its work was aimed at a national audience: films and visual exhibits illustrating what the TVA was doing in its regional planning and construction. Another was adult education for the workers on the dams, who worked only five and a half hours a day on a five-day week (as a way of spreading the work around.)[45]

The educational training program for adult workers was consciously designed to provide an internal ladder within the labor force for ambitious workers, and also, not incidentally, to produce foremen and skilled workers in crafts, in short supply in the Tennessee Valley. The TVA used tests of mechanical aptitudes and ability to follow instructions partly as a way to select trainees (part of the test was adapted to persons with no formal schooling). At Norris, Tennessee, and Muscle Shoals, Alabama, workers were able to request the kinds of classes they wanted. Some took courses to prepare them to become foremen (sometimes this included rotation among different kinds of jobs); to learn skilled trades such as carpentry, electrical work, or auto mechanics; to become engineers' assistants; and to study scientific agriculture. Some workers attended discussions of current economic issues such as rural rehabilitation, cooperative farming, and community organization. Women took sex-segregated courses in the use of new electrical appliances for the home, child study, and crafts. Blacks fared far less well than whites—the TVA bowed to the Southern caste system—but they could take literacy classes and some training in practical trades used in house building. Much of the educational and recreational program of the TVA also reached out to involve the grassroots valley people and to involve them in the planned campaign for modernization. The educator Harold Rugg regarded the TVA as "the finest 'social' laboratory in our country," a planned regional change that should be a model to students everywhere.[46]

The Civilian Conservation Corps

The CCC also had an educational component, although it was less the result of New Dealers enamored of social planning than it was an afterthought about how to fill the empty hours in the camps for young men working on conservation projects. The CCC was a pet project of Roosevelt's, one that blended his concern for preserving nature with worry about the revolutionary potential of unemployed youth, his glorification of the virtues of rural life, and his desire to shape up discontented young men. Administratively, the CCC was a Rube Goldberg invention designed to calm the fears of organized labor while still getting a program into place rapidly. The American Federation of Labor had initially opposed the CCC in the spring of 1933 because it might reduce wages and provide a force of militarized strike-breakers. Responding to those fears, Roosevelt appointed an official of the Machinists' Union, Robert Fechner, to run the program and directed the Department of Labor to recruit the "boys" from unmarried youth eighteen to twenty-five years old. To speed up the building and administration of the camps he placed the army in charge, with the Forest Service and the National Park Service helping with the planning and supervision of the work. When told that this was inefficient, the president countered, "Oh, that doesn't matter. The Army and Forestry Service will really run the show. The Secretary of Labor will select the men and make the rules and Fechner will 'go along' and give everybody satisfaction and confidence." When an educational program appeared in the CCC in 1934, the Office of Education assumed responsibility for choosing the educational advisers. Roosevelt was a master at playing one part of the federal bureaucracy off against the others.[47]

The CCC soon earned a solid record of accomplishment in planting trees, halting soil erosion, building trails and firebreaks, constructing campgrounds, fighting fires, and controlling plant diseases. It also created a legend for itself. Images crowded the mind: young men so eager for a job that they grabbed brooms and swept the recruiting office; scrawny CCC enrollees becoming strong and ambitious; uniformed crews restoring hillsides scarred by fire; the mountain camps with their esprit de corps, their group singing and camp newspaper. It was partly a legend built by and for a middle-class America that wanted to believe in itself again, to think that an era of exploitation was over, that now the society was conserving, not wasting, its resources and that worthy young men once again had a chance if they worked hard. Nothing expressed this ideology better than the CCC's own *Camp Life Reader and Workbook*, a reader for marginally literate corpsmen. It presented a series of lessons on appearance (one was to have clean, pressed clothes and shined shoes), on learning ("every hour misspent is lost forever"), on courtesy ("a gentleman is no sissy"), on thrift ("everyone should train himself to use money wisely"), and on the flag. It also included lessons on how to fell trees and build a house and get a job. When Congressmen and CCC officials talked about the need to train youth in citizenship, this kind of Boy Scout earnestness was usually what they meant.[48]

The actual enrollees were hardly Eagle Scouts. Some camp commanders described them as irresponsible, unhealthy, unclean, and without mental or moral stamina. "First, I want to teach them to wear shoes," commented one officer. An educator who studied corpsmen in Utah and Nevada commented that they lacked moral standards, resented hard work and plain food, and did not understand common courtesy, and that many of them could not be happy "even in their leisure time." Such evaluations from middle-class observers were not surprising, for the CCC youth came predominantly from families on relief; about a third lived in broken families; most were from rural backgrounds; and the average enrollee had finished only eight or nine grades. Relatively few had held jobs, and those had been mostly short-term and dead-end.[49]

Many of the corpsmen could not or did not want to adjust to life in the camps in the woods, far from city lights or even small settlements, run by reserve military officers, and with a schedule that began with reveille at 6:00 A.M., then physical training, barracks inspection, and hard work, broken only by meals and some recreation or training classes in the evening. One in five enrollees deserted or was dismissed; the average term of service (a full term was two years) was about nine or ten months. In its evaluation of the CCC the American Youth Commission commented that the army's mode of operation produced "an authoritarian atmosphere" in which real learning of democratic principles was impossible. Commissioner Studebaker complained in 1935 to a superior that without a better educational program "these boys will leave the camps with a feeling of having been regimented under a government which has recognized a duty to feed its unfortunates but has likewise expected from them in exchange long hours of wearisome labor." Young men kept applying, nonetheless, and over its nine-year life, the CCC enrolled about 2.5 million.[50]

People in the various government departments that ran the CCC had rather different notions of what constituted "education" for youth such as these and what were the major purposes of the Corps. Although the Office of Education and its educational advisers in the camps enjoyed more influence and funding as time went on—gaining authorizations for school buildings and for films and other teaching materials, and some moral and fiscal support from Congress—the real control continued to rest in the hands of the army at the local sites and in Director Fechner at the national level, who together with the president believed that the chief job of the CCC was employment on conservation projects. "The Army is afraid of uplift work," commented one critic, while an officer complained that "we are going to be hounded to death by all sorts of educators instead of teaching the boys how to do an honest day's work."[51]

At stake in the conflict between the factions was not simply control of the camps but different philosophies about what was the best education for the youth in them. Fechner and the army and most of the technical advisers from the Forest Service believed that the best way to learn to be a productive adult was to gain the discipline of hard work, to keep healthy and clean, and to follow orders. "Citizenship courses" to them were a means of promoting "camp responsibility" and immunizing corpsmen against "radicals . . . and those who make trouble." The educators who worked in the CCC in a subordinate role or tried to influence policy at the national level had a very different conception of social education in the camps. Their philosophy stressed self-expression, "pride and satisfaction in cooperative endeavor," better mental and physical health, vocational training and guidance, and appreciation of nature.[52]

Even the educators, however, realized that the training in the camps should not mirror that in public high schools. The corpsmen were mostly refugees from public education and wanted no more of the traditional fare. A CCC adviser in Connecticut asked a thousand enrollees why they had left school; two-thirds said they quit because they did not like it. Whatever classes they took had to come in the evenings, after a day of clearing trails through the buckbrush on a hot slope or digging a drainage ditch. This placed an additional burden on teachers to motivate the corpsmen. But some of the advisers found the rough-and-ready camp life a welcome touch of reality after teaching in public schools. "I wanted a job that needed doing," wrote one. "I was tired of teaching a lot of twaddle that nobody wanted or needed . . . Despite the fact that I was considered liberal and progressive I knew that [educational] tradition held reality outside my door." Others felt that public educators could learn from the CCC how to reach those who were ready to drop out.[53]

In comparison with the elaborate bureaucratic structure of high schools—the grades and credits, the required courses and hall passes—the educational program of the CCC camps was flexibility incarnate. Attendance in courses was voluntary (though technically a law passed in 1937 made education compulsory in the camps and some officials

CCC classroom. Unidentified photo, CCC files, National Archives.

pressured enrollees to attend), and there was great latitude of choice. The educational advisers did not teach most of the courses themselves, though on the average they might teach four or five courses. They asked corpsmen what subjects they wanted to take, and for teachers they recruited the Forest Service and army officers, corpsmen, public school teachers from nearby schools, WPA and NYA employees, and any volunteers that could be persuaded, from garage mechanics to businessmen. Class sizes ranged from about ten to twenty. Some corpsmen attended nearby colleges. The topics studied could be divided into three major groups: remedial teaching for those who were illiterate or had only rudimentary schooling; vocational courses; and avocational instruction. Much of the vocational training took place in conjunction with the work of the camp, and it included

typewriting, drafting, surveying, construction crafts, and driving trucks
and heavy machinery. Roughly a third of the courses were vocational,
a third academic, a fifth remedial, and the rest avocational. By the
late 1930s the educational advisers had far more resources at their
disposal than the 35¢ per corpsman available in the early period;
camps typically had libraries, classrooms, facilities for showing educational films, and an attendance rate of about 90 percent.[54]

This represented progress, but even at its peak the CCC educational program hardly justified the judgment of Studebaker (in one
of his public as opposed to private expressions of opinion) that the
educational program was "one of the most heartening and thrilling
experiences in the history of American education." For him "the
moral and spiritual value" of the CCC overshadowed its contribution
to conservation and work relief. The educational director of the
CCC, Clarence S. Marsh, called the educational program "a great
American folk school, a school whose genius is indigenous to the
native character and culture of communities in which the camps are
located." Corpsmen learned about ranching or mining in the West,
Spanish in the Southwest, and cotton grading in the South. In progressive fashion, students learned skills by doing. Camp shows and
newspapers built an esprit de corps, while youth learned civic skills
by serving on committees. But in fact the educational program remained subordinate to Fechner and the army.[55]

Fechner vetoed most of Marsh's proposals for liberalizing and
enlarging the program. Marsh was clearly out of step with Fechner's
and the army's ideas about citizenship. Camp officials had "an almost
panicky fear of 'agitators' and of books which might stir up uncomfortable discussion," wrote one observer. "One corps area officer
remarked that all writers on sociology were somewhat radical, and
therefore he would approve no books on sociological subjects!" Marsh
finally resigned in a controversy over a social studies series the Office
of Education had commissioned to teach corpsmen about the depression and unemployment. One of these books, called *You and Ma-
chines*, written by William F. Ogburn and enlivened by cartoons,
dealt with some of the negative consequences of industrialization
such as unemployment and the deskilling of labor. This was too much
for Fechner, who banned it as subversive. Attacked by liberals for

violating academic freedom, Fechner explained to the War Department that he was curbing radicals. That settled the matter.[56]

In retrospect, it is difficult to imagine a "folk school" movement, rich in participatory democracy, emerging within a structure dominated by a conservative unionist and the army (whose commander-in-chief at the start was Douglas MacArthur). In the spring of 1935 a play called *The Young Go First* dramatized that incongruity. Its central characters were eight young radicals who went from New York to a camp and found their superiors to be "pinheaded overseers and sadistic disciplinarians, with a few minor alcoholics tossed in for good measure." Others protested the CCC's discrimination against blacks, which took the form of restricting black admissions, not using black administrators, and largely segregating blacks into separate camps despite a specific clause in the CCC act forbidding racial discrimination. Despite such criticisms, however, and despite the failed hopes of educators who sought to transform the CCC educational program, the CCC remained popular with the public and successful in its goals of conserving natural resources and employing young men.[57]

The conservative Fechner-army view of education as work and disciplined routine largely won out in the CCC. Roosevelt himself systematically took their side in conflicts with the subordinate educational division of the CCC. He was committed to the conservation work of the corps and eager that nothing should dilute that. He had often expressed concern about "unrestrained youth" and did not seem to have been interested in the kind of instruction proposed by Studebaker and Marsh for the camps. He did not want the "Negro question" to interfere with the popularity of the institution. He wrote Harold Ickes opposing "Brother Studebaker's idea" of teaching boys during their work hours, adding that if they were really interested in learning, they could read "worthwhile books" on Sundays. In the final years of the program he regarded the CCC as a program that aided the national defense.[58]

The National Youth Administration

Whereas the CCC stressed conservation and the discipline of work, the NYA embodied alternative values. Aubrey Williams, director of the NYA, had such a different conception of both relief and education that it is a tribute to the President's catholicity—or inconsistency—that he could have supported both Fechner and Williams. Both the CCC and the NYA were work-relief projects aimed at youth. But one can hardly imagine a sharper contrast between their directors, their guiding philosophies, or their modes of operation. Fechner was a conservative trade unionist who endorsed the army's hierarchical operating procedures, feared radicalism, and seemed content to work within the racial caste system of the army and the South. Williams was a social worker and lay minister who sought to use the government's resources to bring about social justice, a reformer who sought to bring about racial equality in the NYA, and a flexible politician who sought to work in a pluralistic way with a plethora of grassroots agencies.[59]

Like Hopkins, his boss, Williams sympathized most "with these people at the bottom of the heap" and wanted to redistribute economic and cultural rewards to provide "every young person in America . . . a decent break." A blunt man who spoke his own mind, he thought that teachers should have the courage to present the facts about poverty and the "palpably unfair distribution of wealth" in America and stop "romancing about" the glories of free education—which did not exist for millions of Americans. From his poverty-stricken childhood in Alabama, where he left school to go to work at the age of seven, and from his everyday experience with those on relief, he had a worm's-eye view of the country that was quite different from the view had by executives in corporate offices. He recognized that schooling could promote caste and class distinctions quite as much as it promoted equality of opportunity. Williams satirized the old-fashioned individualistic outlook of business analyst Roger Babson, who had told New England superintendents that bad schooling was "primarily responsible for at least 7,000,000 of the 10,000,000 unemployed in the United States" because educators had not instilled "within the souls of the students the desire to struggle and the willingness to sacrifice." Williams believed that even more and better public education would not solve the basic "youth problem"; the source of that lay in the structure of the economy. By itself, of course, the NYA—with its meager budget and limited mandate to provide relief—could do little to change the basic inequities lamented by Hopkins and Williams.[60]

Few people had a better opportunity to hold up a mirror to the faults of public education than the NYA staff who had daily contact with children from families on relief. Fifty percent of the youth in the work project program of the NYA had not gone beyond the eighth grade. Reporters Betty and Ernest K. Lindley, who traveled all around the country visiting NYA projects, heard from supervisors that the enrollees "have a definite fixation against going inside a school door again." The young people told them why they did not stick with school: "it's like prison"; "they treat you like babies"; "it's just so dead." One could argue that the NYA had in effect done the public schools a favor by absorbing these alienated youths at a time when there were no jobs for them and when there was public pressure to keep them in school. Yet these same youths, the Lindleys wrote, were actively learning that the NYA projects combined work with instruction. But there were other reasons besides alienation for the low school attainment of the poor. Some did not have the money even to buy shoes for school, and many lived in regions that lacked "schools that are passably good by any standard." "Where is the celebrated American school system?" asked the Lindleys rhetorically.[61]

Hopkins and Williams were acutely aware of the defects of schooling for the poor and thus not enthusiastic about an Office of Education plan to train youth in school-based adjustment and guidance centers. They were chiefly concerned, as was FDR, about relieving the massive problem of youth unemployment, which was producing, they thought, a human erosion more serious than the degradation of natural resources. No one knows precisely the dimensions of that unemployment of people aged sixteen to twenty-four, but informed estimates put the number variously at one-fifth to one-third of the age group, with some pessimists arguing that in the worst times the absolute number may have reached seven million. Hopkins's Federal Emergency Relief Administration had experimented in 1933 and 1934 with various work-study plans for college students and work project programs to relieve the unemployment of youth—and to keep more of them out of the labor market—but by 1935 it became apparent to the president and his liberal advisers (including his wife) that a more concerted youth program was necessary. The CCC was expensive—it cost over $1,000 per corpsman per year—and only absorbed a fraction of the male unemployed. Young people were dropping out of college because they could not afford the tuition and quitting high school because their parents could not afford clothing and other expenses. The gap seemed to be growing between the time a young person left school and the time he could find work, and this was producing a new kind of lost generation, some of whom were restless and explosive and many of whom seemed to be losing hope. FDR knew that a youth program might prove controversial with Congress, that political opponents might accuse him of regimenting youth, and that the NEA was suspicious of New Deal youth programs. He decided, therefore, to create the NYA by executive proclamation within the WPA rather than by Congressional authorization.[62]

As director, Williams had to figure how to make the initial appropriation of $50 million—about $10 for each unemployed young person—go as far as possible. He was determined to include women and blacks. In discussing the program with his advisory board Williams advocated an experimental approach. He and his staff, energetic and imaginative, were determined to keep the operation lean. (The administrative overhead for the program was less than 5 percent, though Congressional critics complained that his Washington offices occupied 34,926 square feet.) He sought to keep the actual operation as close to local communities as possible, appointing state NYA directors who requested projects from public and semipublic agencies in localities. He wanted to pass almost all of the funds through to the enrollees themselves, asking the local groups to pay for materials and supervision. The money was to come from the federal government, but the initiative and the design of programs from the grassroots. He was particularly eager to hire blacks as staff and to enroll them in the various programs. To encourage this he created a Division of Negro Affairs within the central office, and leading blacks like Mary McLeod Bethune helped to publicize the NYA within the black community. The NYA helped some 300,000 black youths.[63]

The program of the NYA took two major forms: one was aid to college and high school students, a work-study program to help them earn enough to stay in school; and the other was paid work experience of various kinds for youth who were out of school and who were poor (about 95 percent of enrollees came from relief families).

One way to close the gap between school and job was to extend years of schooling, and high school enrollments did increase through the 1930s. But for an estimated one-quarter of high school students the costs of attending were a serious barrier to completing the secondary grades. For typical NYA families, who had a yearly budget of only $600, assistance was frequently essential. From 1935 to 1943 1,514,000 high school students received an average of $5.41 per month in the NYA work-study program (they worked no more than ten hours per week)—hardly a princely sum, but one that often helped morale and provided funds for clothes, carfare, and school fees. As in Title I of the Elementary and Secondary Education Act of 1965, the funds were allocated to schools according to the number of children from poor families; in the NYA case, the quota of work-study grants was initially 7 percent of the number of youth on relief in the district. Between 6 and 10 percent of secondary students were in the program during its nine years. A larger proportion of college students—12 percent—were in the NYA in the years 1935 to 1937 (somewhat reduced in the period 1938–1943). Some graduate students also received aid, and a special affirmative action fund was set aside to assist promising black graduate students. Partly as a result of this program, about two hundred blacks received Ph.D.s during the 1930s compared with only forty-five for the period from 1900 to 1930. The average wage for college students per month ranged from $11.54 to $12.90, while graduate students earned eight to ten dollars more.[64]

The program was a modest one. In exchange for the NYA grants the high school students served as clerical aides to teachers, landscaped school grounds, and worked in cafeterias, laboratories, and workshops. In some cases they developed recreational facilities or served in school health programs. In higher education the NYA students worked in research projects, served as departmental assistants, did library tasks, or participated in community service jobs. For many the small stipends made the difference between staying in school or leaving, and school officials, who chose the recipients, often praised the contributions they made. But for Hopkins the plan had broader ramifications. One day, he hoped, it would be possible to create genuine equality of opportunity in American education: "That is the crux of the thing; to decide once and for all that this business of getting an education and going to law school and medical school and dental school and going to college is not to be confined to the people who have an economic status at home that permits them to do it." Although Hopkins's dream of equality of opportunity in higher education has yet to be realized, subsequent federal legislation ranging from the G.I. Bill to work-study programs to opportunity grants for poor youths in college eventually did move in the directions he urged.[65]

For poor youths out of school and out of work, the NYA developed several kinds of programs of paid work and training, including community projects, resident centers, and vocational training. In all, some 2,677,000 youths participated in these, of whom 45 percent were female. The average monthly wage ranged from $15 to $22; the initial maximum number of hours per month started at forty-six and then increased markedly after 1938. The highest number of workers employed was 976,000 in 1940–41, reflecting a shift toward preparation for defense production and increased fiscal support from Congress.[66]

The NYA workers performed an enormous variety of services in their local communities, serving needs as perceived by people in grassroots public and semipublic agencies such as park departments, libraries, settlement houses, youth groups like the YMCA, colleges and schools, and local governments. Betty and Ernest K. Lindley vividly described some of these:

Converting a swamp in Fort Morgan, Colorado into a park with a swimming pool and landscaped grounds.
Restocking fish hatcheries in New England.
Making globes and other visual aids for schools.
Working in WPA preschools.
Assisting in hospitals as practical nurses.
Working as interns in government agencies as machine operators and clerks.
Sewing clothes and making furnishings for public institutions.
Building community centers in small towns.
Constructing suspension bridges over swollen creeks in rural West

Virginia, so that children could walk to school in the rainy season. Learning and teaching methods of controlling soil erosion.[67]

The State Administrator for the NYA in Alabama told about projects in his state in 1940. In one area a county school board wanted shelters built for school children waiting for the bus; in another, the welfare department wanted clothing and mattresses sewed for poor clients; a neighboring town wanted furniture constructed for its community house or a first coat of paint for its school. Building roads, renovating civic buildings, building fire trails for the state forestry department—these also kept the NYA workers busy. But it was not just work; it was also an opportunity to learn: "After spending a morning in repairing an automobile for some government agency, a youth employee may spend part of the afternoon learning the theory of auto mechanics . . . A boy on a construction project might learn blueprint reading in a related training class, while a youth on an agricultural project will have classes in the chemistry of soils."[68]

In Alabama and other rural states, where the population was poor, scattered, and often without civic resources to devise useful work projects, the NYA developed cooperative resident centers where rural youth could learn to build houses, farm more scientifically, plan and cook balanced meals, do shop work, can food, sew clothes, and develop other useful skills. About two-thirds of the youths in these resident centers came from the thirteen southern states. Many got adequate food and medical attention for the first time. Two-thirds of the NYA workers in Alabama had not gone beyond grammar school, and most had no opportunity to learn vocational skills in their formal schooling. Workshop projects for black and white youths scattered across Alabama gave them a chance to learn skills like auto mechanics, welding, cabinetry, electrical work, and painting, often by producing goods and services for public agencies and for needy people.[69]

In fact, as charged by its public school critics, the NYA was creating an alternative style of education—in its community projects, its resident centers, and its vocational training and guidance centers— aimed at the poorest of the poor in a redistributive program that cost far less than the CCC. Indeed, through 1940 the NYA had spent only about $325,000,000 compared with the CCC's $2,553,800,000.

Charles Taussig, a friend of Franklin and Eleanor Roosevelt and a prime architect of the program and chairman of its advisory board, summed up its contributions in 1939. It had begun to fill the gap between school and work; it had pioneered in "a new technique in education . . . that is, education through work"; many trainees had found jobs in private enterprise; they had contributed "much socially useful work . . . which will enrich the community as well as the lives of the erstwhile unemployed youth." It had also been criticized for "make-work," for infringing on the domain of the public schools, and for being an entering wedge for socialism. But where the state NYA directors and local agencies had been imaginative, it had opened the way for a new conception of the federal role in the war on poverty. One of these state directors—the Texas leader described in a field report as "easily one of the best men directing one of the best staffs in one of the best programs with the most universal and enthusiastic public support of any state in the Union"—would not forget the lessons the NYA taught. His name was Lyndon B. Johnson.[70]

The Works Progress Administration

Youth was only one of the educational concerns of the NYA's parent agency, the WPA. Hopkins believed in putting unemployed people to work in the way they could contribute most to the public good, and that meant hiring teachers to teach, nurses to attend to the public health, artists to create or perform, and librarians to staff libraries. In 1936, for example, the WPA hired a total of over 100,000 professional and technical workers, including 36,059 teachers, 3,979 nurses, 2,829 artists, 11,820 musicians and teachers of music, 3,514 actors, and 4,846 librarians. Since the WPA had to avoid displacing existing workers, Hopkins sought to supplement rather than replace the existing system of formal schooling. The program focused on adult education and preschool children.[71]

Anticipating the Headstart Program of the 1960s, the Emergency Education Program established nursery schools for the children of the poor and childcare classes for their parents. There were only an estimated 300 nursery schools in the country when the program began, mostly patronized by the upper middle class, but between October 1933 and June 1934 there were 2,979 such schools established. By

A WPA bookmobile in North Carolina. Unidentified photo, WPA files, National Archives.

1938 over 200,000 children had enjoyed the benefit of their services in health, nutrition, supervised recreation and social development, and activities like storytelling, music, and dramatics. Of the teachers, 90 to 95 percent came from the relief rolls. Many of them were unfamiliar with the new work, but funds from the General Education Board and assistance from professional groups helped these people to learn new careers. The program proved to be especially helpful to working mothers, and its parent education and that of allied adult education classes reached hundreds of thousands of families.[72]

The adult education work of the WPA was its biggest educational program. In February 1934 over 40,000 instructors taught over 1,500,000 people, more than the total number of secondary and

collegiate graduates of that year. By 1938 there were 1,542,021 enrolled in these classes. Roughly one-sixth of the teachers and students
were black. The adult education program showed astonishing variety.
To a large degree it reflected what people wanted to learn. Indeed,
those who ran the program in New York City said that they would
try to create any course that ten or more persons requested. The
most important instruction was a campaign to eliminate illiteracy.
The 1930 census had shown that 4.3 percent of Americans (over four
million) were unable to read or write, and it was estimated that over
twice that number were "cut off from written communication or from
information through the printed word." By 1938 the WPA claimed
that its literacy program had enabled a million people "to master a
practical knowledge of reading and writing." That helped to repair
a massive failure of the public educational system, especially for
blacks, but the WPA program went well beyond the fundamentals.
In 1938 over 350,000 people took classes in general academic subjects, 300,000 in cultural and creative work, and 200,000 in occupational classes that supplemented on-the-job training for WPA
workers.[73]

Supplementing these were "worker education" classes that discussed current economic and social issues and other public forums
that attracted 155,000 people. The WPA programs in the arts—
comprising both the creation of artworks and performances in music,
theater, dance, vaudeville, and other popular and folk arts—can be
understood as part of this larger program of popular education. Despite criticism, Hopkins opened wide the door to such popularization
of culture and discussion of public issues, asserting that "what actually *could* be done in such a program has depended to a very great
extent on what our American communities have felt *should* be done."
Those standards varied widely in New York City or Farmer City,
Illinois.[74]

The WPA's direct contribution to public schools, especially in the
poorest sections of the country, provided health services to hundreds
of thousands of school children, constructed furniture and teaching
aids, and provided supplementary teachers, as in a program of remedial reading and mathematics in 259 elementary schools in New
York City. In one of its most far-reaching and successful efforts,

WPA workers used surplus food to feed hot lunches to needy school children, preparing the staggering total of nearly 1.25 billion free lunches by the end of the WPA program. This was not a new idea— it had been instituted in some schools early in the twentieth century— but the WPA succeeded in institutionalizing the practice.[75]

Despite the direct benefits of the New Deal work-relief programs to the public schools and their assistance to the needy, educational leaders expressed reservations about the New Deal style in eduation. As Harry Zeitlin has shown, they were annoyed that the money flowed to the new agencies and not to established school systems. They feared a loss of control and a decline of professional standards as people without proper certification were taken off the relief rolls and put in classrooms as teachers. They didn't know where it would all lead.[76]

Jurisdictional Dispute

Unable to get federal aid for public schools and ineffective in gaining influence over the new federal ventures in education, the educational establishment proved finally to be more potent as a veto group than as a shaper of New Deal policy. The NEA was one part of a coalition that campaigned for the demise of the CCC, the NYA, and the WPA. It had learned that it was only a dream that the federal government would place the money on the stump and run—a message that Robert Hutchins tried to get across to school finance reformers in 1935 when he wrote to Paul Mort, "The Federal Government never has given and never will give money for the support of education without influencing the educational situation in the political unit to which the money is granted." Although the depression and the New Deal programs broadened and liberalized their conception of the proper scope and purposes of public education, educators remained en- amored of their conception of professional autonomy and expertise. If they couldn't control the New Deal educational program, they questioned its worth.[77]

This is not to say that educators were of one mind about the New Deal programs. Some leaders, like Charles Judd, not only admired the New Deal style in education but helped to shape its policies.

A school lunch at Lake Dick (a Farm Security Administration Project). Jefferson County, Arkansas, 1938. Photo by Russell Lee.

Many local educators saw the good that NYA jobs, new WPA coats of paint for one-room schools, and recreation programs were doing in their own communities. And many, even among the national leadership, never gave up hope that FDR would see the error of his ways and support general federal aid, for they believed that educators were preeminently in the business of social betterment.[78]

Could the New Dealers and public educators have cooperated enough to enact federal aid to education? In some respects they were not very far apart in their basic policy orientation. FDR valued state and local control and had no strong desire to intervene in the mainstream of education. He bewailed from time to time the fiscal inequalities between states and regions. Roosevelt and the NEA leaders did not have to like each other. Educators might have gone on believing that FDR was a private school snob—as William H. Kilpatrick thought—and Roosevelt that public school leaders were fussy. But politics can weld strange combinations when leaders share interests and goals. Both the president and school finance reformers recognized that only the federal government could act to equalize the enormous educational disparities between the states, especially between North and South. The region that stood to benefit most from an aid formula based on need was the South, and some southern congressmen did support aid to education, even though they were often hostile to some of FDR's emergency aid programs. But the conservative and independent southern legislators were uncertain allies both for FDR and the NEA.[79]

To win Roosevelt's support, educators would have had to modify some of their favorite claims: that public school people were apolitical; that there must be uniform general aid to all states; that federal funds should not have strings (for example, to be used for nursery schools or for eradicating adult illiteracy); or that school people as professionals had little to learn from the kinds of people FDR sought as advisers (Frances Perkins, Harry Hopkins, Charles Taussig) about programs for youth. They might instead have shown a greater willingness to recognize that relief of poverty and unemployment were more pressing than school retrenchment, to rethink how they were preparing youth for new political and social conditions, to cultivate the kind of political savvy long demonstrated by the American Vocational Association, and to find a compromise on the issue of aid to Catholic schools that so concerned Roosevelt's northern, urban, Democratic contingent.

But all the changes could not have been on one side. Roosevelt talked about states' rights and the virtues of decentralization in education, but he mixed together his own New Deal programs of education like a marble cake alongside the established schools. He talked about the need to help impoverished schools in places like Georgia, his second home, but he followed through only with the scattered work of relief agencies. The president of the University of Wisconsin criticized the New Deal's ambiguous drift in educational policy: "Despite its profound social significance, education has largely been left to shift for itself by a new era politics that purports to put social considerations first. In the face of the seeming disposition of political liberalism to insure everything to everybody, the guarantee of educational opportunity to the children of all classes and all conditions of men clamors in vain for its rightful place on the current agenda of liberal politics, save as it can be made a side-issue to relief."[80]

Roosevelt and the educational establishment probably could not have gotten together on federal aid, for neither side was willing to meet the other's terms. But it was a time when a basic injustice of American education—the gross inequalities of schooling caused by its pattern of finance—might have been addressed, had leadership been more astute and bold on both sides. The New Deal did try, after all, to address other basic unfinished business like social security and labor's right to collective bargaining. The chief losers were the school children and teachers in impoverished states and communities. To have provided adequate schools for them would have cost far less than building battleships.

If the relations between the educational establishment and the New Deal began on the high note that together they might pursue a moral equivalent of war, it went flat in a jurisdictional dispute over who would serve youth. In 1941 the Educational Policies Commission (EPC)—a group that Charles Judd said was "fully authorized to speak for the teachers and administrators of the public schools"— issued a report on the CCC and NYA. It recommended that the agencies should be discontinued and their functions transferred to the public educational system. The government should not try to run its own programs for youth, it said, but should give funds to public schools to carry these out. The solution to the "youth problem" was extended education; the average duration of schooling should be fourteen years. The key to "adaptability, experimentation, and progress" was decentralized control, the key virtue of American public education. The role of the federal government was to provide leadership through research, demonstration projects, and conferences; to pay the states to set up new programs and equalize funding between them; and to create public service jobs when the economy slumped— but not to provide affiliated education. *Leave youth and their training to us* was the clear message. Educators had the solution to the "youth problem," or the gap between school and job: the EPC declared that "there will be no 'out-of-school unemployed youth' for federal agencies to educate, when schools everywhere extend their responsibilities to all young people until they are satisfactorily established in adult vocations" by trained teachers and guidance people.[81]

It was Charles H. Judd who most effectively assaulted the assumptions underlying this view of the public school omnipotent. In an article in 1942 on "the real youth problem" he asserted that school leaders "cannot afford to spend their time in guerilla warfare against federal agencies. Did the schools show in 1933 and 1935 the slightest insight into the youth problem or any disposition to take care of young people who were out of school and out of work?" Is there evidence, he asked, that administrators will spend funds and time giving pupils the needed "skills or orientation of any kind with respect to social institutions"? The EPC pamphlet, he added, "is another of a long series of evidences that a great many school people are suffering from acute intellectual myopia. They see petty issues and completely fail to get any view of the vast social horizon which lies beyond their immediate selfish interests." The commission ignored the real youth problem—"that there has in recent decades been so complete a dislocation of young people in the industrial and economic systems of this country that something new and radical has to be devised." Youth unemployment was a permanent condition, not a temporary aberration, and the key question was the solution to that, rather than jurisdictional disputes. What was needed, Judd said, was "a penetrating analysis of the American industrial system and of the relation of youth to this system. If [the commission] had done so, it would surely have seen that the determination of a future public works program is the really important problem with which the intellectual leaders of the nation must wrestle." The real youth problems lay in structural causes, in the connections between industry, government, and labor. "To hope for an effective solution of the youth problem through an enormously expanded public educational system supplemented from time to time by federal employment may be a credit to one's imagination but certainly not to one's sober, objective thinking."[82]

Judd's analysis was similar to that of Williams and of a principal of a school for working-class boys on New York's East Side, who reported that one of his students told him "that all this vocational guidance was ridiculous as long as no jobs were available." Was more and better schooling really a solution to the adjustment of youth to work? A statistically ambitious and thorough study of employed and unemployed youth in Massachusetts came to an illuminating conclusion. It found that when the job market was so dislocated (49 percent of youth had no regular jobs), there were no significant differences between those who were employed and those who were not. On all the major measures—years of high school training, school grades, teachers' ratings of personality, attitudes toward education— the two groups looked alike.[83]

Thus, school alone did not make much difference in youth's chances for work when the economy was so depressed. That opinion also came through in the many studies conducted by the American Youth Commission, a group sponsored by the General Education Board under the American Council on Education. In its final, often eloquent, report, *Youth and the Future*, the AYC accomplished just what Judd was calling for—a study of the reasons for youth unemployment, together with a careful analysis of public work as a cure. It concluded that the government owed youth not just education but jobs as well, if the private sector failed to generate enough.[84]

The New Deal had made a beginning in putting unemployed youth to work, but it reached only a fraction of those who needed it. The sudden demand for labor and troops in World War II seemed to end the youth problem by eliminating the gap between school and work.

In fact, youth dropped out of secondary school in enormous numbers to go to work or to the armed services. Now workers, not jobs, were scarce. While spending billions for war—on a scale unimagined in the programs for social justice in the 1930s—the Congress killed the CCC, the NYA, and the WPA. The problems they had addressed, and the underlying issues Judd had raised, would remain when the war was over.

4 Behind the Schoolhouse Door

The English supervisor tiptoed into the high school English class in Buffalo, New York, and squeezed his 250-pound, pear-shaped frame into a student seat at the back of the room. A classical scholar, he wrote his observations of classes in Latin or Greek to keep his skills fresh. That year—1937—he had given the new teacher an eighty-page mimeographed syllabus of the high school curriculum, specifying what novels and poems the students were to read and when, the schedule and topics of compositions, and the subjects to treat in grammar. The lesson that day was on *Idylls of the King*, and a sassy pupil did his best to disrupt the class. The teacher tried kindness to quiet him, then resorted to sarcasm. Peering through his thick glasses, his bald head glistening, the supervisor scribbled a note, which he left on the teacher's desk as he tiptoed out. After the class left, the novice teacher looked at the message. It read: "No knight of Arthur's noblest dealt in scorn ignoble."[1]

The students in the east-side Buffalo high school came from a community where nine-tenths of the parents spoke Polish. Some of them complained that their fathers slapped them if they spoke English at home. In the 1930s there was no place for most of them to go but school, for laws compelled them to attend even if it meant repeating the same grades over and over. Half dropped out in the freshman or sophomore years of high school when they reached the age of sixteen. But school was at least a warm place where they could get a free lunch. They scraped the plates clean; for many it was the only full meal they had.

The new teacher was one of the lucky ones from his college class: twenty-two had passed the day-long English teachers' examination for the Buffalo schools, but only a few had actually won teaching positions. He was paid only $1,050 as a "permanent substitute" (a commonly used device to cut instructional costs). It was his job, he knew, to teach the syllabus in the customary way. The students were to read classic authors—Shakespeare, Sir Walter Scott, Emerson; to parse sentences and understand the subjunctive mood; and to write ten compositions per semester, six of them on required subjects. Typically a class consisted of recitations on homework. Corporal punishment awaited those who stepped too far out of line. It was the way it was supposed to be. It was high school.

Across the country, the Nambé school stood in a valley nineteen miles north of Santa Fe, New Mexico, nestled among the adobe houses of the village, by a road lined with old cottonwoods. Dozens of little fields, planted with corn, alfalfa, chiles, peas, and beans, lay alongside the communal ditch that drew water from the Nambé River and the snowfields of the Sangre de Christo Mountains in the distance. Most of the 160 families in the area were descended from the settlers who came from Mexico, the first in 1711. At home and in the village they generally spoke Spanish. Before the crash, the men had gone away to work for wages in mines, railroads, and farms, but the jobs mostly disappeared. Two-thirds of the families were on relief, supplemented by the meager crops they could grow on their subdivided small lots.

In the kindergarten room of the school, thirty-five children sat in a circle on the floor as the teacher unwrapped a package. Inside was a big blue ball. The children learned its English name and the words *roll, throw, catch, play, blue.* Then a group of girls washed doll clothes, set the table, and swept the floor, talking as they worked and played. Next door, in a first-grade classroom filled with picture books, the children told a story about cooking; the teacher put it on the blackboard:

Cooking

The girls made soup.
The boys brought vegetables.
We washed the vegetables.

An informal classroom at the Nambé School. Plate IV, L. S. Tireman and Mary Watson, *A Community School in a Spanish-Speaking Village* (Albuquerque: University of New Mexico Press, 1948).

> We cooked the soup on the stove.
> We ate the soup.[2]

The school lunches, made partly from produce grown in the big garden outside the front door, were a mainstay of the children's diet. Most of them were underweight. In a terrarium in the first-grade room were frogs, turtles, and salamanders (the children feared the salamanders at first as dangerous lizards). The third-graders went on a trip to identify and feed birds they had been reading about. They walked to Ernesto's house to see four women plastering the adobe, and the children helped to mix mud and straw. They wrote a story about their conversation with the school nurse. The older children studied irrigation and put their lessons on conservation to practice by cleaning the irrigation ditches with their fathers and planting eroded gullies. They learned what had caused the flood at Española. Some worked in the NYA wood-carving room, some figured out the mathematics of a terracing project, some played the guitar under the tutelage of the WPA music teacher, some struggled with phonics, some played basketball. The school at Nambé was centered on the everyday life of the community and respected the language and culture of the Hispanos. It was enriched by teachers who also sought to introduce children to the world outside and to skills that would help them to survive.[3]

In the Deep South, the children who went to school in Dine Hollow hoed and picked cotton, tended the young ones while their mothers labored in white people's homes, and roamed about to find sticks for the fireplace when the weather was cold. School didn't start until the cotton was harvested in the fall and ended when children were needed for the planting. Often the school was in session for only five months: the truant officer knew better than to drag children to class when the white plantation owner wanted them in the fields. For many of these children school was the only way out of the drudgery and despair of their daily lives. They would trudge by the side of the red clay roads for miles, angry when the yellow bus went by carrying the white children to their school. Unlike the children of Nambé, many of them feared school: it was a place where the teacher slapped you if you were late, where your mind went blank when she asked you questions, where people made fun of you. Sick and malnourished, many children came to school already defeated. And like the pupils, the teacher and the building symbolized inequality and caste.

The Dine Hollow school was a rundown shack that showed only traces of its ancient whitewash. It stood in a rocky yard crowded with dusty weeds. Inside, four grades assembled, seated on broken benches, a population three times bigger than the school was built to hold. Lacking books or other aids, the weary middle-aged teacher wrote an assignment on the board for the first two grades:

> Write your name ten times.
> Draw an dog, an cat, an rat, an boot.
> Draw an tree, an house, an cow, an goat.
> Draw an book, an apple, an tomato.[4]

She proceeded with the older children to see how well they had memorized an antiquated grammar lesson and spelling rules. Pupils then multiplied and checked their sums by adding on their fingers. A boy in another class tried to repeat a story his group had read:

Fred was a little boy. He went to the city to work for a man. The
man told him if he worked he would pay him. Fred worked three
years. The man paid him only three pennies. Fred said . . . Fred
said . . . The man paid him only three pennies. Fred said . . . [5]

He could not go on. What, indeed, was Fred to say?

The Buffalo English class, the Nambé community school, and the
Dine Hollow school illustrate three of the many faces of public schooling
in the depression: in Buffalo, the persistence of traditional content
and modes of instruction even for new kinds of secondary students;
in Nambé, the attempt to focus a school on the everyday life of a
community; and in Dine Hollow, educational inequality so gross that
one questions whether the term "education" is appropriate.

In earlier chapters we have argued that the 1930s did not constitute
a watershed in the finance or governance of public education even
though it was a time of momentous change in the economy and
federal government generally. In this chapter we inquire into continuity and change in educational practice—in what happened behind
the schoolhouse door. Some have claimed that the depression decade
was a time of vigorous reform in American education. It was a period
when school people found themselves confronted with new kinds of
high school students, pushed or pulled into secondary schools, who
in an earlier time would have been working. It was an intensely
ideological time. The rise of totalitarianism was making Americans
newly conscious of the importance of democratic beliefs and processes, and there was lively debate among educators about how to
relate schools to the larger society and economy. It was an era of
aggressive professionalism in education, when standards for certification and education of teachers and specialists were rising in a
buyers' labor market. But one could also argue that hard times were
not propitious for innovation, that school people had such trouble
merely maintaining earlier gains that they had little opportunity to
experiment, and that what school boards and other power-wielders
in local communities wanted was not advanced ideologies but the
old verities, not fads and frills but the basics. Obviously the question
of continuity and change in educational practice is one of degree,
and in our analysis we link it to another theme of this book: the
inequalities that were part and parcel of the diversity of American

public schooling. How much did the dividing lines of race, class, and gender in the larger society continue to penetrate behind the schoolhouse door to vitiate the promise of equal educational opportunity in the depression years?[6]

Educational Trends, 1920–1950

Change behind the schoolhouse door is harder to measure than aggregated statistical trends of enrollment, graduation rates, school terms, average daily attendance, and per-pupil costs, but the statistics do provide a larger context for appraising educational practice. They at least indicate in a gross way how many pupils were in school for how long and what resources were available for educating them. We have chosen to bracket the 1930s by statistics on the 1920s and 1940s so that the depression years can be seen as part of thirty years of development. The depression decade did not much deflect trends that had been established in the 1920s and that continued fairly steadily in the 1940s. Looking backward, one could say that these long-term trends better predicted what happened to schools in the 1930s than the catastrophic events in the economy or the major shifts in the government outside the schools.

Figure 1 shows the thirty-year trends in enrollment at the elementary and secondary levels. Although the elementary enrollments fell, reflecting a drop in the birth rate beginning in the 1920s, the secondary schools increased until the 1940s. The percentage of persons aged five to seventeen attending school increased steadily each year from 1920 (83.2) to 1940 (94.2); then it dropped slightly during the war years, and then rose again to 92.3 in 1950. As figure 2 illustrates, the young people attending school received a steadily larger number of days of schooling per year (with the exception of a brief dip during World War II). Another measure of the "gross educational product" of those thirty years—shown in figure 3—is the percentage of the population of seventeen-year-olds who graduated from high school. Again except for a dip during the war, this curve moved upward steadily from 16.3 percent in 1920 to 57.4 percent in 1950, with the sharpest proportional growth taking place in the depression years (from 28.8 percent in 1930 to 49.0 percent in 1940). Figure 4 indicates that the elementary pupil-teacher ratio re-

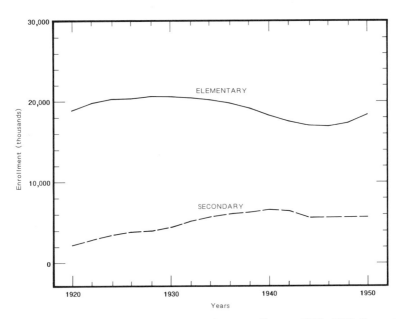

Figure 1. Trends in elementary and secondary enrollment, 1920–1950. Source: *Historical Statistics of the U.S.*, I, 368.

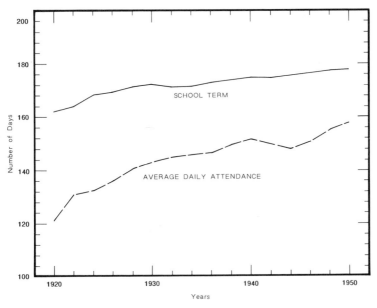

Figure 2. Length of school term and average attendance, 1920–1950. Source: *Historical Statistics of the U.S.*, I, 375.

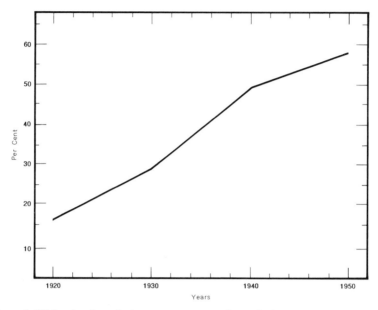

Figure 3. High school graduates as percentage of population seventeen years old, 1920–1950. Source: *Historical Statistics of the U.S.*, I, 379.

mained mostly stable during the three decades; the secondary ratio climbed briefly during the early years of the depression and then continued its long-term modest drop. Finally, figure 5 plots the expenditures per student in average daily attendance. The curve, turning downward only in the harshest years of the early depression, again shows that the long-term upward trend in school finance was only slightly affected by the depression.[7]

The aggregated national figures suggest the overall dimensions of change and stability, but they obscure the enormous differences between districts. An average teacher-pupil ratio, for example, blurs the urban and rural disparities, city classes typically being much larger than those in one-room schools. The variance in per-pupil costs between regions, between black and white schools, and between districts within states was striking. In addition, school finances were more strained than the generally rising per-pupil expenditures would suggest, for enrollments were decreasing at the cheaper elementary level and growing at the more costly secondary level.

During the depression there was a sharp rise in high school at-

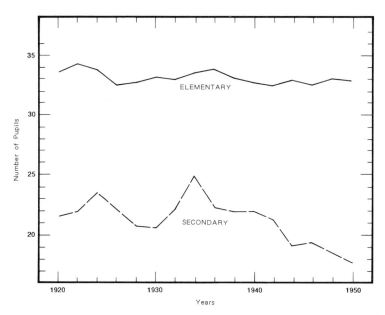

Figure 4. Public school pupil-teacher ratio, 1920–1950. Source: *Historical Statistics of the U.S.*, I, 368.

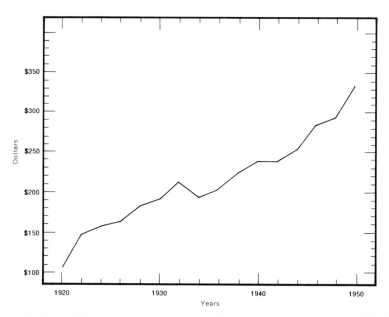

Figure 5. Expenditures per pupil in average daily attendance in constant (1970) dollars, 1920–1950. Source: *Historical Statistics of the U.S.*, I, 373–374.

tendance: pupils who previously would have been in the workforce—
children from poor families—came to classrooms. It would be a
mistake, however, to attribute this increase primarily to the depression, for the curve of increased retention began its rise early in the
twentieth century. The growing proportion of teenagers attending
high school in the period from 1920 to 1940 resulted from the interaction of many factors, among them changes in the labor market
that lowered the demand for youthful workers; a growing conviction
among parents and youths themselves that secondary school would
help them obtain better jobs; compulsory schooling and child labor
laws; declining birth rates, which meant that parents had fewer children to support and needed their children's wages less; and greater
availability of high schools, particularly in small communities. Each
year a larger and larger number of young people progressed to higher
levels of the system. Even major events like the depression and
World War II only marginally affected this long-term trend. In a
regression analysis of the effects of the business cycle and war on
high school attendance from 1910 to 1970, Abbott L. Ferriss has
estimated that the percentage of unemployed people in the labor
force explained only 1 to 3 percent of the variance in the progression
from ninth to tenth grade and from tenth to eleventh grade during
those years. For the passage from eleventh to twelfth grade, however,
the unemployment rate explained 8 percent of the variance in attendance, and the expansion of the military in wartime explained 10
percent. The draft had a greater effect (negative) on enrollments
than did even massive unemployment (positive).[8]

Ferriss does indicate an interesting deviation from the general
upward trend during the 1930s for each high school grade level. He
finds that there was a drop in the rate of increased attendance in the
most severe years of the depression—especially from 1932 to 1934—
and a tendency for attendance to rise when the economy began to
improve. To some degree this finding is counterintuitive. One might
expect youths to attend school when jobs were most scarce and to
seek jobs when employment began to rise. There are at least two
possible explanations for the apparent anomaly. One is that some
families simply did not have the money to pay for even the minimal
costs of attending high school—shoes and clothing, carfare, textbooks. (Recall that one reason for the NYA work-study program for

A high school classroom. Concho, Arizona, 1940. Photo by Russell Lee.

high school students was to give them funds for such purposes and that the agency claimed that its modest subsidies enabled hundreds of thousands of youths to attend school.) Another possible reason is that even in the hardest times youths were sometimes able to find some sort of work—at least part-time—that helped their families to survive. In his sample of California families, Glen Elder found that 72 percent of the boys and 43 percent of the girls in deprived families with unemployed fathers were working at paid jobs, ratios well above those in nondeprived families.[9]

In any case, the rise in high school retention rates during the 1930s convinced many educational policy-makers and practical teachers that they should try to adjust the curriculum to the "new students"— the diverse clientele appearing in secondary classrooms. Powerful influences, however, impeded change in high schools as in the rest of the public school system. And to those elements of continuity and innovation we now turn.

Rhetoric and Reality in Educational Reform

Historians disagree about whether the depression was a high point of reform in public education, a progressive era. One reason they disagree is that the word "progressivism" designated many different ideas and practices—it was, and is, a foggy concept. Another reason is that historians have looked at different kinds of evidence; those who focused on what leaders said, on their rhetoric, often reached different conclusions from those who sought to discover what actually happened behind the schoolhouse door. We shall suggest some of the varieties and progressivism, examine some examples of reform, and analyze impediments to change in the 1930s.

Educators talked a great deal about reform during the depression. As Patricia Albjerg Graham has observed, it was a great age of ideology in education. Journals and conventions and yearbooks of school people resounded with words like "democracy," the "new education," the "project method," and "socialized learning." Whole states—California, for one—climbed aboard the progressive rhetorical bandwagon. The Progressive Education Association (PEA) reached the peak of its membership and influence during the depression decade; it received a large sum from the General Education Board to conduct its noted Eight-Year Study in modern secondary education. The word "democratic" so infused educational discourse, Richard Hofstadter has written, that when school administrators "are trying to assure that the location of school toilets will be so clearly marked that the dullest child can find them, they grow dizzy with exaltation and launch into wild cadenzas about democracy and self-realization."[10]

"Progressivism," then, was fashionable, but what did it mean? It was easier to see what the reformers were against than to specify what they approved, for the prescriptions were legion. They disliked "traditional education," by which they typically meant teaching familiar academic subjects by recitation. A chart on the two kinds of school gave one enthusiast's view (see figure 6).

The Two Extremes

By HELEN HAY HEYL

Supervisor, University of the State of New York, Albany

This chart does not represent the teaching of any school of thought, but merely indicates the two extremes in practice.

Principal credit for the ideas here presented is ascribed by Miss Heyl to Rugg's "The Child Centered School."

TRADITIONAL SCHOOL	PROGRESSIVE SCHOOL
Child is *sent* to school which is *kept* until four o'clock, after which he " explodes into freedom! "	Child goes to school and cannot get there early enough, he lingers in shops, laboratories, yards, and libraries until dusk or urgent parents drag him homeward.
This is a school for *listening*.	This is a school for *working*.
Children are pigeon-holed in long rows of desks.	Children are seated in groups at light tables in comfortable chairs.
Children sit quietly, studying their lessons.	Children sit working at projects, asking questions as needs arise. They " learn by doing " under wise teacher-guidance.
Movement means marching in rows at signal, teacher-directed and teacher-controlled.	Movement means purposeful activity, with consideration for the rights of others, and leads to self-direction and self-control.
Child learns unquestioning obedience to authority.	Child learns obedience through participation.
Keynotes are *memorize, recite, pay attention*.	Keynote: *Experiences leading to growth*.
Child's mind is submitted to the grindstone of an educational discipline which dwarfs his capacity to think for himself.	Child is taught to think, to develop tolerant understanding, to question critically, to evaluate.
AIM: *Mental discipline* which it is believed will produce good citizens.	AIM: *Growth and tolerant understanding* which it is believed will produce good citizens and the improvement of the social order.

Figure 6. Which way is better? The traditional school versus the progressive school. Source: *Journal of Education* (November 7, 1932): 602.

This version of progressivism stressed techniques of instruction that emphasized activity, participation, and "growth." It represented the pedagogical side of reform, which was probably the mainstream of progressivism. But other kinds of reformers also thought of themselves as progressive—social reconstructionists who wanted to use the schools to bring about a new, collectively planned social order; administrators who wanted to produce specialized bureaucracies replete with testing, tracking, and experts in guidance; libertarians inspired by psychological theories that demanded leaving the child alone to follow the trajectory of natural development; and liberals who proposed community-based schools (like Nambé) to assist the dispossessed in regenerating their neighborhoods.[11]

Hardly any of the educational reform ideas in circulation during the 1930s were new, with the possible exception of the radicalism of the social reconstructionists. Almost all of the school districts that were known as centers of progressivism in the depression (to name four: Winnetka, Illinois; Bronxville, New York; Raleigh, North Carolina; and Denver, Colorado) had already begun their reforms in the 1920s or earlier. While the depression stimulated certain kinds of reform—for example, radical views of the role of the school—it dampened others. Libertarian concepts of the freedom of the individual child, which triumphed in the Freudian schools of the 1920s, lost much of their appeal in the socially-minded 1930s. Retrenchment slowed the addition of expensive new social services. And even wealthy suburbs struggled to keep progressive practices alive amid widespread attacks. To the degree that progressive educators succeeded in retaining old programs or installing new ones, they had to work within severe fiscal constraints in most districts. And the success of publicized reforms probably obscured the conservatism of the great mass of American public schools.

As we turn to examples of reform and then to impediments to change during the depression, it is useful to recall that rhetorical shifts can be measured more easily than innovation in classrooms. Many contests were more symbolic than substantive. The reforms called "progressive" started well before the depression. In many communities the shortage of dollars and the outcries against fads and frills in the 1930s stymied even modest advances in a progressive

A first-grade classroom. Norfolk, Virginia, 1941. Photo by John Vachon.

direction, save as such reforms could be advertised as enhancing economy and efficiency. Progressivism seems to have fared best in relatively prosperous states and districts and to have most affected children from favored social classes. Ironically, of course, these were the groups least in need of help, an issue to which we later return in examining the abiding lines of inequality in the society and in the schools.[12]

Examples of Reform

The reformers wrote voluminously about their work. Perhaps the most famous report came out of the Eight-Year Study (1933–1941) led by Wilfred Aiken, the head of a private school. This experiment, more than any other event of the 1930s, gave the depression years a reputation for innovation. Reform-minded secondary schools had chafed for decades under what they called the domination of college requirements—the demand that students take certain courses and be examined on those for college admission. Educational reformers claimed that this severely limited the freedom of high schools to experiment in curriculum and methods. "The reason for the nearly complete failure of the secondary schools to respond to the progressive stimulus," wrote one advocate of change, "seems to lie in the college-entrance requirements, which effectively determine the major part of the secondary curriculum, preserve the crystallization of that curriculum in 16 admittedly artificial Carnegie units, maintain the predominance of the tool subjects, grant to the content subjects only a marginal limbo, and for schools whose students must pass College Entrance Examinations dictate even the specific material to be included in unit courses."[13]

In 1930 the PEA appointed a committee to look into this problem. By 1932 this Commission on the Relation of School and College had persuaded about two hundred prestigious colleges to accept graduates of experimental programs without applying the usual admission standards. As participants it selected at first twenty-seven secondary schools, later enlarged to thirty and then reduced to twenty-nine. The time was ripe for such a test. Colleges, even many of the most eminent, were hurting for students. In the East only Harvard, Radcliffe, and Yale refused to participate. The gamble was a slight one, for participating colleges gained publicity and the commission agreed to select "only schools of highest character and excellence and established reputation." The principals in these select schools would then guarantee the students' abilities, serious interests, and quality of preparation in college subjects.[14]

The secondary schools that participated in the Eight-Year Study were hardly a representative cross-section of American secondary education. They were mostly what would later be called "lighthouse schools" and were selected by the commission from over two hundred institutions nominated because they were well known for their quality as progressive schools. Thirteen were prestigious private schools, six were laboratory schools connected with universities, and ten were public high schools in innovative systems. In Denver more than one high school took part in the experiment, and there the so-called

Aiken classes constituted a kind of school within a school composed of motivated college-preparatory students. The dice were loaded in favor of the success of the undertaking. Not only were the schools outstanding individually, but the opportunity to share ideas and to evaluate their own programs by watching how their students did in college created a larger esprit de corps among them. The study won what for that time were enormous grants from the Carnegie Corporation ($70,000) and the General Education Board ($622,500) and the assistance of a superb evaluation team led by Ralph W. Tyler.[15]

At first the schools diverged widely in what they proposed to do with their new freedom from college requirements, ranging all the way from teaching "The Progress of Man through the Ages" to instruction in "Football from the Spectator's Point of View." This diversity reflected the piecemeal nature and philosophical confusion of much that passed for progressivism. But over time schools participating in the Eight-Year Study converged on certain broad themes in their curriculum and instruction. Most of the schools developed some kind of "core curriculum," or blending of subjects like humanities and social sciences (for example, cross-disciplinary study of modern American culture); most provided for individualized work, especially in the arts; most decreased emphasis on specialized study in foreign languages, mathematics, and the individual sciences; and almost all stressed democratic participation in decision-making. The new methods broke down the distinction between the curriculum and "extracurricular activities"; artistic performance, field trips, community work, and publications were seen as an intrinsic part of the learning process.[16]

The Eight-Year Study enjoyed the sponsorship of the PEA, the financial support of foundations, the sanction of leading colleges, a sophisticated evaluation effort that encouraged self-conscious measurement of results, and a membership of largely elite schools. Not surprisingly, given the upper-middle-class character of most of the schools and the students, the graduates did well in college both in their classes and in their nonacademic ventures. But even the reforms conducted in these schools under such favorable auspices proved to be short-lived; when an investigator visited the schools at the end of the 1940s, he found few traces of the experimental programs.[17]

A great deal of "progressive" innovation took place in scattered, piecemeal fashion. In 1937 and in 1939, for example, 193 teachers in one-room schools in Michigan reported on changes they had made in their teaching as a result of in-service courses they had taken in new ways to teach. Their accounts form a tapestry of what the "new education" meant to rural teachers. Dena Beltman in Fennville put up curtains on the windows and pictures on the walls and put the bolted-down desks on skids so that they could be regrouped. Alice Cross in Bangor helped the children make puppets and write and stage a puppet show on the Pilgrims. The pupils in Ruth Eckert's class in Hudson wrote a school newspaper that they duplicated for the community in hectograph copies. The upper-grade boys in another class made skis from hard maple. Many of the teachers turned over the running of the everyday tasks of the school—making and serving lunch, cleaning up, greeting visitors, preparing for assemblies for parents—to committees of students. Some had science projects that included field trips to collect plants and animals for a nature corner in the schoolhouse. Underlying the new approaches was a common philosophy: that children could learn best through common activities that called on them to develop skills and knowledge of use to them in their own community.[18]

Perhaps more than any other state, California was a pioneer in the new education during the 1930s, and its State Department of Education tried to coordinate innovation. The director of its Bureau of Elementary Education, Helen Heffernan, was an enthusiastic advocate of Dewey's educational philosophy. She used the bureau's publications, state-sponsored conferences, and leagues of cooperating schools to advance the cause of child-centered schooling across the state. To her this meant an activity program adapted to pupils' interests. The state superintendent, Vierling Kiersey, used some of the language of the social reconstructionists about the need for social planning for a new social order and the dangers of selfish individualism, but his vote went for a moderate New Deal program of recovery rather than the more radical vision of Counts. (Kiersey was a Republican, a Mason, and a card-carrying member of the Optimist Club and the Sons of the Revolution—the American Revolution, not the communist.) In California during the 1930s it was fashionable to be "progressive," but that meant a gradual evolution and im-

Children arriving at a one-room school. Grundy County, Iowa, 1939.
Photo by Arthur Rothstein.

Studying insects. White Plains, Greene County, Georgia, 1941. Photo
by Jack Delano.

provement of schools along lines already laid down during the previous two decades.[19]

In 1933 the Association of California Principals called for "A New Deal in Secondary Education," a program of change consonant with Superintendent Kiersey's goals. They called for a new social studies curriculum that would help to prevent another depression, unlike the "socially impotent, politically spineless, and economically innocuous" fare of the past. Kiersey and the principals interested in reform created a Committee on Secondary Education and a group of cooperating experimental high schools to accelerate changes. The latter group was similar in spirit to the Eight-Year Study, for students graduating from the experimental high schools could be admitted to the University of California without meeting the usual requirements if they were recommended by their principals.[20]

Progressivism in secondary education in California meant different things to different people. The State Department of Education estimated in 1938 that one-quarter of four hundred senior high schools had instituted some type of curricular change: integration of social studies and English in core courses; remedial work in language and mathematics; individual guidance and orientation classes. About 75 percent of junior high schools claimed that they had some kind of blending of subjects in combined classes. Partly because of the new kinds of students remaining in high school and the fiscal and psychic costs of repeating grades, ability grouping of students and social promotion became more common. The relatively rich secondary schools of California were also able to add new courses and extracurricular activities. The specific programs advocated by "progressives" gave the state's ambitious school leaders a yardstick by which to measure their achievements. But the historian Irving J. Hendrick has concluded that "aside from a few inspired experiments and some noble statements of intent, the rate of change was not particularly impressive. In fact, charges leveled against the secondary curriculum in the late thirties were very little different from those common several years earlier."[21]

Although some state departments of education, like California's, used their influence to make educational reform attractive, ultimately decisions about educational practice were made in local communities. These decisions, in turn, reflected differences of values, of political cultures, and of distribution of wealth and power at the local level. In their study of Middletown, Robert and Helen Lynd speculated why the waves of change generated by distant forces—federal programs, new professional norms developed in university schools of education and taught to educational leaders, social movements inspired by powerful ideologies—swept through some communities with powerful force and merely lapped at the banks of tradition in others. As the Lynds argued, many factors beyond a general emotional receptivity to reform help to explain why some districts innovate while others do not: "The factors include a community's wealth, the relative urgency with which its different problems press upon it, the tenacity of its traditions, the presence or absence of strong local personalities with an active interest in a particular change, the rate of change in the larger culture surrounding it, and the development in this larger culture of clearly defined and easily transmittable yardsticks by which such relative lags as may exist in local procedures can be recognized."[22]

   In Middletown the Lynds found conflicting forces of educational reform and cultural conservatism. The resulting educational practice they called "change of a 'conservatively progressive' sort." The pressures of new kinds of students in the high schools impelled educators familiar with the "new education" to devise new courses like "shop math" and "business English" and to expand what they called "guidance" and "individualization," following national trends in educational philosophy. But local power-holders wanted to keep costs down by keeping class size high and salaries low. They kept close watch on radicalism in an attempt to preserve the midwestern verities. The resulting system, the Lynds argued, was a characteristic product, "a culture under strain. It has, for the most part, left the central educational train untouched and simply hitched on another boxcar called a 'guidance program.' "[23]

   In a study of four Illinois communities in the 1930s, Arthur Zilversmit has underscored the importance of local wealth and differing political cultures. Of the four, two were wealthy Chicago suburbs (Winnetka and Lake Forest), one a small industrial city (Waukegan), and one a village (Mundelein). Only Winnetka had a thoroughly progressive system, the product of its innovative superintendent Carleton Washburne and an upper-class reformist school board. The political culture of Winnetka reflected the liberal ideology of its elite leaders, who in the second decade of the twentieth century had decided to create a public school system similar in program and spirit to the kinds of upper-middle-class progressive private schools that dotted the wealthy suburbs of the nation at that time. In 1919 the liberal board, largely trained at eastern prep schools and colleges and sophisticated about the new education, invited Washburne to run the schools. The "Winnetka plan," as it came to be called, combined an individualized system of teaching basic skills and knowledge—whereby pupils proceeded at their own rates through programmed texts—with a stress on creative and social learning in groups in a correlated curriculum in art, music, and social education. In the early depression local critics accused the schools of having too many fads and frills and a lack of discipline; they also worried about Washburne's "radicalism." The pace of innovation slowed, but Washburne held his job.[24]

Lake Forest, by contrast, made some rhetorical bows to progressivism but stressed drill and separate disciplines. Instead of building a community house and a publicly owned public utility, as did its neighbor Winnetka, the Lake Forest citizens attended their exclusive social clubs and looked down on Winnetkan women as overly intellectual bluestockings. Both groups were prosperous Republicans, but their commitment to community enterprises was markedly different. Public schools in Lake Forest were for other people's children, not for the elite. "In short," writes Zilversmit, "Lake Forest chose a path of privatism and noblesse oblige while Winnetka committed itself to a pattern of upper class reform."[25]

If the depression had relatively little impact on these rich suburbs, on industrial Waukegan it fell with considerable force. The city had adopted some of the reforms considered "progressive" earlier in the century—art, music, manual training, domestic science, physical education. After a drop in revenues in the early 1930s, funds for these subjects were cut. The board cut teachers' pay by 45 percent, shortened the school year, and enlarged classes. Teaching methods in Waukegan had hardly been progressive in the best of times, but the fiscal crunch forced teachers to adopt the most traditional of methods. One fifth-grade class had only a single copy of the approved textbook. The teacher had to read it aloud to the students.

The village of Mundelein simply continued during the 1930s with its rote methods of the 1920s. "We were supposed to cover the material in a year," said one teacher, "and that didn't leave much time for anything else." Another said that her classroom was like the one she had attended as a girl. Winnetka and the Progressive Education Association were another world to the people who worked in Mundelein.[26]

Impediments to Change in the 1930s

Our reading of the evidence on educational practice during the depression years suggests that there were many more Mundeleins and Waukegans than Winnetkas, many more high school classes like the English recitation in Buffalo than like the progressive ones publicized in the Eight-Year Study. To the degree that there was actual reform behind the schoolhouse door—and there surely was—it followed ideals developed well before the depression. Many of the school systems that did embody "progressive" practices in the 1930s were struggling to maintain the momentum of reforms launched in the second or third decades of the century, often against the opposition of local worthies opposed to innovative subjects. To the extent that the depression itself promoted the adoption of different practices in the schools, reforms tended to be those that promised greater economy and efficiency, such as testing and tracking students and promoting them each year.[27]

In the early years of the depression, in particular, school leaders often complained that retrenchment was forcing a retrogression to the public education of a generation earlier. Less money meant that teachers and students had to make do with old facilities, old textbooks, bolted-down desks. Between 1930 and 1934 the sale of textbooks dropped by about one-third. A survey in one state discovered that one-third of the pupils lacked required textbooks—one in ten did not even have half of those they needed—and that the average date of publication of history books was 1924. The first cuts in programs typically struck the subjects last added and presumably the most modern, such as art and music, manual arts and home economics, physical education and health. And the neediest districts— those where there were the largest numbers of unemployed parents and hungry and sickly children—were the first to eliminate social services centered in the schools: medical and dental care, recreation, and counseling.[28]

Michael W. Sedlak and Robert L. Church have observed, "In spite of the theoretical benefits to be derived from a broad program of social welfare and vocational adjustment services during a period of intense social turmoil, occupational displacement, poverty, and alienation, traditional academic curricula were protected and preserved far more successfully than were the auxiliary services." The high school in District 218, located in a blue-collar white ethnic community outside Chicago, was a case in point. Classes in Latin, advanced mathematics, and ancient history were continued while shop, home economics, physical education, and commerce were dropped or greatly curtailed and shops and cafeterias were converted for use as academic classrooms. Opposition to fads and frills—a common theme in the educational politics of countless communities—meant protecting the established core of the traditional curriculum and the jobs of established teachers of the older disciplines, not only the three *R*s but often traditional college preparatory subjects as well. For all the talk about the importance of the new social studies in the early years of the depression, the number of students taking courses in the field actually dropped from 1928 to 1934, and in the latter year there were many more pupils taking classes in ancient history, medieval history, and modern history than any course dealing with contemporary social science. A survey by the Regents of secondary school curricula in New York state found that in most high schools students could choose only between college preparatory subjects, home economics, and commercial courses; 97 of the 110 cities with a population over five thousand offered no industrial or technical education.[29]

In no domain of public education was the contrast between reformist rhetoric and the reality of schooling more apparent than in "guidance." Vocational and academic guidance was widely advocated as an answer—even the solution—to the youth problem in countless reports, but few youths received it. A detailed survey of sixty-two academic high schools in New York state found that 90 percent assumed "*no active concern for their pupils' vocational adjustment when they leave school*" (emphasis in source). More than half of the New York high school students interviewed in that study said that they chose their courses without anyone's advice, while only about one-quarter said that any school staff member (principal, teacher, or guidance officer) had counseled them. In California—comparatively rich, like New York—only 15 percent of all high schools had a full-time guidance counselor. Middletown, the Lynds reported, prided itself on its plan of individualized guidance, but what this meant in practice was that each high school student saw a counselor for ten minutes each semester. In Maryland, only about one-fifth of 13,528 youths interviewed in the late depression years said that they had received any vocational guidance.[30]

Reformers also claimed that schools should employ psychologically-trained staff to test pupils, to help disturbed students, and to provide a bridge between school and home for truant children. In 1937, however, in cities with a population over one hundred thousand there were only 2.82 psychologists, 0.54 psychiatrists, and 27.55 social workers per 100,000 students. An era of retrenchment like the depression was clearly a time when most school districts could not afford to add or even to retain costly social services like guidance officers or psychologists, whatever the claims of reformers.[31]

But progressive reform, it could be argued, was fundamentally a classroom affair, a new kind of interaction between the teacher and the students. Was change or continuity more characteristic in methods of instruction and in the relations between the teacher, the pupils, and what was taught? Here one is faced with the immense difficulty of generalizing about hundreds of thousands of classrooms. Vivid contemporary descriptions of successful reforms—often written by the teachers or administrators who carried them out—tempt the reader to believe, or hope, that such innovations were sweeping classrooms everywhere. We are skeptical. We suspect that actual changes in instruction were modest and that the traditional teacher-centered mode of drill and recitation remained by far the most common pattern.

Evidence for this tentative conclusion comes from different quarters. Educators commented on the grinding and depressing effect of retrenchment. An urban teacher put it this way: "Then came hard times, delayed pay, added classes, and increased numbers in those classes. Harassed by too heavy teacher loads and too many other duties, joy in our work grew less. We could no longer labor with the spirit of the artist who takes pride in his creation. We were forced to work like mill hands and like them to grind out a certain amount of routine each day." Both surveys at the time and a searching new study by the historian Larry Cuban show that traditional forms of teaching were the typical pattern. And many studies of teachers in the 1930s stressed their limited training, their subjection to constricting community norms for their behavior both in and outside the classroom, and their socialization to familiar patterns of instruction. As Arthur Zilversmit has argued, successful child-centered teaching required a high degree of commitment and sophisticated techniques that presupposed specialized preparation.[32]

The most telling investigation of classroom practice in the 1930s was the survey of schools in New York state known as the Regents' Inquiry, which included several observational studies of instruction in arithmetic, English, and social studies. Even making allowances for the biases of observers—most of them favored the newer methods of the "activity curriculum"—the verdict was quite clear: teachers typically continued to use the traditional teacher-centered instruction. After visiting 320 classrooms, the reading specialists concluded, for example, that 60 percent of the teaching was in the lowest category on their five-point scale: "A narrow, formal type of instruction which was provided during the reading period two or three decades ago, and which gave major emphasis to mastery of the mechanics of reading rather than to the broader ends which reading may serve in child life." Observers in social studies classrooms found that pupils spent over half the time on questions and recitations on the textbook. Teachers in social studies themselves reported that 12 percent of their time was spent on making the assignment, 45 percent on recitation, 23 percent on supervised study, 11 percent on tests, and only 10 percent on all other activities.[33]

Surveys of instruction in rural classrooms had documented that classroom recitation on the contents of the textbook was mainstream educational practice. In Texas, for example, observers who visited 230 rural schools during the 1920s found that the teachers mostly spent the day quizzing individuals or small groups of students on their lessons, breaking up the time into short recitation periods. One-

Children making circles at the blackboard at Lakeview (a Farm Security Administration project). Phillips County, Arkansas, 1938. Photo by Russell Lee.

third of this time was spent on drill, over half on prying out of the students what they had learned from the textbook, and less than 15 percent on other activities. Dire poverty in many rural areas during the 1930s impeded state efforts to upgrade education there, and complaints about the quality of instruction continued to recur.[34]

Using a great variety of evidence—pictures, observers' reports, descriptions by teachers and students, surveys, and other data—Larry Cuban has characterized continuity in classroom practice from the 1920s into the 1930s. He examined how the classroom space was organized (the arrangement of desks, for example), how pupils were grouped for instruction, the nature of talk in the classroom, the movement of students, and various classroom activities. Teachers, he noted, were expected to control the students and to impart skills and knowledge to them. They had to process batches of involuntary students within the boundaries of set spaces and times. From childhood, teachers had been exposed to certain ways of teaching, certain expectations about the roles of teachers. Cuban found only a modest amount of piecemeal change in the years from 1920 to 1940. Teachers adopted some parts of the "new education," those that dovetailed well with their experience and goals and the classroom realities they faced—for example, new ways of grouping students, the blending of two or more subjects, field trips, or class projects. But teacher-centered instruction continued to be the commonest pattern in the 1930s as in the 1920s, according to Cuban. Even where districts sought to install "progressive education," he estimates, the new practices rarely showed up in more than a quarter of the classrooms. The changes least likely to appear were those that "touched the center of the teacher's authority: student decision-making on what content to study; the allocation of time in the schedule; and movement in the classroom without requesting the teacher's permission." High schools were far less likely to change than elementary schools, he found.[35]

It seems likely, then, that whatever the new educational rhetoric, average educational practice was similar to the routines of Hamilton's Lamson Grammar School and the Buffalo English class with their emphasis on academic skills and facts, their bolted-down desks, their teacher-led recitations, and their traditional daily schedules. As late as 1934, 40 percent of *new* desks sold were fixed, not movable. Countless schools had to make do with the old bolted variety, whether they wished to or not. Even New York's professedly innovative superintendent preferred fixed seats, arguing that moving furniture created "noise and confusion. One teacher might want the chairs arranged one way, another teacher another way. Ease is not always productive of attention and concentration."[36]

Teachers *did* differ about how to arrange chairs. In most districts, however, their preferences counted for less than what urban administrators wanted or what the rural community expected. In 1930 over four-fifths of teachers were women. They were disproportionately young, compared with most other occupational groups: one-third of the women teachers were under twenty-five. Elementary teachers typically had little training; two-thirds of them had no more than two years of schooling beyond high school, and only one in ten had completed four years of college. As Willard Waller documents in his brilliant book *The Sociology of Teaching*, outside school—at least in small communities—teachers were expected by patrons to toe the line of the strictest moral standards regarding smoking, drinking, and sex; inside the school, which Waller called "a despotism in perilous equilibrium," teachers were expected to maintain order while giving the young the kinds of instruction familiar to their parents. Under such conditions it would hardly have been surprising if teachers taught as they had been taught.[37]

In the depression decade, moreover, community influentials were often fearful of controversy and wished the schools to inculcate a safe common denominator of conservative values. Teachers knew that if they stepped out of line, applicants were waiting to take their place. They did not need to take loyalty oaths to realize that their freedom of expression was tenuous. Church and Sedlak argue that in the 1930s school people's "primary concern . . . focused on the problem of youth's frustration with an economy in which there was no place for young people. Schools spent even more time and effort on teaching patriotism and respect for the status quo, discouraging students from questioning the system even more than they had in the twenties." Under such circumstances, even supposedly progressive methods could be used to serve conservative ends.[38]

A teacher in Middletown told the Lynds, "I am facing a new problem nowadays: My pupils insist on raising questions that I dare not let them discuss though my conscience demands that I not clamp down on their honest questions. The things they say continually keep me on pins and needles for fear some of them will go home and tell their parents. I have an uneasy furtive sense about it all." The schools there became caught in the middle of cultural and political conflict. The concept of "education for individual differences" came during hard times to clash with the symbols and folklore of solidarity and patriotism, the beliefs by which adults made sense of their lives and which they wished to have inculcated in their children. "Children encouraged to think," wrote the Lynds, "are inclined to poke a finger through the paper wall and look in at the realities within." There

TO MAKE THE SCHOOL STRIKE UNPOPULAR THE SCHOOL AUTHORITY MUST STRIKE BACK!

Local school leaders often preferred the woodshed to the counselor's office as the place to deal with student dissent. "It becomes a ridiculous spectacle," editorialized the *American School Board Journal*, "on the part of the pupil to enter upon a demonstration which holds that he is wiser than the school authorities." Source: *American School Board Journal* 86 (March 1933): 15.

were signs that the businessmen on the school board and other influential groups in the community were having doubts about any new
philosophy that would lead to uncomfortable questions about the
social order. "The same controls that are at present closing so firmly
about 'labor troubles' as a threat to 'the life of the city' will close
about the 'philosophy' of the schools," they observed. And that
would mean that "education for individual differences" would not
permit "the right to be 'different' as regards the broadening area of
issues and activities which Middletown regards as central to its group
welfare." The decentralized nature of the political economy of
schooling—and those who controlled it at the local level—set limits
on the extent of real change that could be permitted, whatever the
rhetoric of the progressives.[39]

Abiding Inequalities: Class, Race, and Gender

In Elmtown High School, in a large midwestern town, even the hooks
for coats were segregated by social class, not by law or school rules
but by the peer culture of the students. The boys and girls who arrived
from their neighborhood across the canal in shabby clothes with
homemade haircuts knew that they were to place their jackets on
the hooks in the busy hallway; the prosperous youths who drove to
school had their own corner in the cloakroom. The high school itself
was an old firetrap with narrow corridors and dark rooms, most of
it built in the 1890s. Equal opportunity in secondary education in
Elmtown usually meant making the choices dictated by social class
backgrounds—doing what your friends did and what your parents
expected, which generally turned out to be the same thing. Students
from the upper stratum typically took the college preparatory track,
those from the middle tended to favor the commercial course (especially the girls), and working-class students (when they attended
high school at all) mainly entered the general track. Students and
teachers in the academic and vocational tracks belonged in many
ways to distinct worlds, both in and out of school. School grades
were closely correlated with family status.[40]

Conservative and high-status men on the school board ran an
educational system that reflected the distribution of power and privilege in the community. Caught between professional norms and the

need to hold his job, the superintendent found it convenient to ignore infractions of rules by the prosperous and to land hard on the working-class pupils. When Frank Stone, Jr., arrived late in his father's Cadillac, the superintendent told him to sit in his office rather than going to detention hall; "Boney" Johnson, a rebellious son of a worker in the fertilizer plant, found the principal and the superintendent waiting after school to escort him to detention. Boney quit school.[41]

"Frankly, for a lot of us there is nothing here but just going to classes, listening to the teacher, reciting, studying, and going home again," said one lower-middle-class girl. "We are pushed out of things." Students from the higher classes won most of the awards and scholarships and dominated the extracurricular activities, except for sports. "You can't understand those kids unless you can get into their gangs," commented one teacher. In the school the gangs that prospered were composed of the privileged.[42]

Study after study of local communities like Elmtown showed how social stratification outside school influenced what happened inside. Despite the rhetoric of democracy so prevalent among progressives during the depression decade, socioeconomic class remained a key dividing line in the school and in the larger society. A Gallup Poll in 1940 demonstrated that not only social scientists but also a large segment of the population perceived class bias in public schools. One question asked: "Some people say that teachers favor the children of parents who have the most money or the best position in the community. Do you agree?" Forty-seven percent disagreed, but 40 percent of the representative sample did agree, with the largest assent being among low-income groups, farmers, and southerners. Another question probed attitudes toward bias in high school curricula: "Do you think that our present high school programs are planned mainly for the students who are going on to college, or for those who are not going on to college?" Thirty-nine percent said high schools were designed for both groups, 34 percent for "college only," while only 8 percent thought high schools mostly served those not going to college. A further question concerned help to poor families: "If a family is so poor that they have to keep their children out of high school, do you think that they should be given aid by the government so that the children can attend high school?" Seventy-two percent of the whole group said yes, but an interesting split occurred among the younger members of the sample: 81 percent of the lowest-income youth agreed, while only 57 percent of the upper-income youth approved the plan.[43]

In 1937 Aubrey Williams commented to the New York United Parents Association: "I often wonder why educators do not spend more of their time discussing the great spread of family income. There is no use talking to a boy in South Carolina about going to school when the average income of his father is $129 a year." Indeed, the income spread—or maldistribution of both income and wealth— did persist throughout the depression, little affected by New Deal policies. (Relief measures and social security may have raised the floor a bit, but they did not substantially change the relative position of classes or do much to promote class mobility.) In 1929, 65 percent of families and unattached individuals earned less than $2,000, a figure that increased to 77.7 percent in 1935–36 and dropped to 58.9 percent as wartime prosperity began in 1941; in 1935–36, 43.5 percent of households earned less than $1,000. By almost any standard of poverty this meant that at least a third of the nation was, as FDR said, "ill-fed, ill-clothed, and ill-housed." But the top layers of the population remained comparatively rich throughout the 1930s. In 1929 the bottom 40 percent of the population earned only 12.5 percent of the total family income and in 1941 only 13.6, while the top 20 percent commanded 54.4 percent in 1929 and 48.8 percent in 1941.[44]

Williams was right: unlike social scientists of the 1930s, educators did not like to talk about socioeconomic class. Indeed, one reason why educators objected to his NYA was the fact that it was explicitly aimed at youth from relief families. School people preferred to think of public education as class-blind. In a sense they were right, despite the great disparities of schooling for children of different classes. What they meant by class-blindness was basically two things: that public schools took all comers, from every social group (in fact were required to do so by law); and that in classrooms teachers had an ideology of treating every child fairly. "I treat all my children alike"— this norm of fairness was a tenet of professionalism supported by the expectations of parents and children. If one were to look only within individual classrooms, one might conclude that public schools were more egalitarian than any other major institution. This is not to say that schools were in fact unbiased in their operation, for they were not, but simply that on a comparative scale they were probably more equitable than other organizations that mixed classes, races, and the two genders.[45]

But if one were to look further, one would not only find many subtle discriminations within the classroom and the school but also a set of largely unintended consequences of regarding public schooling as a class-blind enterprise. The norm of fairness may have blinded educators and other Americans to the larger context and meaning of class disparities and to the actual conflicts of interest between those on the top and those on the bottom of American society. Teachers who struggled conscientiously to be equitable within their classrooms may not have perceived inequities between schools or even within tracks students pursued within schools. Middle-class in background and attitudes, many teachers had little firsthand knowledge of the desperate circumstances of daily life in their pupils' families, circumstances that constricted both present and future. If all students had an equal chance to succeed in the classrooms of class-blind schools, it seemed, all could one day have equal opportunity in life later as adults. Committed to the efficacy of education, striving for fairness in their own teaching, teachers could thus perpetuate a kind of professional parochialism with respect to the class-bound nature of American society.[46]

This ideal of fair treatment, then, could actually contribute to the justification of unequal rewards and the maldistribution of wealth. If everyone competed under fair conditions in school, then faith in education buttressed societal inequalities by postponing real reform and making structural economic change unnecessary. Study after study of high school students and their parents showed that they believed that more schooling would help them succeed in later work. This vocational motive was the prime incentive to attend school. High school dropouts and graduates interviewed during the depression in New York state illustrate this point; they were overwhelmingly convinced of the value of schooling, even though graduates in the sample had no greater likelihood than dropouts of having jobs during the drastic unemployment of the 1930s (though the kinds of jobs held by the two groups differed). Here is what the interviewers found:

The young people interviewed were asked whether they thought themselves better off than boys and girls who had had no high school training. More of the pupils who had left before graduating than of the graduates expressed some doubt, but the overwhelming majority of both groups answered yes—often with the expressed or implied comment that the question was somewhat absurd: "Anybody ought to know that the longer he stays in school the better off he will be." As many as a third of these boys and girls, whether they had graduated from the high school or not, were hoping to be able to continue their school work some day. Though their notions as to when and how they would go back were usually nebulous in the extreme, their faith in the value of schooling was obvious.[47]

Such a conceptual linking of high school to jobs had two important consequences. First, it narrowed and vocationalized what education meant. Of the New York youth still in high school, 60 percent said "that they would drop out if they thought that their schoolwork would not improve their vocational chances." Second, it reinforced the traditional view that in America success or failure depended on individual effort and that if one did not advance in life it was one's personal fault, not the result of a rigged social order. Ironically, the same study in New York concluded that "whether boys and girls just out of school succeed in getting jobs depends chiefly on luck, accidental contacts, and 'personality'." Such factors were, of course, often linked to class origins—to middle-class modes of self-presentation, for example—and class origins, in turn, strongly influenced whether students would complete high school. Employers may not have paid much attention to school grades or school recommendations, but there were differences in the kinds of jobs available to high school graduates and to dropouts. Employers gave preference to graduates for white-collar jobs, whereas in blue-collar jobs dropouts outnumbered graduates. "So far as there exists a caste system in present-day industry," observed Francis T. Spaulding, "that system tends to distinguish roughly between young people who have finished high school and young people who have not." Under the severe unemployment of the 1930s, schooling could not guarantee jobs, but high schools did help to sort young people for different occupational destinies. In this sense the faith in education had some substance.[48]

In his book *Youth Tell Their Story*, Howard M. Bell presents powerful evidence linking the class background of Maryland youth to their educational attainment. These data are given in table 6. Despite the intent of educators to provide a class-blind education in the classroom, then, it is clear that the inequalities embedded in the social system exercised a powerful effect on how much schooling

Table 6. The percentages of out-of-school youth of various groups who did not go beyond the eighth grade

Classification of youth	Percentage of each group
All nonstudents	39.1
Employed	37.2
Homemakers	41.9
Unemployed	42.6
White	33.2
Negro	68.4
Female	32.8
Male	45.4
Nonrelief	34.4
Relief	68.2
Number of living children in parental family:	
One	22.2
Four	35.0
Seven	52.4
Nine or more	66.1
Father's occupation:	
Professional–technical	7.6
Office	11.1
Sales	14.2
Managerial	16.2
Skilled	32.5
Domestic–personal	39.1
Semiskilled	43.0
Farm owner–tenant	48.8
Unskilled	66.1
Farm laborer	86.3

Source: Bell, *Youth Tell Their Story*, p. 58.

individuals actually received. And that educational attainment, in turn, had a direct correlation with the types of jobs that youth were able to find, as shown in table 7. Thus socioeconomic background powerfully determined how much education people received, and schooling was a potent sorting system allocating individuals to the labor market. Behind the schoolhouse door, as outside, class was a powerful determiner of life chances. Yet because of the fact that public schooling was theoretically equally available to all, it was natural for those on the bottom to blame themselves: "Without school, you're no good. My father and mother had none, and I know what that has meant to them." Or a comment from a laborer who left after sixth grade: "I wish I'd a went higher. You can't get a job lots of places without a high school education."[49]

One way that educators blurred the actual functioning of class in shaping experiences in school and later in the labor market was the categorization of "innate abilities" of individual students. For example in Detroit—where educational testing became a religion—educational planners believed that students could be divided into three major groups: those with abilities to deal with abstractions, those who combined abstract abilities with "motor" abilities, and

Table 7. Median school grade completed by employed out-of-school youth according to the youth's occupational field

Youth's occupation	Median grade	Number of cases on which median is based
Professional–technical	15.4	409
Office–sales	12.1	1,548
Managerial[a]	11.4	254
Skilled	10.2	242
Semiskilled	9.8	1,474
Domestic–personal	9.2	670
Relief projects	8.1	334
Unskilled	7.5	1,041
Total	10.5	5,972

a. Includes farm owners and managers.
Source: Bell, *Youth Tell Their Story*, p. 94.

those who chiefly were "hand-minded" (or had "motor" abilities). Figure 7 indicates how educators in Detroit thought that these three categories of students should be tracked in school and into different kinds of jobs. Within the vocational program of the Detroit schools, educators further subdivided pupils into five groups, ranging from those who presumably could only "work at (and be fairly well satisfied with) simple manual tasks under pretty complete supervision" on through groups with rising levels of skill and initiative to those who could not only supervise others but invent "amazing new contrivances." Such a division, which paralleled the deskilling of labor in industry and the separation of the planning of work from its execution, psychologists portrayed as the result of the inherent aptitudes of individuals rather than of the deliberate new social relationships of production in advanced industry. In this manner they managed to disguise—albeit unwittingly—the actual class structure not only of work but of the educational system itself.[50]

Race interacted with class in determining educational opportunities behind the schoolhouse door, for the great mass of blacks were poor. In the South racial differences in schooling were made visible in a dual system of education in which there were massive differences in the resources offered blacks and whites. In the North the differences were sometimes more subtle, more like class differences among white youth. But everywhere being born black made a vast difference in a child's life chances, in school and out.

Mainstream educational leaders, especially in the North, tended to downplay differences of race, making blacks an almost invisible presence in public schools. The "normal" pupil was typically portrayed as white. Two yearbooks of the American Association of School Administrators illustrate the point. They deal with topics that directly concerned blacks: *Youth Education Today* (1938) and *Schools in Small Communities* (1939). The book on rural education ignored blacks entirely, however, and illustrated its tale with bucolic photographs of swimming holes and country stores and a poem by James Whitcomb Riley; nothing could have been further from the consciousness that informed the documentary writings and pictures on black sharecroppers. The book on youth did mention that one-tenth of young people were black, but then ignored them for the rest of the book (which portrayed well-dressed and well-scrubbed middle-class

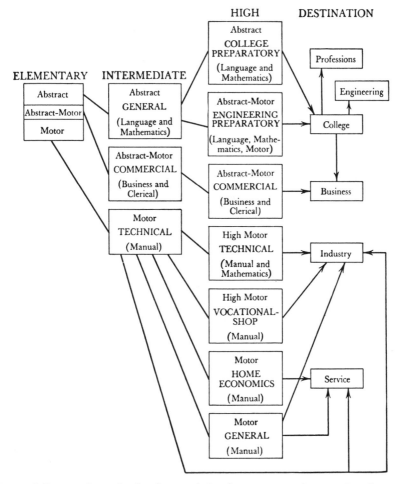

Figure 7. Routes through school to work for three presumed types of students, Detroit Public Schools. Source: Detroit Public School Staff, *Frank Cody*, p. 265.

whites). This neglect of blacks did not result from lack of studies of their situation—the 1930s were an era of eloquent analysis of the caste system and what it meant for young blacks. Rather, blacks were in this case out of the angle of vision of school administrators: invisible.[51]

At times educators seemed insensitive to their own stereotypes. At the 1937 NEA convention in New Orleans, for example, black delegates were segregated from whites, and the superintendents were regaled with a pageant called "The Glory of Dixie" in which "Negro voodoo dancers raised the primitive note of the Congo amidst the refinement of old plantation life." The black scholar Horace Mann Bond commented sardonically about a grandiose breakfast where "real Negro 'mammies' furnished incidental entertainment." And this convention was to honor the hundredth anniversary of Horace Mann's common school crusade; they chose to do this, said Bond, not by honoring his abolitionist principles but by recommending "that he be made a postage stamp."[52]

In some cases school leaders went well beyond simple neglect or stereotype. The national education honorary society, Phi Delta Kappa, which enrolled a large number of educational leaders, had a clause in its constitution specifying that "only white males of good character shall be eligible to membership in this fraternity." The white-only provision was challenged in the 1930s, but unsuccessfully, and the clause still sat in the constitution in 1939. The NEA, likewise, had segregated southern branches and proved so inhospitable to blacks that they formed their own state and national organizations. Black educators severely criticized the NEA for abandoning their interests when trying to gain passage of federal aid. Charles H. Thompson wrote that "the Harrison-Black-Fletcher Bill made its debut, but it came out garbed in soiled linen. It is hoped that the N.E.A. in the future will emulate their many sister organizations which have refused to sacrifice principle for a questionable (in fact unjust) expediency." In order to satisfy the southern sponsors of the bill, he argued, the NEA had refused to safeguard disbursements to black schools: "I am unable to see how or why anyone can seriously contend that Negroes have any reasonable chance of obtaining anything like an equitable share of the funds proposed under this Bill."[53]

In a series of essays dealing with Dewey, Counts, Rugg, and Kilpatrick, Ronald K. Goodenow has argued that even the social reconstructionists tended in the 1930s to favor a gradualist approach to racial justice, advocating educational means of changing white attitudes and failing to appreciate the need for more direct legal and political action. Rugg applauded the Tennessee Valley Authority but failed to indict the caste system it left intact. In his textbooks he talked in stereotypical terms of the "contributions" of blacks but slighted the socioeconomic roots of their degradation. Kilpatrick thought blacks and whites were to be reconciled through better "intercultural education" and through evolutionary changes in attitudes; he repeatedly counseled blacks against legal actions that might upset whites. Counts had documented unequal education for blacks in powerful empirical studies and was one of the few northern white leaders to call for desegregation and equity for blacks, but his desire for solidarity in the 1930s was "to push him," says Goodenow, "in the direction of seeing race and ethnicity in terms of dangerously unhealthy divisiveness." As a result of his concern for core values that would hold the nation together, his earlier structural analysis of the effects of poverty and caste for blacks became blurred. Even Dewey, who had been a founding member of the National Association for the Advancement of Colored People and spoke out against racism throughout his long life, shared the tendency of other social philosophers in education to stress changes in psychological attitudes as a cure for racism, to proclaim democratic ideology an antidote to prejudice and a source of consensus, and, in Goodenow's words, to "downplay racism's material and structural causes."[54]

Southern educators, drawing on the new ideas of northern progressives and often enlisting them as consultants, developed their own version of progressivism that preserved the caste system. Such states as Virginia, Alabama, and Mississippi climbed aboard the bandwagon of the new education, proclaiming that they were promoting cooperative planning, socialized learning, and even equality of opportunity. Georgia made clear what equal opportunity meant within its caste system, which placed a white race "a thousand years" advanced over a black race that was "a constant menace to the health of the community, a constant threat to its peace and security, and a constant cause of and excuse for the retarded progress of the other race." Blacks should learn cooperation by raking lawns and shining shoes; college was not for them. Their destiny was useful service to the "community" and loyalty to the existing order.[55]

The black scholars Horace Mann Bond, W. E. B. DuBois, Doxey Wilkerson, E. Franklin Frazier, Carter C. Woodson, Charles S. Johnson and others had a quite different idea about what was wrong with black education and what to do about it. In many ways people like Bond were the true social reconstructionists of the time because they had a firsthand and accurate knowledge of the underside of American society and a realistic understanding of how great a task it would be to bring about real social justice. Bond knew better than any of the Teachers College group that "the schools have never built a new social order, but have always in all times in all lands been the instrument through which social forces were perpetuated."[56]

During the 1930s black social scientists produced brilliant studies that linked black education to social structure. Some of these books— especially those on contemporary youth financed by the American Youth Commission—combined statistical analyses with poignant and penetrating ethnographies. Bond's path-breaking historical studies analyzed how the economic and political oppression of black Americans shaped their education. Other works probed the psychological effects of caste discrimination on black children. In his study *Special Problems of Negro Education* prepared for the President's Advisory Committee on Education and published in 1939, Doxey A. Wilkerson summarized the statistical effects of the powerlessness of the black caste on schooling in the South.[57]

Taken cumulatively and drawing on the different vantage points of history, sociology, anthropology, psychology, and education, these investigations told a coherent story of the results of oppression. The disenfranchisement of blacks in the South meant that the white-controlled state legislatures, county boards of education, and local authorities systematically starved appropriations for black schools. While white educators reformed schooling for whites by building new high schools, busing white children, improving the qualifications of teachers, creating programs of skilled vocational training, lengthening the school terms, and consolidating rural schools in new quarters, blacks fell further and further behind, with the result that by 1934 black children received "a smaller proportion of the public funds in the Southern states," wrote Bond, "than they have at any time in past history." The depression hit blacks with special force precisely because their school budgets had so little fat (86.3 percent of their budgets went for teachers' salaries, as compared with 78.9 percent for white schools).[58]

Wilkerson's survey of black education in the southern states demonstrated these inequalities in the mid-depression years. About 47 percent of black pupils were in the first two grades of school, compared with 28 percent of whites. Only 19 percent of blacks aged fourteen to seventeen were enrolled in high school, in contrast to 55

A new central high school for blacks. Greene County, Georgia, 1941.
Photo by Jack Delano.

percent of whites. Blacks constituted over one-fourth of the students
but received only 3 percent of the transportation budget and 12
percent of the total revenues. Blacks received only 46 percent of the
federal funds for vocational education that were legally due them.
The educational results of all this fiscal starvation, in all the Dine
Hollows of the South, were there for anyone to see. Here is a description of a typical school in East Texas:

> The building was a crude box shack built by the Negroes out of
> old slabs and scrap lumber. Windows and doors were badly broken.
> The floor was in such condition that one had to walk carefully to
> keep from going through cracks and weak boards. Daylight was
> easily visible through walls, floors, and roof. The building was used
> for both church and school. Its only equipment consisted of a few
> rough hewn seats, an old stove brought from a junk pile, a crude
> homemade pulpit, a very small table, and a large water bar-

rel . . . Fifty-two children were enrolled. All these crowded into a single small room with benches for but half that number. The teacher and pupils had tacked newspapers on the walls to keep the wind out. Rain poured through the roof, and school was dismissed when it rained. No supplies, except a broom, were furnished the school by the district during the year.[59]

Such were the educational conditions to which powerlessness, caste, and discrimination had reduced a large proportion of southern blacks. What faith could blacks place in the glorious American tradition of state and local control of education? The eminent white educators who made up President Hoover's National Advisory Committee on Education thought that even the "perplexing" problem of "negro education" would be solved by local initiative. In 1931 it commended the "impressive advance made by the colored people" together with the aid of "patriotic leaders of both races" and private philanthropy. The committee declared that state and local autonomy, coupled with modest general federal aid, "will in the end result in more lasting benefit to [blacks] than would federal action directed toward supplying quickly any special educational facilities for the Negro under federal supervision or administration." Writing in a more liberal political climate and buttressed by the kinds of data Wilkerson had amassed, FDR's Advisory Committee recommended that federal grants must be equitably divided between black and white schools, without supplanting funds already spent for black schools. But that federal aid, so desperately needed, was not to come until much later. The federal educational aid that did reach blacks came mostly through the WPA and the NYA.[60]

In the meantime, blacks realized that they themselves must press for justice and improve their own schooling. Indeed, the depression years were a period when, despite the obstacles, blacks did make modest advances. As we have indicated, half a million adult blacks learned to read and write under the WPA programs, radically reducing black illiteracy. The number of blacks attending high school more than doubled from 1930 to 1940 while the number of graduates tripled. The percentage increase in black enrollment in those years was nearly double that of whites. But blacks were still far behind whites—and in any case, where did schooling lead for them?[61]

Black educators knew perfectly well that schooling was only part—and usually a small part—of the total education of blacks; one of the great virtues of their broad-angled scholarly lens was that it encompassed the whole process by which the young "learned their place" in the caste system and the dire constraints on black political, social, and economic life both before and after schooling. Schooling alone could not, they knew, rectify a racist and class-biased society, but it could give blacks an appreciation of their heritage, survival skills, an understanding of the nature of an oppressive society, and a long-term strategy for changing that society and their own role in it. Honest social education might also one day help to solve the white problem. The black educator Walter G. Daniels wrote:

> As long as Negroes are the victims of lynching, police brutality, disfranchisement, residential covenants, higher rents, segregation, poor housing conditions, unsanitary living conditions, meager recreational opportunities, and other forms of discrimination, the social-civic aim of education is defeated. The community must demand that the school provide education that will eliminate these handicaps and develop a minority strategy which will ameliorate the undesirable conditions. The school and community, however, are under the domination of the historical tradition which would rather perpetuate these conditions, are controlled by vested interests which have preconceived ideas of what the schools should do, or are governed by political forces which are probably apathetic to the needs of an important minority. Education should begin now to change the standards, ideals, and behavior of the next generation of white citizens.[62]

It was not only the black social scientists and educators who advanced black education in the depression but also many thousands of black parents in poverty-stricken communities who contributed time and effort and their meager funds to build or repair schools, board teachers in their homes, and pay for school equipment. The NAACP aided leaders at the grass roots to get what was legally due them by seeking to convince "the mass of Negroes themselves that they are part of the public which owns and controls the schools" and by giving advice on their legal rights. In the depression decade the NAACP launched successful attacks on segregation that eventually led to the Brown decision in 1954. It also fought for equal salaries for black and white teachers. Blacks in northern cities, less subject to intimidation and reprisal than those in southern towns but still facing severe discrimination, organized to prevent segregation, win better facilities, oppose textbook stereotypes, and secure more equal access to vocational programs.[63]

In Harlem, for example, blacks actively protested what they regarded as Jim Crow education in the nation's largest city. Following a serious riot, the mayor appointed a committee to investigate the condition of the schools. The report confirmed facts already known to the blacks who lived there: that classes were crowded, often reaching fifty or more pupils and with an average of forty-five; that the buildings were obsolete and old, several of them firetraps, some with outdoor toilets and poor ventilation; that there were no nursery schools in Harlem despite the fact that there were high proportions of working mothers living in the ghetto; that lunchrooms and gymnasia were totally inadequate; that there were minuscule playgrounds, poor medical and dental assistance despite severe need, no child guidance bureaus, and too few visiting teachers to link home and school; that Harlem youth were shunted to vocational high schools and denied access to nearby academic high schools; and that all too many teachers regarded assignment to Harlem schools as a form of punishment. Parents and teachers organized to pressure the Board of Education for changes. Improvements came very slowly and parsimoniously. It was uphill work.[64]

New York prided itself on its "progressive" classrooms and its "activity program" that was extended to 10 percent of its schools in the 1930s. An average Harlem school as described by a reformist teacher, was the polar opposite of the progressive ideal:

> A typical Harlem school is like a prison, and a badly run one at that. Even the most diligent scrubbing cannot really clean a building built in the 70s or 80s; that there is not diligent scrubbing the odor of ages in the lunchrooms and the rubbish accumulated under benches testify. The children have none of the *joie de vivre* popularly associated with their age, and tuck their rachitic legs under benches too small for them in rooms unadorned, bleak and dingy. Teachers, trying to cope with classes whose numbers average slightly more than even those in other overcrowded sections, with children who have eye defects and toothaches and empty stomachs, suffer from

frayed nerves and give way to harsh-voiced impatience . . . Some bring with them indifference, some prejudice. Discriminatory practices are supposedly dealt with by the authorities; yet one teacher who snapped, "How dare you talk like that to a white woman?" was still teaching in the same school weeks after the incident.[65]

New York was hardly atypical; similar classrooms, similar attempts to segregate blacks by zoning or other methods, similar injustice, could be found in cities across the nation.

The dividing lines of class and race entered the schoolhouse as potent determinants of educational opportunity. So did those of gender, though the issue of differentiation by sex rarely surfaced as a policy question, however pervasive sex stereotyping was both in secondary classrooms and in the sexual division of labor in the economy. Even liberal New Dealers like Aubrey Williams, who was acutely aware of injustice produced by the divisions of class and race and worked diligently to reduce inequality, tended to accept the structuring of opportunity by gender. While the NYA did include females, unlike the CCC, its work and training programs usually relegated them to women's work like sewing, cooking, child care, and secretarial and clerical functions; the WPA, likewise, typically followed the sexual division of labor and sex-typed interests in its emergency education program. The school systems that had the most "progressive" differentiation of instruction tended to have the most sexual segregation in classes. It was thought to be newsworthy, if not funny, when in 1937 "home economics and manual training classes at Roosevelt High School, Dover, Ohio, changed places for a two-week period, the girls wielding hammer and saw while the boys attempted to control needles and thimble."[66]

The "youth problem" of the 1930s, like the problem of attracting and teaching "hand-minded youngsters" through vocational schooling in the early twentieth century, was seen more as a male issue than as a female one. The most visible symbols of "youth astray"— young hoboes riding the rods, youth attracted by political activists, delinquents, gangs on street corners—were typically young men. Because girls could help around the house and were not thought of as permanent breadwinners (though women did increase their comparative share of the job market during the depression), "the social pressure to seek work is not as great," said the American Youth

Commission, "and there is less stigma attached to failure in the search." But the actual problem of finding jobs for girls was "very nearly as compelling" as for boys, the commission argued. The percentage of unemployed girls was often larger than that of boys, both for whites and blacks, and when they found jobs, girls typically worked less steadily and for about one-third the male weekly salary.[67]

In the disabled society of the depression, when people were struggling to survive, when educators were trying to keep the schools on course despite retrenchment, when families sought to keep their collective lives intact, it was not surprising that there was not widespread questioning of gender bias or attacks on sex stereotyping and the sexual division of labor. At such times people often seek continuity rather than change in the deepest dimensions of their lives, and gender roles constitute one such deep dimension.[68]

Public education was deeply embedded in American society. In the final chapter we shall review how it was that schools continued to develop in familiar ways in the 1930s even under the impact of the greatest economic catastrophe America had ever known. Its finance and governance, its ideology and patterns of educational practice all remained largely intact. Part of the embeddedness of schooling reflected the deep and abiding inequalities of class, race, and gender that structured the larger society. These inequalities, too, persisted and presented a challenge to those who would have the nation realize its dreams deferred.

5 Then and Now in Public Education

In the past decade, the mid-1970s through the mid-1980s, public educators have had to learn how to cope with three kinds of scarcity: pupils, money, and public confidence. Of the three shortages perhaps the most unsettling has been the decline in confidence in a profession that for so long had millennial aspirations of service to the nation. In 1961 half of American teachers said they "certainly would" enter the classroom as a career if they were starting over again; by 1981 that percentage dwindled to 22, while the percentage saying they would not, or probably would not, teach again increased from 11 to 36. The psychic as well as the material rewards of teaching declined in the 1970s. Administrators who had been trained to manage growth found that they had to superintend decline. If expansion had meant success, did dwindling numbers of students and dollars mean failure? Just when they were being asked to do more with less, changes in governance seemed to rob local administrators of the autonomy they desired in making decisions. Everyone wanted to run the schools: courts, state legislatures, federal officials, special interest groups, teachers' unions. Everyone wanted to give marching orders, but no one wished to buy the boots. And no one seemed pleased with the results of schooling, not even educators.[1]

Dropping elementary enrollments, tax resistance, retrenchment, demands for greater efficiency, and public complaints about fads and frills were hardly new in educational history. The educators of the Great Depression would have found these trends entirely familiar. But they would have thought their peers in the 1980s incredibly affluent in comparison with the 1930s and the economy of the 1980s healthy by comparison with the maelstrom that had followed the great crash of 1929. Confronting high schools jammed to the corners with new students, the educators of the depression period might have wondered why a pupil shortage was a problem rather than an opportunity. Struggling to consolidate small schools, they saw school closings as a professional reform, not as an invitation for community conflict and an obituary for struggling superintendents.[2]

For their part, the educators of the 1980s might have looked with envy on the educators of the 1930s. Never before or since were teachers better paid in comparison with the average wage-earner than during the catastrophic year 1933. Teachers and administrators, specialists and generalists on school staffs, were largely united in a common professional front, adept in publicizing the schools and in gaining new money from the state legislatures. Local control of schooling remained strong. And despite grouses about unnecessary expenditures, the public maintained its historic faith in the value of the common school and in the dedication of teachers.[3]

In many respects the worlds of the educators of the 1930s and the 1980s were far apart. However painful to their victims, the recessions of recent years were minor in comparison with the economic collapse of the early 1930s. Many depression-era Americans believed that economic growth had permanently slowed and would have found the vast surge of development after 1941 astonishing. Political changes in the last generation—collective bargaining, new activism of the courts, federal and state legislation, militant social movements—fundamentally altered how educational decisions were made. Low-power groups that had once been largely excluded from the shaping of educational policy demanded that their interests be served. In the Sputnik and Reagan eras schools became an arena for debate about the nation's standing in international competition, whether military (with Russia) or economic (with Japan and western Europe). In successive decades the rhetoric of reform shifted from meritocratic to egalitarian to meritocratic, while schools were variously criticized for being too lenient or being too rigid. This cyclical character of reform suggested to some observers that the 1980s bid fair to reinvent the 1950s, while the gains in opportunity for the poor and minorities in the meantime were threatened or even seen as a problem.[4]

Although the hard times educators faced in the 1930s and in the last decade differed, in both periods educators confronted the politics of scarcity. What do these times of scarcity tell about the relation of schools to the rest of society? What hard educational choices have Americans made in hard times?

Public Schools in the 1930s: Embedded and Unequal

In our introduction we asked whether the depression years constituted a watershed in American public education. The simplest answer—which needs some qualification—is no. In comparison with the private economy, in which employment and the GNP fluctuated radically, public schooling remained remarkably stable in funding. The depression did not deflect much the long-term trends of institutional expansion from 1920 to 1950. Set against the transformation of the functions and scope of the federal government in the New Deal, the governance of public schools changed very little. Even when school income remained stable or dropped in absolute terms, the dollars bought more because of declining prices—a sharp contrast with the inflation of the last decade. The politics of scarcity was sometimes heated in the early depression, but for the 1930s as a whole it turned out to be the politics of compromise and continuity more than of conflict and change. Despite challenges, the ideology of public education was more reaffirmed than transformed. Public confidence in the schools remained strong. And educational practice behind the schoolhouse door showed more stability than innovation.

The picture needs some shading, however. As we have shown, nationally aggregated statistics mask vital regional, state, and local variations. The depression hit some districts far harder than others. The degree of dislocation in the schools reflected the general economic health of communities, their distribution of wealth and power, and the political cultures that influenced decisions about education. Another shading is chronological: in most districts outside the poorest communities, the depression did not really bite into educational budgets until 1932; the hardest retrenchment came in the next two years; and then most districts began a long, slow climb resembling the pre-1929 trajectory of fiscal and institutional growth. The years from 1932 to 1934 or 1935 were also the period of the most widespread questioning of the legitimacy of the American political economy generally, and specifically of the role of schooling within that social order.

The history of public schools in the Great Depression might be summarized as one of short-term dislocation and long-term continuity. Set in the perspective of long-term trends from 1920 to 1950, two characteristics of the public schools stand out: their embeddedness as an institution in the larger society and—often disguised or ignored within this embeddedness—significant inequality in the provision of public schooling.

How can one explain the embeddedness of public education— the relative continuity of ideology, of educational practice, and of finance and governance—when so much else was in flux during the depression? Part of the answer can be found in the attitudes of the public toward the schools. A Gallup Poll conducted in 1939 gave evidence of strong public support for education. Here are some sample questions and answers from a national cross-sample of adults:[5]

"Do you think young people today are getting a better education in school than their parents got?"	Yes—better	85%
	About the same	6%
	Poorer	7%
	No opinion	2%

"Many people say there is too much importance placed on education these days. Do you agree or disagree?"	No	73%
	Yes	21%
	No opinion	6%

"How do you feel about the amount of tax money now being spent for schools here—would you say it is too much or not enough?"	Not enough	19%
	About right	47%
	Too much	14%
	No opinion	20%

Such positive results accord well with a study of newspaper editorials on education during the early depression, which found strong support for teachers and for the general value of schooling (even though editors freely criticized "fads and frills" and certain peripheral parts of the system). People blamed financiers rather than the schools for the depression; schools were part of the solution, not the problem.[6]

Part of the stability of the educational system derived from a faith in schooling that remained largely unshaken by the depression. In their study of Middletown during the midst of the depression, Robert and Helen Lynd found that the people of the city, whatever the confusion caused by the gap between their traditional beliefs and the everyday lives they led, were united in their faith in education. "Middletown reaches with eagerness, albeit an eagerness tempered with caution and apprehension over the unfamiliar, for what it conceives to be its children's good. If adult Middletown sees its own hope for the immediate future as lying in hard work and making money, it has been wont to see in education the Open Sesame that will unlock the world for its children." In a time of frightening changes, many people wanted public schools to preach the familiar verities and to keep potentially restive youth in line. From left to right, critics of public schools were more likely to argue that there was not enough education (especially in depressed regions) or that it stressed the wrong things—not that education was unnecessary or did not make a difference in people's lives.[7]

A second and related source of stability resulted from the nature of the "market" that the educational profession served. Educators were fond of saying that children only grow up once and can't wait for their education, whereas the governments can, if need be, wait to fill potholes in streets and build highway overpasses. By the 1930s eight years of compulsory elementary education had become a normal part of the life-cycle of the young, except in especially deprived regions such as black areas of the rural South. The prospect of eliminating elementary education for fiscal reasons provoked an outraged response and prompt federal action to supply teachers. And during the depression decade there was strong pressure to make secondary education more universal, partly as a way of keeping youth off the labor market. Thus, even amid declining elementary enrollments there was a determination to keep the system expanding through

Dick and Jane's message to rural schoolchildren. Williams County, North Dakota, 1937. Photo by Russell Lee.

promoting the growth of high school enrollments. Even when funds lagged, demand held high.

A third cause of embeddedness lay in the sources of school finance. Despite the inadequacies of the local property tax as a means of supporting education, particularly in poor states and communities hit hard by the depression, it continued to provide a stable source of revenue in most places. When coupled with the increased buying power of the deflated dollar, the local property tax served middle-

and high-income districts reasonably well throughout the 1930s, especially after the dismal years from 1932 to 1934–35. Such a system, of course, preserved the highly unequal status quo in school finance in which the quality of schooling reflected local property wealth. Districts that enjoyed an independent status as governmental and fiscal agencies—that is, were not parts of the local government and raised income from state-mandated tax levies—had legal protection for revenues and did not face tax-cutting competition from other local agencies. They were a protected domain. Unlike most other local agencies, schools also had special standing as a *state* function only delegated to local districts. This gave education some additional legal claim on state funds. Hence educators flocked to state capitals for new funds, and state aid to public schools nearly doubled during the depression.[8]

A fourth source of stability lay in the character of the educational profession itself. Educators came from socially conservative backgrounds and were expected to meet strict standards of propriety in their communities. They sought to anchor their occupation in a prudent form of professionalism. During the twentieth century there had been a steady trend toward raising standards of certification for teachers, administrators, and specialists. Such prescribed training served several purposes beyond the usually expressed function of improving instruction (important though that was): it limited access to the occupation; it legitimized specialized expertise; and it enhanced educators' legal and professional authority. In 1930, as we have seen, the standards of training and certification were still rudimentary, especially for elementary teachers, but those standards rapidly rose during the depression. Between 1930 and 1940 the average length of schooling for teachers increased by one year; between 1935 and 1937 alone, twenty states raised the requirements. Faced with a glut of applicants, many cities imposed stiff examinations in addition to state certification requirements. "Those of us who managed to pass the teaching test in New York City were regarded as excellent prospects by the families of our girl friends," recalls one depression-era teacher. In cities especially, teaching conferred reasonable pay, security, and "an aura of authority" that few contested.[9]

Higher standards of entry and specialized certificates for positions on the hierarchical ladder were only one part of the campaign to

professionalize work in education and to give school people greater
autonomy and authority in their domain. Educators also sought to
create a united front among all educational workers in the name of
professionalism and in defense of a common occupation in which
they had invested. During the depression, in fact, little infighting
took place between teachers and administrators, specialists and classroom teachers. In contrast with many other sectors of labor-man-
agement relations—where there were sit-down and industry-wide
strikes and bitter conflict—educators tended to rally under a common
banner. The NEA resembled a company union, dominated by administrators but increasingly responsive in the 1930s to the needs of
teachers on issues like tenure, retirement funds, academic freedom,
and controlled participation in policy-making.[10]

Here and there—as in Chicago and Gary, Illinois, and Jessup,
Pennsylvania—teachers became militant when they did not receive
their pay or sought the restoration of salary cuts. Some protested
reactionary local boards or tax-cutting businessmen. Some factions
in the American Federation of Teachers opposed school administrators and demanded greater freedom of political action for teachers.
In such places as Detroit, teachers became active in school politics
to a degree uncommon before the 1930s. There and elsewhere educators rallied in defense of academic freedom. By and large, however, teachers were concerned about holding their jobs, willing to
take salary cuts or larger classes without active protest, and disposed
to act in common with administrators in the name of a selfless and
united "profession." In winning public support for the schools through
public relations techniques and in securing state legislation for laws
raising certification standards or tenure safeguards, this unity was
probably a political asset. In a time when there was a surplus of
teachers in most fields, dissidents needed unusual courage to speak
out. Unemployed urban teachers were the ones most likely to be
radical.[11]

This successful quest for increased professional autonomy not only
made educators more united politically in defending the schools from
retrenchment but also helped to increase the insulation of schools
from rapid changes in other parts of the social system. As distinctive
institutions, schools had a trajectory of development that resisted
deflection. Monumental clashes between the political parties typically

had little impact on public education. In hard times schools prospered more than the private economic sector. Major new technologies of learning, such as films and radio, penetrated the classroom but little. Although schools both reflected and shaped developments in the larger society, they had an internal logic and momentum of their own. The structure and processes of instruction, responsive to the need to process batches of students while teaching them certain required knowledge and skills and keeping them under control, changed only slowly, as we have suggested in our discussion of educational practice.[12]

There was great inequality in the resources available for educating children. Between regions and states, within states between districts, within districts between schools, and even within classrooms between children of different backgrounds, the differences in educational resources were marked: in the quality of buildings, the training and skills and attitudes of teachers, the imaginativeness and rigor of the curriculum, and the connection of what was learned to opportunities in later life. This diversity stemmed in large part from what was purported by many to be the glory of the American pattern of schooling: its decentralized political economy of governance and finance. The funds available were largely a function of local wealth or poverty; the disposition of that income depended heavily on the local political culture. The disparities in the education of Americans resulted not only from unequal wealth in different communities but also from the way in which community influentials made decisions. Here is James S. Coleman's analysis of leadership in local districts (he is speaking of a later period, but his analysis coincides with similar studies of the 1930s):

> In local communities, the political structure is most often dominated by the property-owning classes, including the social and business elite of the community. As many community studies have made clear, communities, both suburban and independent, and small or medium-sized cities, are not governed through a strong competition by political parties, but are governed by an oligarchy among whose members there is more consensus than conflict. In addition to interests in universal education . . . these men have three interests which together lead in the direction of a system of preferential or differentiated education. The first is a desire for

their own children to have maximum benefits from the educational system. The second is to keep low property taxes, from which education is largely financed. Both these interests lead to the concentration of children in schools according to background (whether through concentration of residence or through selection), and greater educational effort expended on children from better backgrounds. A third interest, that of maintaining the social order, or the social structure of the community, without the disruption caused by high social mobility, is also held by consensus in such oligarchies, and reinforces the pressure toward differential educational opportunity.[13]

Partly as a result of such political economies of schooling in local districts, actual schooling during the depression continued to reflect the abiding dividing lines of race, class, and gender that marked the larger social structure. Working-class youth did gain greater access to secondary schools, blacks made some important gains in literacy and other educational measures, and there was increased rhetoric about schools as democratic institutions. But *inequality* of educational opportunity remained a prominent feature of an educational system predicated on fairness of treatment, even in an era when economic disaster made desperate the lives of millions of people on the bottom of the social system. Indeed, the most successful efforts to reach the dispossessed took place mostly outside the mainstream of public education, in New Deal programs such as the WPA and the NYA.

Embeddedness and inequality, then, are themes that emerge from the history of public schools in the Great Depression. That terrible dislocation did not severely deflect long-term trends in public education, but this does not mean, of course, that schools are impervious to major social changes. Those long-term trends themselves result from a complex of factors—demographic, economic, ideological, political—and trends even in so persistent an institution as the public schools can be altered. Do Americans now live in a time when the public school is in an authentic crisis?

Facing Scarcity in the 1970s and 1980s

The fluctuations of the economy during the 1930s were vastly more serious than in the last decade. The economic downswing of the early depression, in particular, created a genuine emergency in school funding. But deflation of prices was easier to cope with in planning budgets than inflation, school governance was largely unaffected by the depression, enrollments grew steadily, and public confidence and professional morale remained high. Of the three shortages confronting educators in the 1980s—students, dollars, and public confidence and professional morale—the school people of the Great Depression faced only one: money. Could it be argued, then, that educators today in a new era of scarcity face a potentially more serious crisis than in the 1930s, especially if the downward trends continue unabated in an "age of slowdown"? It is difficult to separate the "hard data" on dollars and students from the "soft data" on morale and confidence, for they have been inextricably intertwined and enmeshed in the pervasive uncertainty that dogged those charged with planning for the future of public education during the last decade.

The Pupil Shortage

Educators were mostly taken by surprise by the pupil shortage of the 1970s. So, for that matter, were many demographers. In 1960 two experts predicted elementary and secondary enrollments for 1980. Their low estimate was 52,452,000, their high estimate 63,077,000. In fact, 42,917,000 students actually turned up in classrooms in 1980. Women of childbearing years, whose numbers increased sharply in the 1960s and 1970s as the postwar population bulge reached adulthood, were not having the predicted number of children. That fact was becoming apparent by the mid-1960s, but educational administrators were preoccupied with other matters: with desegregation, with new compensatory programs emerging from the war on poverty, with new curricula, with student unrest, with the four Bs—buildings, bond issues, buses, and budgets. They were still trying to build enough classrooms for what *Life* magazine had called in the 1950s a "tidal wave of students" that flooded the schools after World War II. They had little lead time in which to adjust to demographic changes, for it took only five years to grow kindergartners.[14]

Little did educators know in 1970 that a decade later school board members would rank declining enrollment as their number one concern. Indeed, 10 percent of Colorado superintendents surveyed in the early 1970s did not even know that the numbers of students were dropping in their districts. Taken by itself, the decrease in enrollments might have been a fine opportunity to improve schooling, and in many districts it was just that. School people had been struggling to find enough space and teachers ever since 1945. Fewer students meant more room for remedial classes, extracurricular activities, and offices for administrators of the new federal and state programs. It meant less crowded classrooms and hallways, more opportunity for individualized attention to pupils.

The declining numbers of students also helped to produce a surplus of teachers. This meant that administrators could choose between applicants rather than scurrying about to find enough people to staff classrooms. Thus far the drop in pupils was a net gain. But as we shall see, the decline in enrollments also brought other, less welcome developments. Educators accustomed to managing expansion at first found mild contraction a benefit, but they were ill prepared to cope with the effects of a more massive pupil shortage.[15]

Before looking at those problems of decline and the responses of educators it is useful to examine demographic patterns. Figure 8 shows the actual national enrollment trends from 1960 to 1980 and projections for the decade 1980–1990 (given the cloudiness of demographic crystal balls, these predictions need to be approached cautiously). School people did not and will not face smooth patterns of growth and decline but rather *fluctuating* enrollments, first rising on the secondary level while falling on the elementary, and then reversing those trends. Furthermore, there have been striking regional variations. Enrollments reflected not only different birth rates but also migration of families with children. Overall, the sunbelt gained in population while the snowbelt lost it. In the decade 1970–1980 all of the nine states that gained pupils were in the South and West, save New Hampshire. Nationally, the average loss of students was 10.7 percent; 16 northern states lost 15 percent or more.[16]

Within states, what kinds of school districts were most likely to lose pupils? All of the twenty-seven largest American cities had shrinking public school enrollments in the period from 1968 to 1975. Of these only seven lost less than 10 percent; fifteen lost more than 15 percent; and eight lost more than 20 percent. In plains and mountain states like Iowa and Colorado rural schools tended to show the

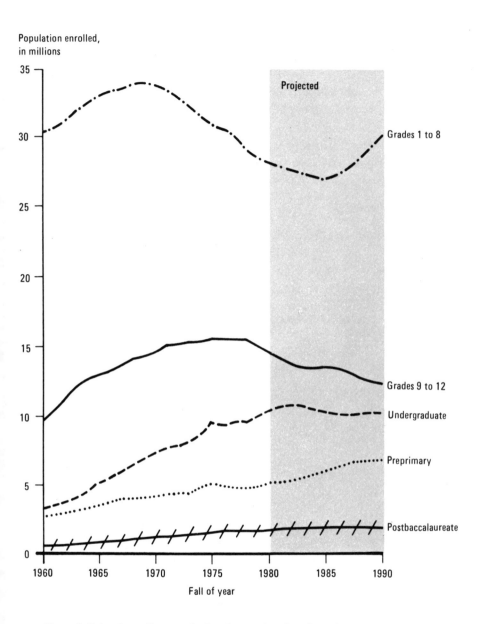

Population enrolled,
in millions

Projected

Grades 1 to 8

Grades 9 to 12

Undergraduate

Preprimary

Postbaccalaureate

1960   1965   1970   1975   1980   1985   1990

Fall of year

Figure 8. School enrollments, by level, actual and projected, 1960–1990. Source:
NCES, *The Condition of Education, 1982*, p. 11.

greatest decreases. Certain kinds of suburbs also experienced decline in students: those like Levittown, New York, which filled up with veterans after World War II who bought homes cheaply, raised their children, and stayed on to live there; wealthy suburbs like Palo Alto, California, where homes became too expensive for all but very prosperous young parents to buy; and inner-ring suburbs like Livonia, Michigan, where out-migration of families with children to larger homes in semirural areas depopulated the schools by 26 percent between 1961 and 1978. A study of declining enrollments in Michigan, Missouri, South Dakota, and Washington found the shrinkage greatest in districts with fewer than five hundred pupils and in those with more than ten thousand, although losses occurred all across the spectrum. In general, the districts that lost students in those states and in Iowa were 25 percent above average in local property wealth, a factor that helped them to cope initially with the fiscal strain induced by the shrinking enrollment.[17]

The drop in students affected different kinds of districts in quite different ways. One survey of districts with declining enrollments in Colorado, for example, found that costs increased, pupil-teacher ratios grew smaller, and student achievement and retention increased. A similar picture appeared in rural environments in Iowan declining districts. Wealthy suburbs could profit from surplus space and staff. But the effects of enrollment decline sometimes produced severe cuts in state funds per pupil, which in turn devastated local finance. Livonia, Michigan, for example, received $325 from the state for each student in attendance but lost $1,400 for each student deducted from the rolls.[18]

Educators had learned how to manage expansion but not contraction. Even in the 1930s, when the birth rate slumped, rising enrollments at the secondary level meant that the total number of students in public schools increased and staff not needed in the early grades might shift upward. But by 1970 high school enrollments had already expanded to include almost all of the age group; graduation rates remained in the 1970s at a high plateau of about 75 percent. Expanding systems offered opportunities for ambitious school people to climb the ladder into higher positions as administrators and specialists or to move about freely to other districts. But in declining school systems people tended to be less mobile both vertically and horizontally, thereby removing one incentive for able people to enter or remain in the profession. Younger teachers frequently had to be fired—"reduction in force" was the euphemism used to describe this painful process.[19]

In many states and districts financial stringency coincided with the decline in students, which increased uncertainty in planning for the future. State aid was typically tied to average daily attendance. Fewer students meant fewer dollars at a time when a larger proportion of school budgets came from state treasuries. As the number of students declined, citizens became increasingly reluctant to pass new bond levies at the local level or to raise taxes. Why should a smaller school population require more money, many people asked. It was a reasonable question, but the process of adjusting to decline was not the same as adjusting to expansion, only in reverse. Drops in the number of students typically did not occur neatly in one school ripe for closure; rather, it was a few in this classroom, a few in that. Because districts, honoring the principle of seniority, usually fired the younger, less well paid teachers, average salaries of teachers increased. Districts had fixed costs that could not be avoided simply by not purchasing textbooks or paper. Federal and state governments mandated certain new programs for the handicapped, for example—without providing sufficient funds to pay for them. Inflation and particularly the oil crisis ballooned everyday costs that could not easily be prorated to enrollment. And complicating all this fiscal uncertainty, as we shall show, were the tax revolts at the end of the decade that put caps on taxes and spending. As a result, the 1970s and 1980s were an era in which planning was exceedingly difficult.[20]

Where enrollment declines were sharp, school administrators found that merely trimming district-wide costs was not sufficient to balance budgets. It became necessary also to close schools. Since elementary and high schools were reasonably self-contained cells of the larger structure called a district, it had been relatively easy to add them during the period of expansion. But closing them inflamed intense emotions. People had a deep investment in *their* neighborhood school and often the political clout to back up their sentiment. Closing schools became the hottest of political hot potatoes in countless towns, suburbs, and cities.

There was a certain irony in all this, for closing schools had in the

Busing children at a consolidated school. Ross County, Ohio, 1940. Photo by John Vachon.

past been a sign of professional wisdom. Between 1929–30 and 1970–71 the number of elementary schools dropped from 238,306 to 65,800 and the number of one-room schools from 149,282 to 1,815. That kind of school closing had been called consolidation of rural schools. Most rural people had not liked the process—largely forced on them by state legislators and professional experts—but people in the countryside typically lacked the political power to stop it, especially in areas of declining population.[21]

Educators typically preferred to justify such rural school closings in the language of professional expertise and rational decision-making—that made the process seem less political. They had also cut budgets during the depression by invoking the canons of "scientific management." In the 1980s as in the 1930s experts in school administration wrote countless articles and handbooks on rational strategies of retrenchment. But the actual politics of school closings, as William L. Boyd discovered, was "far more a 'divide and conquer' than a 'plan and agree' process." In prosperous suburbs, rich in managerial talent, different factions used elaborate statistics and rational models to show why *their* neighborhood school should not be closed and another selected. Blue-collar communities, less accustomed to the corporate planning model and more openly "political" in their decision-making, engaged in bargaining. Big-city school boards often stalled in school closings until they were on the verge of receivership; it was easier to obscure deficits and harder in an intensely pluralistic climate to arrive at consensus. In many districts, decision-makers were likely to pick the least powerful neighborhoods for school closings, and in practice that often meant shutting schools in poor sections. This in turn removed a source of stability in neighborhoods where disintegrating influences were strong. In any case, school closings were a political arena in which there were clear-cut winners and losers, and it is not surprising that school board members and superintendents found their work increasingly arduous.[22]

The Dollar Shortage

The pupil shortage contributed to the fiscal strain that appeared in American schools in the 1970s, but an emerging dollar shortage resulted from other causes as well. At first glance, public education appeared to have fared relatively well financially during that decade. From 1970 to 1980 the per-pupil expenditures jumped (in constant dollars adjusted for inflation) from $1,680 to $2,169. Far more stable than the private economic sector—which was beset by slowed economic growth, surges of unemployment, the oil crisis (which lowered real national income), inflation, and foreign economic competition— public schools seemed in the 1970s, as in the 1930s, remarkably immune to the sharp ups and downs of private business. The rise in local property values and inflation-driven increases in sales and income taxes sustained their income. The rise in per-pupil expenditures, however, did not mean prosperity for educators, for inflation and rising energy costs in particular ate away school budgets. The real earning power of teachers fell 15 percent during the decade.[23]

Figure 9 shows the rapid absolute rise in revenues from local, state, and federal sources from 1959–60 to 1978–79. In the latter year state subsidies exceeded local ones for the first time in history, while federal aid continued to increase throughout the period but at a lower rate than state and local expenditures. This relative prosperity gave school administrators far larger budgets than the educators of the 1930s had enjoyed. But the tax-paying public was growing restive.

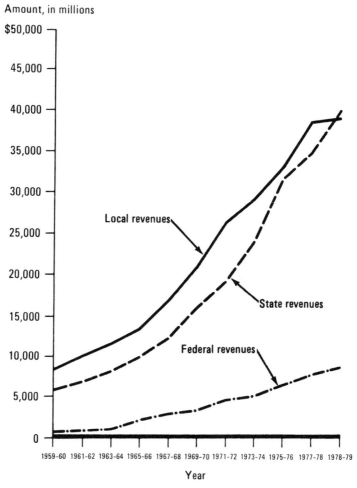

Amount, in millions

Figure 9. Revenue receipts of public elementary and secondary schools, 1959–60 to 1978–79. Source: NCES, *The Condition of Education, 1982,* p. 57.

Fewer and fewer citizens were telling the Gallup polltakers that they would be willing to pay more taxes, and they acted on their conviction: the rate of failure of local bond levies increased from 25 percent in 1964 to 54 percent in 1974. Rising home values and higher property taxes were making many people house rich but cash poor. This was especially true in the West, where 44 percent of people surveyed in May 1978 declared the local property tax to be the least fair of all the taxes they paid.[24]

Thus the stage was set for what happened on June 6, 1978, when California voters overwhelmingly approved Proposition 13, a constitutional amendment hailed or attacked at the time as the beginning of a nationwide "tax revolt" at the state level. Columnist Russell Baker quipped, "After Proposition 13 there were only about four liberals left in the country." This amendment limited property taxes to 1 percent of property value and put a cap on assessments. Its effect was to reduce average property taxes by 57 percent and to cut tax revenue by about $7 billion. In the summer that followed, members of a network of advocates of tax and spending limits initiated forty-four propositions in twenty-seven states. By November 1978, there were fiscal control measures on the ballot in seventeen states. Eight of thirteen tax limitation measures passed and four of seven expenditure limits.[25]

Were Proposition 13 and its varied offspring "the most important U.S. political-economic event of 1978, perhaps even the 1970s," as one economist asserted? Subsequent studies of the actual impact of such measures showed that their effects varied widely, but one common element was that they created uncertainty and undermined the ability of educators to plan ahead. Tax limitation and control on spending generally succeeded in cutting property taxes or slowing the growth of state and local spending, but at first most of them did not produce major cutbacks in public services. In 1978 the only state where the tax limitation threatened to cut deeply into services was Idaho. A poll of people interviewed after voting on Proposition 13 showed that over 70 percent believed that public services would not be cut. In fact, a large state budget surplus did enable the California legislature to bail out most of the local agencies, including the schools (though we will indicate in a moment some negative results as well).[26]

California was comparatively lucky; when Proposition 2½ hit Massachusetts schools, there was no state surplus. As inflation continued and the recession deepened throughout the country, the hardest-hit states cut deeply into school budgets. Michigan's governor ordered a 25 percent cutback for fiscal 1981 and called for a property tax amendment to slash revenues by $200–$290 million; in Iowa and Kentucky and Missouri the governors ordered cuts in 1981. By that year seventeen states had passed measures to set limits on taxation or spending. In several states, as in California and Massachusetts, the changes had the effect of limiting the autonomy of local districts in spending and in many cases increased state power by shifting the tax burden upward. In other states that did not have such legal caps on public funds, and in the federal government, the tax revolt had the effect of sending a message to officials and lawmakers that people wanted economy in government spending.[27]

The effects of all this on educators went well beyond the impact of fiscal strain. The tax and spending caps not only hastened retrenchment—already under way because of declining enrollments, inflation, and local resistance to bond levies—but also deepened the sense of vulnerability of educators already shaken by a decade of declining public confidence. Two case studies—of California and Massachusetts—illustrate this.

In the campaign for Proposition 13, school people were not exempt from charges by tax-cutter Howard Jarvis that they, like other public employees, were "bureaucrats at the public trough." Strikes, collective bargaining, and infighting within the educational profession had undermined the traditional image of teachers as disinterested public servants. Throughout the spring of 1978 educators were uncertain about where their paychecks would come from the next year, for the proposition would have cut about 60 percent of their expected revenues, and state aid was uncertain. They felt the abrupt ups and downs of a fiscal yo-yo. Before the March 15 legal deadline for notifying teachers of possible layoffs, almost thirty thousand teachers received notice of possible dismissal. In a decade full of "shock and overload" for educators in the state, and at a time when they were being asked to carry out a multitude of new tasks amid great flux in governance and finance, this was a final blow for many. In San Francisco alone, 2,200 teachers—half the staff—received notices. The president-elect of the San Francisco teachers' association observed that "all this is tearing the district apart. People are tired and demoralized." A study by the California State Department of Education on the effects of Proposition 13 concluded: "While the most difficult to pinpoint and describe . . . nebulous feelings of frustration and discouragement may in the long run have the greatest effect on elementary and secondary education in California, because they can lead to reduced efficiency, a high attrition rate among personnel, and a general defeatism among a group of employees who have been, traditionally, hard-working, altruistic, and reliable." A survey of teachers in 1979 found that Proposition 13 had torpedoed morale; almost 63 percent of them reported lower morale, and only 3 percent higher. Many teachers—including California's Teacher of the Year for 1978—were looking for another job.[28]

To compensate for the slack in the property tax the California legislature funneled $2 billion from its surplus into a bail-out for school districts. This represented some 90 percent of the planned 1978–79 budget, forcing elimination of some programs, the loss of 938 positions, and cuts of 63 percent in construction and equipment. Smaller districts, such as La Honda-Pescadero, had few options for economies: that district was forced to cut its administrative staff to a superintendent who doubled as high school principal while one principal supervised two elementary schools twenty miles apart. It also had to cut back on library service, adult education, supplies and equipment, and health and community service programs, while increasing class sizes. It was a pattern of cutbacks that depression educators would have recognized.[29]

An unintended consequence of Proposition 13 was a greatly increased role for the state as school finance became to all intents a state function. As a school board publication put it, "the ultimate cut is in local control." The finance plans adopted by the legislature, partly in response to court demands for greater equalization of funding under the *Serrano* decision, "leveled up" the bottom but did not leave much discretion for districts to raise extra funds locally. In addition, as school funding became more closely tied to sales and income taxes, it became more sensitive to swings of the economy— a fact that would become painfully apparent when state surpluses disappeared as the recession deepened. By February 1983 California and twenty-one other states faced deficits.[30]

When Proposition 2½ hit Massachusetts in 1980, the state had such high public expenditures that it was coming to be known as "Taxachusetts." The ballot initiative, approved by 59 percent of the voters, required all communities to bring down their property tax rates to 2½ percent of full market value if they exceeded that ratio, dropping their levies by 15 percent a year until they reached that level, and then only raising taxes by no more than 2½ percent a year. Since schools were heavily dependent on property taxes, they were especially hard hit. Another provision of the initiative abolished the fiscal autonomy of local school districts; instead of setting a budget total to be approved by the local government, they were required to work within appropriations approved by the town or city and retained authority only over the line items. Although school systems had consumed only 47 percent of local revenues prior to Proposition 2½, they suffered two-thirds of the municipal budget cuts (this resulted in the dismissal of 10,300 people). In these local political conflicts, schools suffered disproportionately. Of the 182 towns and cities that had to reduce expenditures, the big cities were hurt the most.[31]

Public schools, already reeling from the effects of high energy costs and expensive new programs mandated but not fully funded by the state or the federal government, were forced to make deep cuts in programs and services and to lay off staff and teachers. Firing teachers in mainline subjects was typically last in the list of priorities, according to two investigators who studied budget-cutting.[32]

Case studies of two Massachusetts districts, Natick and Brookline, suggest how deeply the budget knife cut. Natick faced a 15 percent cut after already closing three schools and not replacing fifty-four teachers in the previous four years. The first step it took in cutting its budget was to close two more elementary schools and one of its three junior high schools, and to lay off 24 percent of its professional staff and 30 percent of its support staff. People hired to help students with special needs—reading specialists, speech and language therapists, counselors, and others—were slated for dismissal. Fees were imposed on participants in programs that had formerly been free. Improvements in the system slowly built up over the previous generation disappeared in a matter of months as the district coped with Proposition 2½.[33]

In Brookline an anguished superintendent also witnessed the dismantling of a fine system he had labored for eighteen years to build. The first year he fired 127 out of 790 employees, including 68 professionals, closed two schools, required fees for summer schools and sports, and slashed supplies and modernization of buildings. And that was only the start. "We've peeled off the outer part of the onion and preserved the core," he said. "I'm upset about what I know we'll have to cut next time . . . There's too much human pain associated with cutting." Energy costs and minimal raises for teachers would absorb more than the 2½ percent permissible increase, he knew. What might come next? "Home economics, arts programs, music, foreign language, maybe the teacher-pupil ratio." But the real costs of retrenchment went beyond slashing programs. The good people who were going could simply not be replaced, he feared, and the biggest challenge was "how to keep morale up in the face of real gloom."[34]

Natick and Brookline were prosperous communities, better able than most to absorb tax cuts. As in the Great Depression, the dollar shortage in schools generally hit hardest the parts of the country where unemployment was highest and therefore taxes most onerous. Although schools in general are vastly better financed today than in the 1930s, there are some sections of the country where whole industries have been in a depression, not simply in a temporary recession. This is true, for example, of part of the automobile and steel industries and the lumber industry. In 1983 the unemployment rate in Flint, Michigan, was 22.0 percent; in Birmingham, Alabama, 15.9 percent; in Youngstown-Warren, Ohio, 21.1. The effects of economic dislocation in such communities reach everywhere, including the schools.[35]

The depressed state of Michigan is a case in point. State school officials there predicted that about one in ten districts might go bankrupt in 1982, while the president of the Michigan Federation of Teachers said, "I'm afraid that school closings may become just another everyday event in 1982." Since 1971 public school support has dropped from 29 percent of the state budget to 15 percent, and in 1981 local voters voted against four-fifths of requested millage increases. "Schools are no longer the sacred cows they were through the 1960s and 70s," observed a state senator. "Unfortunately, public perceptions of schools now center on crime and violence, declining test scores, teacher salaries, and strikes. These perceptions have shaken the security blanket that once encapsulated education." While budgets for prisons and social welfare were rising, those of schools were dropping.[36]

The Shortage of Public Confidence and Professional Morale

The dollar shortage was clearly related to a pervasive shortage of public confidence in the schools. In recent years public education has suffered fiscal inflation and ideological deflation. The schools have always faced critics; teachers have always complained about the low pay and low social standing accorded their high calling; but never before has public education fallen so far so fast in public regard. During the hard times of the 1930s, as we have said, the treatment of teachers and the schools in newspaper editorials was largely positive, and public opinion about the worth of public education was very favorable (even though many people complained about specific issues, like "fads and frills"). In 1946, 87 percent of Americans polled by George Gallup said that they were satisfied with the school their child atended. When asked to criticize the schools, 40 percent could not even think of one thing wrong, and the rest mostly complained of crowded buildings, not enough teachers, and an inadequate curriculum. Only 8 percent thought the teachers were doing a poor job, while 60 percent said they were doing good work. In 1955, 67 percent of Americans told Gallup that they would "be willing to pay extra taxes, if the extra money were used to raise the salaries of school teachers." In 1980 only 30 percent declared themselves willing to raise taxes. As late as 1969 three out of four had answered yes to the question "Would you like to have a child of yours take up teaching in the public schools as a career?" By 1982, however, the public had lost much of that confidence in schools and in teachers. When asked to rate the nation's public schools that year, only 2 percent gave them an A and 20 percent a B, while finding a multitude of problems. They blamed school people for poor discipline, students' use of drugs, poor curriculum and academic standards, unmotivated or untalented teachers, and a host of other problems highlighted in the media. It had been an article of faith that education was improving with every generation. By the 1980s that faith was severely shaken.[37]

The decline of confidence in public schools was only part of a more general erosion of trust in most public institutions, a development that some political observers call a crisis in the legitimacy of the modern state. Studies of popular confidence in government have shown a sharp drop of those Americans who "trust" government, from 58 percent in 1958 to 19 percent in 1978, while those who were "cynical" grew from 11 percent to 52 percent. Watergate and the Vietnam war certainly contributed to this disillusionment. But this is not simply an American development; it is common in most industrialized democracies.[38]

It is likely that part of the general malaise stems from higher public expectations of government—a reflection, perhaps, of the very kind of welfare capitalism inaugurated during the New Deal. This produces a loss of credibility when the state fails to deliver the benefits and moral leadership the people demand. Often citizens see the problems of government quite differently than do officials. In education, for example, Americans polled by Gallup rate as most serious the problems of discipline, drugs, low academic standards, finances, the securing of good teachers, and racial integration. By contrast, educators see other problems as more pressing: fiscal stress, declining enrollments, governmental interference with local autonomy, requirements in special education, and the opening of better communication with the public. Such disparate perceptions of what is wrong help to account for the disenchantment of the public and the low morale of professionals.[39]

This bifocal vision occurs again when teachers and the lay public are asked to explain why teachers become dissatisfied and leave the profession. When teachers were asked what were the most discouraging parts of their work, 66 percent pinpointed "public attitudes toward school" and 60 percent "treatment of education by the media." Low salaries were fourth in their list of grievances, while student discipline came sixth. The general public placed poor discipline first and salaries second. Clearly there was some misperception here.[40]

How and why did the shortage of confidence in public education occur? Though the answers to that question are bound up with the larger issue of declining trust in all branches of government, it is worthwhile to seek more proximate influences. We will examine four possible candidates: real or perceived faults in the schools; the politicization of education; the results of overpromising by reformers of the 1960s; and the attack on the assumptions that underlay the public philosophy of education—the traditional creed that public education is a public good.

One approach to understanding public disenchantment with the schools asserts that public schools have indeed declined in performance and quality—that the American people see real faults that need to be corrected before public education will again warrant support both fiscal and ideological. Critics point to declining test scores (at least in the upper grades of the system), violence and vandalism, neglect of the "basics," the proliferation of unnecessary electives, and generally an amoral and disorganized school climate summed up under the rubric "poor discipline." The media and popular novels have stressed such issues and have rarely given much attention to positive steps to remedy problems. Books and films exposed violence, the foibles of bureaucracy, and drugs and sex.[41]

Another way to understand public disenchantment with the schools focuses on the way schools have become battlegrounds of contending forces, reversing a long tradition in which schools supposedly reflected only those values Americans held in common and were thus "above politics." The media have given disproportionate attention to conflict: white against black, liberal against conservative; teacher strikes and political militance, which called into question the older image of the schoolmarm as selfless public servant; controversies over bilingual education, religion in the classroom, sex education, and other curricular questions; and court cases that affected school policies on issues as diverse as student rights, integration, prayer, women's sports, and special education. If educators sometimes felt themselves buffeted by these conflicts and conflicting mandates—thereby losing some of the autonomy they had once enjoyed—lay citizens who observed such conflicts saw the consensual character of education change into angry contests over who got what, when, where, and how. Education seemed to become a distressingly "political" domain.[42]

These two developments—accusations that standards and discipline were falling and increased political conflict—may indeed have lowered public confidence in the schools. So, too, the overpromising about the results of educational reform that characterized the euphoric early stages of the war on poverty and the liberal domestic phase of the Great Society programs of the 1960s. It seemed for a time that equalized educational opportunities and reforms in instruction could remedy basic social and economic problems. In this faith in schooling, advocates of reform echoed the more optimistic claims of educators of the 1930s who hoped that better schooling could eliminate the causes of depression and poverty and—in Counts's version—even build a new society. In the heady days of the 1960s both social scientists and reformers within the federal government shared those earlier liberal assumptions that equalized schooling could realize the promise of American life. And a whole brigade of educational reformers followed one another in succession, claiming that their particular innovation—performance contracting, open classrooms, programmed instruction, career education, or compensatory instruction—would solve persistent educational problems. It was a great age of panaceas.[43]

Overpromising generated skepticism and disillusionment. Scholars and publicists chipped at the roots of fundamental beliefs about education. During the depression liberals had attacked the inequalities of public education, radicals had called on teachers to use the schools to bring about a new socialist order, and conservatives had protested what they regarded as costly educational sideshows in the public schools. They did not, however, question the fundamental value of the school system. But in the late 1960s and 1970s scholars across the ideological spectrum raised basic issues about public education. Liberals began to wonder if equalizing educational resources would make much difference in educational outcomes—did more money improve education? A related question was whether schools did much—or could do much—to reduce inequalities of opportunity and achievement in later life. Debates raged over whether desegregation improved education. Radicals sought to demonstrate that schools preserved the inequities endemic to capitalism and to demystify faith in education. Conservatives attacked waste and inefficiency in education provided by the state, arguing that competition in a free market for educational services would improve schooling. Some of them advocated vouchers or tuition tax credits that could assist parents to send children to private schools. One result of all the criticisms was that the traditional civic aims of public schools—the creation of citizens who shared a sense of common purpose—became eclipsed. And the older concept of public education as a common good in itself, worthy of loyalty, found few articulate advocates in an era of politicization and disillusionment. Whether observers blamed bloated capitalists or a bloated state for the ills of education, the net result was the same: public schools were under attack.[44]

The loss of confidence in public schools heightened educators' sense that they had lost an autonomy they once enjoyed. Their low morale stemmed in part from a feeling that they were being blamed for conditions over which they had little influence. Uncertainties made planning ever more difficult. Demographic changes, for example, produced fluctuating enrollments and an increasing number of adults who were not parents and who were thus less committed to sustaining public schools. Inflation, recession, and unemployment produced acute fiscal stress. Schools served students from impoverished backgrounds and from inner-city families condemned to joblessness or underemployment for generations. The violence, drugs, and alcoholism that were rampant in the larger society invaded all kinds of classrooms.[45]

Changes in the governance of education also lessened educators' feeling of professional autonomy. Federal and state governments, responding to social movements and interest groups, and to a disenchanted public, created dozens of categorical programs, required accountability and competence testing, and regulated education at the local level to a degree never before known. The courts became much more active in a whole variety of domains: racial desegregation, school finance, student rights, the classification of pupils, discipline, services to the handicapped, and even the regulation of sports. In a litigious and regulatory age, it seemed to some educators that everyone and no one was in charge and that professionals had lost the ability to exercise their traditional discretionary powers.[46]

And on top of all this was the insecurity produced by fiscal uncertainty. Teachers felt overloaded and anxious. When retrenchment hit their schools, they found that they had to work harder as support staff were fired and survivors were expected to do more with less.

Fear hit many members of the staff each spring when "pink slip" time arrived and people received notices that they might be fired. Once secure, the occupation of teaching was now chancy; once honored as selfless service even though underpaid, the calling now failed to command the public's trust.

It is easy to imagine a future in which public schools will become a declining industry, moving unsteadily from crisis to crisis, beset by scarcities and challenges known and unknown. But American public education has survived hard times before, and an alternative future seems at least as plausible as one painted in these grim colors.

Public Schools—Still Embedded?

If one takes a long-term view of educational history, an alternate sense of the future of public education suggests itself to the vision of continuing crisis and decline in the 1980s. From this historical perspective a striking feature of American public schools has been their stability, and at times resilience, even in periods of great social stress. They have been institutions deeply embedded in American society.[47]

For over 150 years America has had public schools and recurrent depressions. But during the periodic downswings—some of them severe—as a rule school enrollments and school terms increased, attendance rose, and expenditures (in constant dollars) held steady or even improved. In these depressions state governments often reformed school finance, passed child labor or compulsory attendance laws, and pursued educational innovation. Such economically distressed periods were also frequently times when educational leaders strengthened the ideology of public schooling. During the Panic of 1837, for example, Horace Mann argued that better education would bring both individual success and economic growth. Calvin Wiley claimed that the Panic of 1857 had increased public confidence in the schools "by the contrast which the stability of its resources and the certainty of its operations have presented to the fluctuations and embarrassments of all other interests." Shortly after the economic roller coaster of the Panic of 1873, a sophisticated businessman observed that "the common schools are the one thing in regard to which there is no division of opinion in America. The people of this country cling to them and lavish appropriations upon them in the firm belief that they are the ark of the national salvation." And as we have shown, even in the worst of times—the 1930s—public education not simply survived but expanded.[48]

Is the situation similar in this decade, an era of slowdown? We doubt that it is basically different and suggest that schools are still deeply embedded in the society, even though no one talks now about the schools as "the ark of the national salvation." In saying this we surely are not suggesting that people concerned about public schools should relax and be complacent, letting the momentum of history take its course. The three shortages we described have complex interactions; low teacher morale, for example, connects closely to lack of funds and confidence and affects the quality of instruction (which may further depress public confidence—and so it goes). And drift now would endanger the meager gains of the last generation in achieving the hardest goal of public schooling: equality.[49]

Nationwide, enrollments will increase in the near future at the elementary level and will probably continue to decline during the 1980s at the high school level. Many of the most difficult adjustments have already been made, however, and the slowdown in population growth has some benefits both for public education and for the economy. Fewer dollars will be needed for new school buildings, and space which has recently been in short supply at the secondary level is now available. Many observers have concluded that the much-touted "youth problem" of the 1960s and 1970s was in part an artifact of the enormous increase in the age cohort, and present problems of unemployment stem in part from the inability of the economy to absorb those large numbers of young adults. The decline in high school (and probably college) graduates may alleviate overall unemployment in the next decade, although structural causes of unemployment may persist.[50]

The dollar shortage poses greater problems as the federal and state governments face deficits and as tax revolts reduce the ability of local districts to levy property taxes. The percentage of the gross national product devoted to education has been declining from its high of 8 percent in 1975 (up from 3.4 percent in 1949). But even in the serious recession year of 1980–81 the expenditure per pupil in average daily attendance jumped 12.2 percent over the previous year, to $2,350.

Retrenchment in the 1980s starts from a much higher level of general support than in the depression or even in the recent past. The number of teachers per one thousand pupils jumped, for example, from 44.8 in 1970 to 53.3 in 1980. Costs of instruction during that decade dropped proportionally to the costs of administration and ancillary services, meaning that there was more slack in the system as a whole. Despite the pain of budget-cutting, then, the schools are now better positioned to maintain the central core of instruction than they were in the depression, and some observers have argued that focusing on basic subjects would in fact relieve schools of attending to what they regard as secondary functions. The problem with this reasoning, as we shall suggest, is that retrenchment tends to hit most severely districts in depressed communities that need social and educational services—health care, nutrition, help in learning English—the most (as was the case during the 1930s). But taking the public schools as a whole, it appears that the dollar shortage will force painful readjustments rather than major surgery.[51]

The shortage of confidence in public education is more nebulous than the demographic or fiscal issues. Was the confidence expressed in the 1930s a function of modest expectations? It is hard to know what "confidence" really means, or indeed to know how to interpret expressions of public opinion in polls—does skepticism reflect the higher expectations of a more knowledgeable and better educated public, one that has been disillusioned by glimpses behind the scenes offered by investigatory media? People who write about the decline of faith in public institutions often disregard the evidence that citizens distrust certain private agencies even more than the public ones. In 1980 respondents to the Gallup Poll ranked labor unions, television, and big business near the bottom of their confidence list, while another poll placed law firms last. Yet this lack of "confidence" does not mean that such organizations are not powerful and viable institutions. Politicians court labor unions, people watch endless television, big business remains the most potent force in American society, and applicants vie eagerly for admission to law schools. It is clear that governmental institutions continue to have prestige and clout even though people may be cynical about them. Underpaid ministers and priests whose congregations are dwindling, on the other hand, may find it cold comfort that they rate highest in public confidence.[52]

Indices of declining confidence in public education, then, may not accurately augur the future of the institution. It is useful, moreover, to probe the meaning of the polls on education. When asked which institutions best served the public interest, public schools came second only to the churches and led (in order of confidence) local government, state government, the courts, and the federal government—suggesting that people most trusted the agencies closest to hand. The evidence is strong that Americans are just as convinced as ever of the importance of education both for the welfare of individuals and for that of the nation (although their commitment to *public* schools may be more tenuous). In 1982, Gallup asked this question: "In determining America's strength in the future—say, 25 years from now—how important do you feel the following factors will be?" Here are the results:

	Very important (%)
1. Developing the best educational system in the world.	84
2. Developing the most efficient industrial system in the world.	66
3. Building the strongest military force in the world.	47

Almost twice as many Americans ranked schools above defense as essential for the strength of the nation—scarcely a trivial estimate of the collective importance of education. And year after year on the Gallup Polls citizens show that they think schooling is crucial to individual careers. In 1982, for example, four-fifths answered "extremely important" to the question "How important are schools to one's future success?"[53]

What is one to make of the "decline in confidence" in public education, then, if schools rank second to churches as institutions serving the public interest, seem more important than factories or armies in creating a strong society, and are regarded as vital to individual advance? Are these the signs of an institution that has lost "legitimacy"? We doubt it. Rather, we suspect that the low grades Americans now give their schools result from a decline in deference for professionals and for a "sacred" institution and from higher expectations that prompt more analytic scrutiny of results from a more critical public. There are many forms of "legitimacy," and perhaps schools and other institutions have largely lost the deference toward authority that marked more traditional times. But this is not necessarily a civic misfortune, though it may be hard on professional morale. While citizens may have less regard for educators, they still care deeply about education.

Caring about education in an age of slowdown can mean many things, however. It can mean that parents will seek the best schooling for their own children by moving to districts that are still thriving or by sending their children to private schools, augmenting the slowly but steadily increasing enrollment in the private sector. It can mean that policy-makers will channel funds to the technical and scientific training of talented youth as a means of meeting foreign economic competition. It can mean concentrating on easily measured cognitive gains of those most easy to teach while slighting the special educational programs aimed at the hard-to-teach and the underserved. For all their failings, public schools may still be the most egalitarian institutions in American society. To the degree that there is a crisis in public education, it may be one that faces those on the bottom of society.

Scarcity and Equality

Speaking of public secondary education, David K. Cohen and Barbara Neufeld argue that "the problems we see now are in good measure the result of past educational successes." The redistribution of funds to the needy, increased educational attainment among youth from poor and minority families, new protections of student rights, willingness to address controversial issues, attempts to adapt the school curriculum to a pluralistic population, sensitivity to ethnic and linguistic differences, attempts to remedy bias by gender, efforts to desegregate schools—these were the fruit of a generation of deliberate campaigns to render schools more equal and just. Such reforms were the educational deposit of powerful social movements that swept across American society in the 1960s and early 1970s. But seen from the middle-class perspective of most educational policy-makers and of the most influential segment of public opinion, such changes created new problems of curriculum fragmentation, real or apparent decline in academic performance, and social unrest in the schools.[54]

In a competitive and hierarchical society, such paradoxical results were to be expected, for as Cohen and Neufeld write, "equality is at once an achievement to be celebrated and a degradation to be avoided." As schools tried to assist more heterogeneous and needy students, the task of educating all grew harder and the results more ambiguous. The efforts on public attitudes toward education were mixed, for people made both a calculus of private advantage and of social conscience. As Cohen and Neufeld say,

> Public schools are one of the few American institutions that try to take equality seriously. Yet their service in this cause has been ambiguous and frequently compromised, for the schools are a public institution oriented to equality in a society dominated by private institutions oriented to the market. In the schools America seeks to foster equality—and individual Americans seek to realize it. But in the market, Americans seek to maintain their economic and social position, thereby contributing to inequality even if they individually wish the reverse. This paradoxical relation between education and capitalism has had an enormous impact on the schools and on the role education plays in American life.[55]

Distrust about public schools, then, may reflect ambivalence about the results of pressing for greater equality in schooling.

Even in prosperous times, when redistributive educational programs meant giving the needy a larger share of an expanding pie, national political support for reforming the education of the poor stemmed from a coalition of liberals in Congress (allied with policy-shapers from the foundations and academia) who were responding to protest movements of minorities and to urban unrest. In few state legislatures were there powerful lobbies for the dispossessed, even in the heyday of the Great Society. At the local level minorities organized to press their case for integration, more ethnic history, hiring of blacks or Hispanics, and similar demands, but often they were less effective there than at the federal level or in the courts. Activist lawyers and judges used the legal system to bring about changes in state school finance, classification of pupils and testing programs, desegregation, and other measures designed to equalize education. In almost every domain of government, achieving equity was hard work, even when the economy was booming.[56]

In severe recession and retrenchment, hard times exacerbate the difficulty of retaining or expanding gains in social justice. Politicians may have been willing, even eager, to take credit for increasing funds for equalizing schools, adding new jobs and programs, and giving side payments in legislation to educational interest groups. When the task was cutting rather than augmenting budgets, however, fewer political leaders wanted to get involved. Today better education is associated with solving the economic crisis and modernizing industry, but little political mileage remains to be gained from improving the education of the poor. There is a widespread impression that too much attention has been paid to the poor and minorities, that existing programs to help them have "failed," and that it is time to get on with the task of doing a better job of educating the "mainstream student" and the gifted—preferably with few added funds. Thus the cycle of attention has come around from concern for equity for dispossessed groups to concern for efficiency and quality. Once again, as in the Sputnik era of the 1950s, worries over foreign competition spur concern for the talented.[57]

How much actual residue has a generation of federal efforts to redistribute resources actually left in the schools? During the New Deal most of the government's efforts to help children and youth—mostly outside but partly inside the schools—were targeted toward the poor and minorities. In the 1960s and early 1970s the Congress did finally get around to providing federal aid to public education through ESEA and other acts. Much of this effort was aimed at the poor and the educationally disadvantaged, especially through Title I of ESEA. The funds appropriated under this program for 1978–79 averaged almost 3 percent of total school budgets for elementary and secondary education that year. (About 95 percent of those funds went to the early years of elementary schools, where achievement scores remained steady or improved.) For the most part the largest sums proportionately went to the poorest states. All of the southern states except Florida received 4 percent or more, with the largest percentages going to Mississippi (9.86 percent) and Arkansas (7.03 percent), two of the poorest rural states. Since the big cities housed a large proportion of poor and minorities, they also received a disproportionate share of Title I funds. Big cities with high or medium-high rates of black and poor children, for example, received almost double the state average of federal money per child.[58]

Such a redistribution of educational resources had been a goal of advocates of federal aid for decades. But the federal programs fell far short of bringing about equity between the states; impoverished southern states like Mississippi still lagged far behind. State expenditures remained strongly correlated with income per capita in 1976–77 after a decade of federal aid, and disparities between states were still substantial. The most economically disadvantaged states by and large still spent the least on schooling.[59]

Another important form of educational inequality stemmed from disparities of taxable property between districts within individual states. The cherished principle of local control and finance meant that the quality of education available to students was in part a function of local wealth. Prior to the 1970s state legislatures had resisted attempts to narrow the gap between high-spending and low-spending districts, in part because people in prosperous communities had more political clout than those in poor ones and in part because of the powerful ideology of decentralized governance. The impetus for the reform of state school finance came not from legislators or local educators but from a sophisticated national network of public interest lawyers, foundation officials, and university social scientists. Moving from state to state, their usual strategy was to challenge unequal finance in the courts and to use judicial decrees to force legislatures to reallocate dollars for schools.[60]

This well-intentioned campaign had ambiguous results, especially for the poor and minorities whom finance reform was primarily designed to help. It soon became clear that creating meaningful fiscal equality was far more difficult than arguing for it in the abstract. In many states the majority of the poor and minority students lived in high-wealth, high-expenditure urban districts, so that a plan that took money away from the big cities and gave it to suburbs with a meager property base could hurt groups most in need. State aid that simply allotted the same funds for each child ignored the facts that local instructional and living costs differed greatly and that the costs of educating children with special needs effectively—the handicapped, the children of non-English-speaking parents, the poor—were higher.[61]

Beyond these questions about the impact of school finance laws on underserved pupils, there is considerable doubt about the degree to which the reforms actually lessened the great disparities between districts. One study found only minuscule differences between 1969–70 and 1976–77 in interdistrict inequalities within states. Most states did not change significantly, six showed greater disparities, and six fewer. Some case studies of school finance suggest that the new laws did more to equalize tax burdens for property owners than they did to redistribute resources to the children who needed them most.[62]

It would be a great mistake, then, to assume that the school finance and other equity reforms of the last generation give cause to be complacent about equality of educational opportunity. Such reforms as did occur came largely from the pressures created by the great social movements of the period (the campaigns for justice for blacks, women, Hispanics, and others), from liberals in Washington, and from networks of elite reformers like the school finance coalition Today there are other social movements and elite coalitions—like the tax reduction and spending limit groups—pushing in opposite directions, and the national administration has placed equity concerns low on its educational agenda. In state governments, Lorraine M. McDonald and Milbrey W. McLaughlin found, there are few spokespeople or organized constituencies working for equality. Indeed, they found that support for redistributive social goals was generally low in the political cultures within which state legislators worked and that the programs that most helped the poor and minorities had been urged on the states by the federal government in the past. This suggests that if Congress and the federal administration were to turn over all Washington dollars to states with no strings attached, the pre-reform business as usual might take precedence over categorical programs for the needy. Now that federal and state governments face deficits and budget-cutting it is unlikely that questions of social justice in education will be salient.[63]

The main reason that social movement leaders and reformers turned to the federal government and the courts in the 1960s and 1970s was that they perceived the states and the local districts to be unresponsive to their demands for change. This unresponsiveness to those on the bottom of society was one reason why New Dealers chose to bypass local educators in setting up educational programs for the underprivileged. Despite all the changes in governance in recent years, the key everyday decision-makers in public schooling remain today at the local level.

These local political economies of education continue to differ widely, as they did in the 1930s cases described by Zilversmit. Charles Bidwell and Noah Friedkin, for example, have studied what happened in Michigan when local systems responded to the governor's demand that they cut back by 10 percent in their budgets. They analyzed a key element in retrenchment—how schools allocate staff—and found an interesting pattern. About 40 percent simply assigned staff on the basis of enrollment, making no distinction between individual schools on the basis of how the pupils were achieving; 30 percent assigned more teachers to those schools where the students were not performing well; and 30 percent allocated extra staff to the schools where pupils were already scoring above average.

In three exploratory case studies they probed why local districts behaved in these distinct ways—in an even-handed, treat-them-all-alike fashion; in a compensatory mode to help those who needed added assistance the most; or in a way that favored the high achievers. What they discovered was three distinct political cultures in three local communities that chose the different ways to assign staff. The city that provided additional teachers for the neediest students had a long tradition of leaders who shared a redistributive conception of public education. The district that assigned more teachers to the high-achieving schools was marked by conflict between groups in which the richest and most powerful faction won. The third case was a large suburb that lacked the "good works" ideology found in the first and the spoils system of the second; it regarded school politics as a marketplace of influence in which the simplest solution was to provide staff to each school in proportion to enrollment.[64]

We argued earlier that public schools are institutions deeply embedded in American society, comparatively stable under stress. They are not, however, one unified and equal system. They reflect a multiplicity of aspirations and vested interests. They exist in some communities wrenched by recession and decay and others prosperous beyond the imagination of most Americans. Public schools have long been part of an energizing dream of social justice, but hard times and a conservative political climate threaten to dim that vision. Americans now face the prospect that an appalling number of children may grow up in poverty in the wealthiest nation on earth. Immigrants, many of them without resources, are flooding the nation in numbers rivalling those of the early twentieth century. Teenage unemployment among minorities in depressed cities is at near-depression levels. Rural poverty among dispossessed people is not less severe than urban, only more remote from the television cameras that focus on soup lines and people sleeping on hot-air gratings on the sidewalks.

Education alone will obviously not solve such problems, but it has been one means of redistributing a rudimentary form of opportunity. Scarcity today poses hard choices amid the paradox of seeking to make the school an agent of equalization in a struggling market society.

Notes

Introduction

1. David Tyack attended the Lamson Grammar School during the depression.

2. Charles S. Johnson, *Growing Up in the Black Belt: Negro Youth in the Rural South* (1941; reprint ed., New York: Schocken Books, 1967), pp. 109–112; Progressive Education Association, *Thirty Schools Tell Their Story* (New York: Harper & Brothers, 1943), p. 581.

1. Maelstrom, 1929–1934

1. Black social worker quoted in Studs Terkel, *Hard Times: An Oral History of the Great Depression* (New York: Pocket Books, 1978), p. 113: U.S. Bureau of the Census, *Historical Statistics of the United States: Colonial Times to 1970* (Washington, D.C.: Government Printing Office, 1975), I, 224, 135, 241, 239, 236; Broadus Mitchell, *Depression Decade: From New Era through New Deal, 1929–1941* (New York: Rinehart, 1947), p. 438.

2. Louise V. Armstrong, *We Too Are the People* (Boston: Little, Brown, 1938), pp. 16, 27; Ann Banks, ed., *First-Person America* (New York: Vintage Books, 1981), p. xii.

3. Malcolm Cowley, *The Dream of the Golden Mountains: Remembering the 1930s* (New York: Viking, 1964), p. 154, chap. 14; Dixon Wecter, *The Age of the Great Depression, 1929–1941* (New York: MacMillan, 1948), pp. 36, 211, 88.

4. Terkel, *Hard Times*, p. 123.

5. Arthur M. Schlesinger, Jr., *The Crisis of the Old Order, 1919–1933* (Boston: Houghton Mifflin, 1957), pp. 170, 172.

6. Terkel, *Hard Times*, pp. 112–113; Cowley, *Dream*, pp. 23, 22; David A. Shannon, ed., *The Great Depression* (Englewood Cliffs, N.J.: Prentice-Hall, 1960), p. 45.

7. Sidney Fine, *Frank Murphy: The Detroit Years* (Ann Arbor: University of Michigan Press, 1975), pp. 249–250.

8. Mother quoted in Dorothea Lange and Paul S. Taylor, *An American Exodus: A Record of Human Erosion* (New York: Reynal and Hitchcock, 1939), p. 14; Howard M. Bell, *Youth Tell Their Story* (Washington, D.C.: American Youth Commission, 1938), p. 29; Erskine Caldwell and Margaret Bourke-White, *You Have Seen Their Faces* (New York: Duell, Sloan and Pearce, 1940).

9. Terkel, *Hard Times*, pp. 71–75.

10. Roy E. Stryker and Nancy Wood, *In This Proud Land: America 1935–1943 as Seen in the FSA Photographs* (Greenwich, Conn.: New York Graphic Society, 1973), pp. 18, 19; Joe Klein, *Woody Guthrie* (New York: Ballantine Books, 1980), pp. 113–114, 118, 121, 126.

11. Terkel, *Hard Times*, pp. 487–488; Shannon, *Depression*, p. 140.

12. Terkel, *Hard Times*, pp. 116–117; Shannon, *Depression*, pp. 147–149; Robert S. Lynd and Helen Merrill Lynd, *Middletown in Transition: A Study in Cultural Conflicts* (New York: Harcourt, Brace, 1937), p. 145; Glen Elder, *Children of the Great Depression: Social Change in Life Experience* (Chicago: University of Chicago Press, 1974), pp. 53, 146–147.

13. Wecter, *Depression*, pp. 36, 211, 88.

14. Childs as quoted in Shannon, *Depression*, pp. 85, 75; Arthur M. Schlesinger, Jr., *The Coming of the New Deal* (Boston: Houghton Mifflin, 1958), pp. 198, 275.

15. Cowley, *Dream*, p. 30; Edmund Wilson, *The American Earthquake: A Documentary of the Twenties and Thirties* (New York: Farrar, Strauss, 1958), p. 313.

16. Terkel, *Hard Times*, pp. 248, 249; Michigan man quoted in Armstrong, *People*, p. 30; Schlesinger, *Crisis*, chap. 26.

17. Terkel, *Hard Times*, pp. 321, 338–360; Shannon, *Depression*, pp. 111–135; Cowley, *Dream*, passim; Wilson, *Earthquake*, part 2; Schlesinger, *Crisis*, pp. 207, 222.

18. Terkel, *Hard Times*, pp. 344, 355–356, 389.

19. Schlesinger, *Crisis*, pp. 4–5.

20. Ibid., pp. 181–198.

21. Edward A. Krug, *The Shaping of the American High School, 1920–1941* (Madison: University of Wisconsin Press, 1972), pp. 234–236; C. A. Bowers, *The Progressive Educator and the Depression: The Radical Years* (New York: Random, 1969), pp. 14–19; Frederick L. Redefer, "Resolutions, Reactions and Reminiscences," *Progressive Education* 26 (April 1949): 188.

22. George S. Counts, *Dare the School Build a New Social Order?* (New York: John Day, 1932).

23. George S. Counts, "Dare Progressive Education Be Progressive?" *Pro-*

gressive Education 9 (April 1932): 257–263; Bowers, *Progressive Educator,* pp. 98, 15.

24. W. S. Deffenbaugh and Emery M. Foster, *Some Effects of the Economic Situation on City Schools,* Circular no. 79, 1933 (Washington, D.C.: Government Printing Office, 1933), pp. 2–3; Department of Superintendence (hereafter cited as DS), *Official Report, 1932,* pp. 291–299; DS, *Critical Problems in School Administration,* Twelfth Yearbook (Washington, D.C.: Department of Superintendence, 1934), p. 60; DS, *Educational Leadership: Progress and Possibilities,* Eleventh Yearbook (Washington, D.C.: Department of Superintendence, 1933), p. 102.

25. Raymond E. Callahan, *Education and the Cult of Efficiency* (Chicago: University of Chicago Press, 1962).

26. David Weglein, "Report of the Committee on School Costs," DS, *Official Report, 1932,* pp. 204, 205; DS, *Official Report, 1931,* pp. 276, 304; David E. Weglein, "How Shall the Crisis be Met by School Officials?" DS, *Official Report, 1932,* pp. 86–87, 90, 86–91; Edwin C. Broome, "The Crisis Defined," DS, *Official Report, 1932,* pp. 79–81; Weglein, "Report of the Committee on School Costs," pp. 289–311.

27. Harold G. Campbell, "The Contribution of the Public Schools," DS, *Official Report, 1934,* p. 21; Charles R. Judd, "Education, the Nation's Safeguard," DS, *Official Report, 1932,* p. 31; Joseph M. Gwinn, "The State of Public Education," *Sierra Educational News* 29 (November 1933): 7; NEA Journal as quoted in H. E. Buchholz, "The Pedagogues at Armageddon," *American Mercury* 29 (June 1933): 131–132.

28. Gary superintendent quoted in *Social Frontier* 1 (February 1935): 33–34.

29. Allen W. Beach, "A Study of Welfare Work in the Schools of California" (M.A. thesis, Stanford University, 1933), pp. 90–96; Terkel, *Hard Times,* pp. 445–446; Shannon, *Depression,* pp. 51–52.

30. Edgar Knight, "Academic Freedom and Noblesse Oblige," *Teachers College Record* 37 (December 1935): 184–185; Krug, *Shaping of the American High School,* p. 238; Cowley, *Dream,* chaps. 3–4.

31. Bowers, *Progressive Educators,* pp. 80–87, 29–30, 98; Jesse Newlon, in "Panel Discussion," NEA, *Addresses and Proceedings, 1935,* p. 554; Peter A. Soderberg, "Charles A. Beard and the Public Schools, 1909–39," *History of Education Quarterly* 5 (December 1965): 241–252.

32. On radical thought generally, see Richard H. Pells, *Radical Visions and American Dreams: Culture and Social Thought in the Depression Years* (New York: Harper Torchbook, 1974).

33. Bowers, *Progressive Educator,* pp. 80–88, 108–110; Ronald Goodenow and Wayne Urban, "George S. Counts: A Critical Appreciation," *Educational Forum* 41 (January 1977): 167–174; George Counts, *The Selective Character of American Secondary Education* (Chicago: University of Chicago Press, 1927).

34. "1,105,921," *Social Frontier* 1 (January 1935): 6; C. A. Bowers, "On

Writing Context-Free History," *History of Education Quarterly* 19 (Winter 1979): 500–501.

35. National Advisory Committee on Education, *Federal Relations to Education,* Committee Findings and Recommendations (Washington, D.C.: National Capitol Press, 1931), pp. 17–18.

36. The Advisory Committee on Education, *Report of the Committee* (Washington, D.C.: GPO, 1938), pp. 33–34.

37. See George Counts, *Selective Character.*

38. Newton Edwards, *Equal Educational Opportunity for Youth: A National Responsibility* (Washington, D.C.: American Council on Education, 1939), pp. 2–14.

39. Charles Beard and William G. Carr, "The Schools Weathering a Storm," *Journal of the National Education Association* 24 (May 1935): 150–151.

40. Edwards, *Equal Educational Opportunity,* pp. 37, 40, 70, 68; chap. 4.

41. Ibid., chap. 4.

42. Advisory Committee on Education, *Report of the Committee,* pp. 9, 17; Edwards, *Equal Educational Opportunity,,* p. 91.

43. National Advisory Committee on Education, *Federal Relations to Education,* part 1, p. 107; Rex David, *Schools and the Crisis* (New York: Monthly Review Association, 1934); Mississippi agent as quoted in Doxey Wilkerson, *Special Problems of Negro Education,* U.S. Advisory Committee on Education, Staff Study, No. 12 (Washington, D.C.: GPO, 1938), p. 289.

44. Avis Carlson, "Deflating the Schools," *Harpers* 147 (November 1933): 705–713.

45. Research Division, NEA, "Current Conditions in the Nation's Schools," *Research Bulletin* 11 (November 1933): 102, 104.

46. W. S. Deffenbaugh and Emery M. Foster, *Some Effects of the Economic Situation on City Schools,* U.S. Office of Education, Circular No. 79, 1933 (Washington, D.C.: GPO, 1933), pp. 2–3; DS, *Critical Problems,* p. 60; DS, *Educational Leadership,* p. 102.

47. Stillman, "Fascism," pp. 132–134; F. L. Bird, "American Cities Face 1932," *National Municipal Review* 22 (February 1933): 51–52.

48. *Historical Statistics,* I, 368, 379–380, 375; Weglein, "School Costs," pp. 204, 205.

49. For example, see William John Cooper, *Economy in Education* (Stanford, Calif.: Stanford University Press, 1933); Henry H. Linn, *Practical School Economies* (New York: Columbia University, Teachers College Press, 1934); F. E. Henzlik, *Practical Economies in School Administration* (Lincoln: University of Nebraska Press, 1932); Weglein, "School Costs," pp. 204, 205.

50. Deffenbaugh, *Depression,* pp. 24, 19–20; Erick L. Lindman, "Are Teachers' Salaries Improving?" *Phi Delta Kappan* 52 (April 1970): 420. Teacher Salaries from U.S. Office of Education, *Biennial Survey of Education,* 1928–

30, vol. 2, p. 76; *Biennial Survey of Education*, 1930–32, chap. 1, p. 74; *Biennial Survey of Education*, 1932–34, chap. 2, p. 66.

51. George Strayer, "Educational Economy and Frontier Needs," DS, *Official Report, 1933*, pp. 138–146; "Current School Facts," *Phi Delta Kappan* 15 (February 1933): 137; "The Program of Public Education during Period of the Depression," *Phi Delta Kappan* 15 (April 1933): 165–167.

52. Sedlak and Church, "Social Services," pp. 40–59; Nelson B. Henry, "What the Depression Has Done to the Schools," *Public Management* 16 (June 1934): 204–208.

53. Bruce Smith, "What the Depression Has Done to Police Services," *Public Management* 16 (March 1934): 68, 69; Percy Bugbee, "What the Depression Has Done to Fire Departments," *Public Management* 16 (June 1934): 175–179; L. H. Weir, "What the Depression Has Done to Parks and Recreation," *Public Management* 16 (August 1934): 227–234; W. F. Walker, "What the Depression Has Done to Health Services," *Public Management* 16 (November 1934): 360–366; R. L. Duffus, *Our Starving Libraries* (Boston: Houghton Mifflin, 1933); Julia Wright Merrill, "What the Depression Has Done to Public Libraries," *Public Management* 16 (May 1934): 135–139; Glen E. Hoover, "How Much Shall Be Spent for Libraries?" *Public Management* 15 (September 1933): 272–274; Bernard Berelson, *The Library's Public* (New York: Columbia University Press, 1949): 90–91; John Boynton Karser, "Surveys and Salaries," *Bulletin of the American Library Association* 28 (April 1934): 177–194; American Library Association statement quoted in *National Municipal Review* 221 (November 1932): 626.

2. Educators and the Politics of Money

1. Henry Filer, "Organizing within the State for Better Schools," NEA, *Addresses and Proceedings, 1934*, pp. 66–68.

2. Ibid., pp. 65–69; for an account of a battle for more state funds led by a Minneapolis school board member, see N. B. Schoonmaker, "Public Schools and Politics," *American School Board Journal* 89 (November 1934): 15–16.

3. Filer, "Organizing," pp. 68–69.

4. Mary K. Herrick, *The Chicago Schools: A Social and Political History* (Beverly Hills, Calif.: Sage, 1971), p. 187, chap. 10; Robert J. Braun, *Teachers and Power: The Story of the American Federation of Teachers* (New York: Simon and Schuster, 1972), pp. 42–48; Lyman B. Burbank, "Chicago Public Schools and the Depression Years of 1928–1937," *Journal of the Illinois State Historical Society* 64 (Winter 1971): 378–379; *Tribune* quoted in Charles R. Foster, *Editorial Treatment of Education in the American Press*, Harvard Bulletins in Education, No. 21 (Cambridge, Mass.: Harvard University Press, 1938), p. 114.

5. "Suggestions toward Resolutions, American Education Week Mass Meetings, November 8," *Texas Outlook* 18 (October 1934): 26.

6. "Idaho," *Social Frontier* 2 (November 1935): 58.

7. Glen Frank, "Balanced Budgets and Unbalanced Lives," *Texas Outlook* 17 (June 1933): 6; Roscoe Pulliam, "Let Us Take the Offensive," *Phi Delta Kappan* 16 (October 1933): 84, 86; Ross Stegner, "Schoolmasters and School Wreckers," *Texas Outlook* 18 (February 1934): 20.

8. Edward C. Elliott, "In Testimony of Dr. Ellwood P. Cubberley and Capitalizing the Frontier Crisis," DS, *Official Report, 1933,* p. 159; *Texas Outlook* 17 (January 1933): 131–132.

9. Frederick H. Bair, "The Future of Education," DS, *Official Report, 1937,* p. 85.

10. David Tyack and Elisabeth Hansot, "Conflict and Consensus in American Public Education," *Daedalus* 110 (Summer 1982): 1–26.

11. Charles H. Judd, "Education," in President's Research Committee on Social Trends, *Recent Social Trends in the United States* (New York: Whittlesey House, 1934), chap. 6.

12. Ellwood P. Cubberley, "Independence in School Government a Necessity," *School and Society* 37 (March 4, 1933): 266, 269.

13. "Real Estate Boards Plan Drive for Reform of Local Taxation," *Business Week* (January 6, 1932): 9; "Illinois Taxes Incomes to Relieve Property-Holders," *Business Week* (February 24, 1932): 19; also, see account of California reform below.

14. W. S. Deffenbaugh, *Effects of the Depression upon Public Elementary and Secondary Schools and upon Colleges and Universities,* U.S. Office of Education, Bulletin No. 2, 1937 (Washington, D.C.: GPO, 1938), pp. 37–43; Educational Research Service, NEA, *State School Legislation, 1934,* Circular No. 3, 1935 (Washington, D.C.: NEA, 1935); David Tyack, "Toward a Social History of Law and Public Education," in David Kirp, ed., *School Days, Rule Days,* forthcoming.

15. National Advisory Committee on Education, *Federal Relations to Education,* Committee Findings and Recommendations (Washington, D.C.: National Capitol Press, 1931).

16. Ralph Dickerson Schmid, "A Study of the Organizational Structure of the National Education Association, 1884–1921" (Ed.D. dissertation, Washington University, 1963); Edgar Wesley, *NEA, the First Hundred Years: The Building of the Teaching Profession* (New York: Harper & Brothers, 1957); Corinne Gilb, *Hidden Hierarchies: The Professions and Government* (New York: Harper & Row, 1966).

17. Gilb, *Hierarchies;* David Tyack and Elisabeth Hansot, *Managers of Virtue: Public School Leadership in America* (New York: Basic Books, 1982), part 2.

18. Hollis Caswell, *City School Surveys: An Interpretation and Appraisal* (New York: Teachers College, Columbia University, 1929).

19. Belmont Farley, "The Citizens Conference on the Crisis in Education," *School and Society* 37 (January 21, 1933): 79–84; George H. Dern, "Value of Education to Business," *Texas Outlook* 16 (July 1932): 21.

20. For a brilliant study of the business of textbooks see Frances Fitzgerald, *America Revised: History Textbooks in the Twentieth Century* (Boston: Little, Brown, 1979); and for a modern analysis of the influence of private agencies in public education see David K. Cohen, "Reforming School Politics," *Harvard Educational Review* 48 (Fall, 1978): 431.

21. For an analysis of why business exerted this dominant influence in politics, see Charles E. Lindblom, *Politics and Markets: The World's Political-Economic Systems* (New York: Basic Books, 1977), chaps. 13, 14.

22. W. W. Charters, Jr., "Social Class Analysis and the Control of Public Education," *Harvard Educational Review* 23 (Fall 1953): 268–283; August B. Hollingshead, *Elmtown's Youth: The Impact of Social Classes on Adolescents* (New York: John Wiley & Sons, 1949), pp. 124–125; Progressive Education Association, *Thirty Schools Tell Their Story* (New York: Harper & Brothers, 1943), p. 6.

23. On the issue of pluralist political responses within capitalism more generally, see Theda Skocpol, "Political Responses to Capitalist Crisis: Neo-Marxist Theories of the State and the Case of the New Deal," *Politics and Society* 10 (1980, no. 2): 155–201; William L. Boyd, "The Public, the Professionals, and Educational Policy-Making: Who Governs?" *Teachers College Record* 77 (1976): 573.

24. *Texas Outlook* 17 (February 1933): 39.

25. Commission on the Social Studies, *Conclusions and Recommendations of the Commission* (New York: Charles Scribners' Sons, 1934), p. 16.

26. Charles Beard, "The Quest for National Security," NEA, *Addresses and Proceedings, 1935,* p. 510; Peter A. Soderberg, "Charles A. Beard and the Public Schools, 1909–39," *History of Education Quarterly* 5 (December 1965): 252.

27. Robert C. Binkley and Mervyn Crobaugh, "The High Cost of Economy," *New Republic* 73 (January 25, 1933): 285–286; "Where the Money Comes From—and Goes," *New Republic* 88 (September 2, 1936): 99; Howard K. Beale, "Forces That Control the Schools," *Harper's Magazine* 169 (October 1934): 603–616; S. Alexander Rippa, "Retrenchment in a Period of Defensive Opposition to the New Deal: The Business Community and the Public Schools, 1932–1934," *History of Education Quarterly* 2 (June 1962): 76–82; "The Attitude of Two Service Organizations toward Retrenchment in Education," *School Review* 42 (January 1934): 2–8.

28. *Idaho Journal* as quoted in *Texas Outlook* 17 (December 1933): 20–21. In 1933 John Dewey told the NEA that the chief foe of public education was the Chamber (William Dow Boutwell, "The Minneapolis Meeting," *School and Society* 37 [March 18, 1933]: 347). For persistence of tax leaguers, see "The Retrenchment Drive," *Frontiers of Democracy* 6 (April 15, 1940): 196–197. On

big business opposition, see Rex David, *Schools and the Crisis* (New York: Monthly Review Association, 1934), pp. 25–28; for local tax leagues, see Hal Stead, "Adventures of a Tax Leaguer," *Saturday Evening Post* 206 (November 11, 1933): 29–30, 90–92.

29. "The Discussion of the Yearbook," *Social Frontier* 1 (April 1935): 4–5; *Phi Delta Kappan* 18 (September 1935): 34; *NEA Addresses and Proceedings, 1935,* pp. 538, 541, 556, 538–539, 540–545, 557.

30. "National Educational Policy," *Social Frontier* 1 (March 1935): 3–4.

31. Ibid., p. 4; "The Liberal Superintendent," *Social Frontier* 1 (March 1935): 5–6.

32. "National Educational Policy," pp. 5–6, 7; "Who are the Friends of Human Rights?" *Social Frontier* 1 (October 1934): 23.

33. "Liberal Superintendent," pp. 5–7; "Friends of Human Rights?" p. 23.

34. For a balanced and perceptive appraisal of the arguments advanced by the reconstructionists, see John Dewey, "Education and Social Change," *Social Frontier* 3 (May 1937): 235–238.

35. Harold J. Laski, "A New Education for a New America," *New Republic* 87 (July 29, 1936): 343–344.

36. Ibid.; see similar critique by Eduard C. Lindeman, "Historians Turn Prophets," *Social Studies* 25 (October 1934): 279–281, and also note more practical objectives to the report by school people in the same issue.

37. Laski, "A New Education," pp. 343–345.

38. Laski, "A New Education," p. 345; John L. Childs, "Mr. Laski's Half Truths," *Social Frontier* 3 (October 1936): 16–18; for other radical writings on education and capitalism, see Theodore Brameld, "American Education and the Class Struggle," *Science and Society* 1 (Fall 1936): 1–17; David, *Schools and the Crisis*, pp. 45–46; Earl Browder, "Education an Ally in the Workers' Struggle," *Social Frontier* 1 (January 1935): 22–24.

39. Dixon Wecter, "Reading, Riting, and Revolution," *American Mercury* 41 (June 1937): 192–198; Harold Rugg, "This Has Happened Before," *Frontiers of Democracy* 7 (January 1941): 108; *New Republic* 87 (March 6, 1935): 86.

40. "The Matthew Woll Incident," *Social Frontier* 1 (February 1935): 33.

41. "Liberty in the U.S.A.," *Social Frontier* 3 (November 1936): 63—from a report of the American Civil Liberties Union called *How Goes the Bill of Rights, New Republic* 86 (March 25, 1936): 178–179.

42. Blanton quoted in *New Republic* 87 (July 8, 1936): 253.

43. Edward A. Krug, *Shaping the American High School, 1920–41* (Madison: University of Wisconsin Press, 1972), pp. 11–14, 234; M. B. Schnapper, "Legionnaires and Teachers," *Social Frontier* 4 (January 1938): 123, 120–124; "But," *Frontiers of Democracy* 6 (October 15, 1940): 5.

44. S. Alexander Rippa, *Education in a Free Society: An American History* (New York: David McKay Company, 1967), pp. 263–269.

45. Ibid., 269–276.

46. Howard K. Beale, *A History of Freedom of Teaching in American Schools* (New York: Charles Scribners' Sons, 1941): 270–271; Merwin K. Hart, "Let's Discuss This on the Merits," *Frontiers of Democracy* 7 (December 1940): 82–87; Alonzo F. Myers, "The Attack on the Rugg Books," *Frontiers of Democracy* 7 (October 1940): 17–19; Roger N. Baldwin, "Gilt-Edged Patriots, Presenting the New York State Economic Council and its Presiding Genius, Merwin K. Hart," *Frontiers of Democracy* 7 (November 1940): 45–57; Rugg, "This Has Happened Before," pp. 107–108.

47. Jerome Davis, "The Teachers Struggle for Democracy," *New Republic* 88 (March 15, 1939): 161–163; "Teachers on the March," *Social Frontier* 2 (October 1935): 5–6; "Superintendents' Meeting," *Social Frontier* 2 (April 1936): 204; *New Republic* 87 (March 11, 1936): 122; Beale, *History of Freedom of Teaching,* pp. 264–276; "Professional Security," *Social Frontier* 1 (October 1934): 9.

48. "Professional Security," p. 9.

49. *New York Sun,* January 16, 1935, as quoted in *Social Frontier* 1 (February 1935): 33–34. Wirt was also opposed to the New Deal—see Ronald D. Cohen and Raymond A. Mohl, *The Paradox of Progressive Education: The Gary Plan and Urban Schooling* (Port Washington, N.Y.: Kennikat Press, 1979), pp. 151–154. At the end of the decade there was an antiradical backlash against the reconstructionists—see William F. Russell, "Education for the Middle of the Road," DS, *Official Report, 1937,* pp. 102–110; "Democracy or Chautocracy?" *New Republic* 30 (August 30, 1939): 90; James Wechsler, "Twilight at Teachers College," *Nation* 147 (December 17, 1938): 661–663, and reply by Teachers College Professors, *Nation* 147 (December 24, 1938): 703.

50. Educational Policies Commission, *A National Organization for Education* (Washington, D.C.: NEA, 1937), pp. 13–16, 39; NEA, *Addresses and Proceedings, 1935,* p. 557; "The Discussion of the Yearbook," *Social Frontier* 1 (April 1935): 4–5.

51. Superintendent as quoted in Krug, *Shaping the High School,* p. 251; Frederick M. Hunter, "Education's Most Dangerous Rival," NEA, *Addresses and Proceedings, 1935,* p. 124. For newspaper commentary in Texas on the idea of teachers directing a new social order and a teacher's skepticism, see "Schools and Politics," *Texas Outlook* 17 (July 1933): 21.

52. Frederick H. Bair, *The Social Understandings of the Superintendent of Schools* (New York: Teachers College Press, 1934), pp. 102, 101, 27; chap. 7.

53. Ibid.; Frederick H. Bair, "The Superintendent as Social Agent," *Phi Delta Kappan* 17 (January 1935): 85–88.

54. See indexes of *American School Board Journal,* 1930–1940. On teachers of the time being subordinate to the community, see Willard W. Waller, *The Sociology of Teaching* (New York: J. Wiley and Sons, 1932), and August de Belmont Hollingshead, *Elmtown's Youth: The Impact of Social Classes on Adolescents* (New York: J. Wiley, 1949), chap. 3. For conservative ideology, see "Lack of Education: A Cause of Bankruptcy," *Texas Outlook*

17 (May 1933): 17; "School or Jail?" *Texas Outlook* 18 (February 1934): 51; George H. Dern, "Value of Education to Business," from *Colorado School Journal* and reprinted in *Texas Outlook* 16 (July 1932): 21, 47; J. Edgar Hoover, "The Task of the Teacher," *Phi Delta Kappan* 21 (March 1940): 329–330.

55. On "democratic administration," see Thomas G. Fleming, "Management by Consensus: Democratic Administration and Human Relations, 1929–1954" (Ph.D. dissertation, University of Oregon, 1982), pp. 110–141; Fred J. Kelly, "Administration of Education in a Democracy," *Phi Delta Kappan* 21 (May 1939): 409–413.

56. John K. Norton, "Report of the Joint Commission on the Emergency in Education," DS, *Official Report, 1933,* p. 293; H. J. Miller, "Reducing Public School Costs," *National Municipal Review* 21 (January 1932): 8–9.

57. Raymond Callahan, *Education and the Cult of Efficiency: A Study of the Social Forces that Have Shaped the Administration of the Public Schools* (Chicago: University of Chicago, 1962).

58. "State Educational Committee Report," *Texas Outlook* 16 (December 1932): 5; "Local Activities," *Texas Outlook* 17 (July 1933): 28; Norton, "Report of Joint Commission," pp. 283, 292.

59. Norton, "Report of Joint Commission," pp. 274–278; Norton, "Looking Ahead toward Educational Recovery," DS, *Official Report, 1935,* p. 151; "Report of the Resolutions Committee," DS, *Official Report, 1933,* pp. 301–302.

60. For an example of a popular article defending schools, see Maxine Davis, "The Little School House in the Red," *Reader's Digest,* 24 (March 1934): 46–48 (originally published in *McCall's Magazine*); John A. Sexson, "Public Relations," DS, *Official Report, 1938,* pp. 158–159; for a high-pressure business approach, see Merle Sidener, "Interpreting the Schools to the Public," DS, *Official Report, 1934,* pp. 49–52.

61 Frank A. Jensen, "Interpreting the Schools to the Public," DS, *Official Report, 1934,* pp. 163–168.

62. Norton's views as represented in NEA, *Evaluating the School Program* (Washington, D.C.: NEA, 1933), p. 4; Ben G. Graham, "The 1934 Yearbook on Critical Problems in School Administration," DS, *Official Report, 1934,* p. 35. See also Thomas W. Gosling, "Public Relations—the Responsibility of the City Superintendent," DS, *Official Report, 1933,* pp. 277–278.

63. NEA, *Evaluating the Program,* pp. 19, 90–91, 112.

64. "City Hall Costs Us 4.7%; The Rest Is Cooperative Services," *Business Week* (May 4, 1932): 28.

65. Foster, *Editorial Treatment of Education,* pp. 190–191, 35, 39.

66. Ibid., p. 121.

67. Ibid., pp. 110–116.

68. William G. Carr, "Educational Policies Commission," NEA, *Addresses and Proceedings, 1940,* pp. 883–884.

69. John A. Sexson, "The Educational Policies Commission," NEA, *Addresses and Proceedings, 1936*, pp. 463–467.

70. Willis A. Sutton, "Report of the Educational Policies Commission," NEA, *Addresses and Proceedings, 1937*, pp. 849–852; John A. Sexson, NEA, *Addresses and Proceedings, 1938*, pp. 854–859.

71. Educational Policies Commission, *A National Organization for Education* (Washington, D.C.: NEA, 1937); Frederick M. Hunter, "We Chart Our Future Policies," NEA, *Addresses and Proceedings, 1936*, p. 41; see also *Leaders in American Education*, National Society for the Study of Education, 70th Yearbook (Chicago: University of Chicago Press, 1971), pp. 70–75.

72. Two EPC volumes, written by Beard and Carr, exemplify the EPC's style of analysis: [Charles Beard], *The Unique Function of Education in American Democracy* (Washington, D.C.: NEA, 1937); [William Carr], *The Purposes of Education in American Democracy* (Washington, D.C.: NEA, 1938).

73. William G. Carr, "School Legislation as a Factor in Producing Good Schools," *American School Board Journal* 81 (December 1930): 37; Carter Alexander, "Can a School Executive Afford to Ignore the Law?" *Nation's Schools* 9 (March 1932): 29.

74. "Real Estate Boards Plan Drive for Reform of Local Taxation," *Business Week* (January 6, 1932): 9; "Illinois Taxes Incomes to Relieve Property-Holders," *Business Week* (February 24, 1932): 19. For elitist views of politics from Harvard and Stanford deans, see: Henry W. Holmes, "Politics and the Schools," *North American Review* 239 (March 1935): 162; Ellwood P. Cubberley, "Independence in School Government a Necessity," *School and Society* 37 (March 4, 1933): 266, 269.

75. Willard W. Patty, "The Educator and Legislation," *Phi Delta Kappan* 17 (January 1935): 82–83; "Should the Teachers Stay out of Politics?" *Texas Outlook* 18 (January 1934): 30.

76. Deffenbaugh, *Depression*, pp. 37–42; Ward W. Keeseker, *A Review of Educational Legislation, 1935 and 1936*, Bulletin No. 2, 1937 (Washington, D.C.: GPO, 1937); Tax Foundation, Inc., *Facts and Figures on Government Finance*, 12th ed. (Englewood Cliffs, N.J.: Prentice-Hall, 1963); "Five Years of State School Revenue Legislation, 1929–33," *Research Bulletin of the National Education Association* 12 (January 1934).

77. Judd, "Education," 368–370; Robert Lowe and Craig Richards, "Public Schools in the Depression: Why Teacher Tenure?" (colloquium paper, Stanford University, 1979); Lucien B. Kinney, *Certification in Education* (Englewood Cliffs, N.J.: Prentice-Hall, 1964).

78. Irving G. Hendrick, "The Impact of the Great Depression on Public School Support in California," *Southern California Quarterly* 54 (1972): 177–195; Arthur M. Schlesinger, Jr., *The Politics of Upheaval, 1935–36* (Boston: Houghton Mifflin, 1960), pp. 112–123: *Los Angeles Examiner* as quoted in *Texas Quarterly* 18 (October 1934): 35.

79. Elmer H. Staffelbach, "California Tax Crisis: 1933," *Sierra Educational*

News 29 (February 1933): 17–32; Vierling Kiersey, "The Challenge of the New Day," *California Schools* 5 (September 1933): 299; Willard E. Givens, "The Public Schools Belong to the People," *Sierra Educational News* 29 (January 1933): 17.

80. Staffelbach, "California Tax Crisis," pp. 26–29.

81. Hendrick, "Impact of Depression," p. 19; Willard E. Givens, "The Public Schools Belong to the People," *Sierra Educational News* 29 (January 1933): 17.

82. Hendrick, "Impact of Depression," pp. 184–185; Willard E. Givens, "Fundamentals of Public School Education," *Sierra Educational News* 29 (February 1933): 15; *Los Angeles Times* as quoted in Hendrick, p. 189.

83. Hendrick, "Impact of Depression," pp. 184–188.

84. Kiersey, "Challenge of the New Day," pp. 297–303; Kiersey, "Confidence Restored," *California Schools* 7 (June 1936): 187; Hendrick, "Impact of Depression," pp. 187–195.

85. Charles B. Stillman, "Financial Fascism in Control," *Phi Delta Kappan* 15 (February 1933): 133; Herrick, *Chicago Schools,* chap. 10.

86. Testimony of Chicago principal, as quoted in David A. Shannon, *The Great Depression* (Englewood Cliffs, N.J.: Prentice-Hall, 1960), pp. 99–103.

87. Stillman, "Financial Fascism," p. 133; teacher as quoted in Michael W. Sedlak and Robert L. Church, "A History of Services Delivered to Youth, 1880–1977," Final Report to the National Institute of Education, Contract No. 400-79-0017, p. 48.

88. Teacher's observation: Herrick, *Chicago Schools,* p. 210; school board member quoted in Anon., "Spasmodic Diary of a Chicago School Teacher," *Atlantic Monthly* 152 (November 1933): 524.

89. Herrick, *Chicago Schools,* pp. 212, 210–213; "Spasmodic Diary," pp. 523–526.

90. Hutchins quoted in Herrick, *Chicago Schools,* p. 215, and Herrick's remarks, p. 213; Sedlak and Church, "Social Services," p. 53.

91. Jeffrey Mirel, "The Politics of Educational Retrenchment: Detroit, 1929–1935" (unpublished paper, University of Michigan 1982), p. 10; Sidney Fine, *Frank Murphy: The Detroit Years* (Ann Arbor: University of Michigan Press, 1975), pp. 253 ff.

92. Mirel, "Retrenchment," pp. 10, 65; Detroit Public School Staff, *Frank Cody: A Realist in Education* (New York: MacMillan, 1943), pp. 265, 315.

93. Detroit Staff, *Cody,* pp. 437, 481–482, 487.

94. Mirel, "Retrenchment," pp. 32, 23; Detroit Staff, *Cody,* p. 435; on the political activism of teachers, see Jeffrey Mirel, "Out of the Cloister of the Classroom: Political Activity and the Teachers of Detroit, 1929–39," forthcoming in *Journal of the Midwest History of Education Society* (Summer 1983).

95. Mirel, "Retrenchment," pp. 44–50.

96. Mirel, "Retrenchment," p. 65.

3. A New Deal in Education?

1. Caroline Bird, *The Invisible Scar* (New York: David McKay Company, 1966), pp. 34–35; Works Progress Administration, *Inventory: An Appraisal of the Results of the Works Progress Administration* (Washington, D.C.: GPO, 1938), p. 40; Margaret O'Brien Steinfels, *Who's Minding the Children? The History and Politics of Day Care in America* (New York: Simon and Schuster, 1973), pp. 66–67.

2. Frank E. Hill, *The Schools in the Camps: The Educational Program of the Civilian Conservation Corps* (New York: American Association for Adult Education, 1935), pp. 22–23.

3. Betty and Ernest K. Lindley, *A New Deal for Youth: The Story of the National Youth Administration* (New York: Viking, 1938), pp. 70, 90–93.

4. Richard S. Kirkendall, "The New Deal as Watershed: The Recent Literature," *Journal of American History* 54 (March 1968): 839–852; Jerold S. Auerbach, "New Deal, Old Deal: Some Thoughts on New Left Historiography," *Journal of Southern History* 35 (February 1967): 18–30; Theda Skocpol, "Political Response to Capitalist Crisis: Neo-Marxist Theories of the State and the Case of the New Deal," *Politics and Society* 10 (1980, no. 2): 155–202; U.S. Bureau of the Census, *Historical Statistics of the United States: Colonial Times to 1970* (Washington, D.C.: GPO, 1975), II, 1102, 1104.

5. Willard E. Givens, "New Deal a Raw Deal for Public Schools," *NEA Journal* 24 (September 1935): 198.

6. Harold G. Campbell, "The Contribution of the Public Schools," DS, *Official Report, 1934,* p. 21; Lotus D. Coffman, "Education of Unemployed Youth," *School and Society* 38 (October 14, 1933): 486; *Texas Outlook* 17 (September 1933): 42; *Texas Outlook* 18 (January 1934): 39; Edward A. Krug, *The Shaping of the American High School, 1920–1941* (Madison: University of Wisconsin Press, 1972), pp. 228–230.

7. Givens, "New Deal a Raw Deal," p. 198; Willard D. Boutwell, "The Minneapolis Meeting," *School and Society* 37 (March 18, 1933): 344: Stephen Kadesch, "A Comprehensive Program of Education," NEA, *Addresses and Proceedings, 1934,* pp. 627–628; "President Roosevelt Supports Federal Aid," *NEA Journal* 27 (September 1938): 164.

8. *NEA Journal* 23 (February 1934): 51; William D. Boutwell to Mr. Strauss, July 1, 1935, as quoted in Morris L. Appell, "Franklin Delano Roosevelt and Education" (Ph.D. dissertation, Ohio State University, 1947), p. 213.

9. Letter of Fred Morrell, official of the CCC, to G. L. Maxwell, secretary of the Educational Policies Commission of the NEA, October 28, 1941, as quoted in Harry Zeitlin's excellent thesis "Federal Relations in American Education, 1933–1943: A Study of New Deal Efforts and Innovation" (Ph.D. dissertation, Columbia University, 1958), p. 313.

10. Paul R. Mort, *Federal Support for Public Education: A Report of an Investigation of Educational Need and Relative Ability of States to Support Ed-*

ucation as they Bear on Federal Aid to Education (New York: Teachers College Bureau of Publications, 1936), p. 5, chap. 1; U.S. National Advisory Committee on Education, *Committee Findings and Recommendations* (Washington, D.C.: GPO, 1931), pp. 38–39.

11. Mort, *Federal Support for Public Education*, p. 1, chap. 1.

12. "President Roosevelt Supports Federal Aid," *NEA Journal* 27 (September 1938): 163–164; *Phi Delta Kappan* 19 (May 1937): 386–387.

13. Mort, *Federal Support for Public Education*, pp. 23, 29, 25–26.

14. Zeitlin, "Federal Relations in Education," chap. 7.

15. Martha H. Swain, *Pat Harrison: The New Deal Years* (Jackson, Miss.: University of Mississippi Press, 1978), p. 210, and NEA praise of Harrison quoted p. 217; Zeitlin, "Federal Relations in Education," chap. 7, p. 259; Arthur M. Schlesinger, Jr., *The Politics of Upheaval* (Boston: Houghton Mifflin, 1966): 139, 415; *Congressional Record,* 75th Congress, 1st Session, vol. 81, part 1, February 3, 1937, pp. 775–777; part 2, March 4, 1937, pp. 1872–1873; part 9, pp. 463–464, 593–594; 3rd session, vol. 83, part 6, May 4, 1938, pp. 6238–6239; part 7, June 7, 1938, pp. 8351–8353.

16. The Advisory Committee on Education, *Report of the Committee* (Washington, D.C.: Government Printing Office, 1938), pp. 53–54, 71, 47–95.

17. Zeitlin, "Federal Relations in Education," pp. 263–268, 269, 271–273.

18. Gilbert E. Smith, *The Limits of Reform: Politics and Federal Aid to Education, 1937–1950* (New York: Garland, 1982), pp. 11–12, 83; Swain, *Harrison,* pp. 211–218; also see citations in note 15.

19. FDR as quoted in Appell, "Roosevelt," pp. 134, 193.

20. Eleanor Roosevelt quoted in Zeitlin, "Federal Relations in Education," p. 267, note 78; Appell, "Roosevelt and Education," pp. 133, 137, 142–143, 146.

21. On Roosevelt as a political leader, see James McGregor Burns, *Roosevelt: The Lion and the Fox* (New York: Harcourt, Brace, 1956).

22. WPA, "Inventory"; Kadesh, "A Comprehensive Program," pp. 627–628; Arthur M. Schlesinger, Jr., *The Coming of the New Deal* (Boston: Houghton Mifflin, 1958), chaps. 16, 19, 22; Swain, *Harrison,* 218.

23. Timon Covert, *Federal Grants for Education, 1933–34,* U.S. Office of Education Leaflet No. 45, 1934 (Washington, D.C.: GPO, 1934), pp. 8–9, 10–11.

24. David Rison, "Federal Aid to Arkansas Education, 1933–1936," *Arkansas Historical Quarterly* 36 (Summer 1977): 192–200.

25. Covert, *Grants;* Melvin R. Maskin, "Black Education and the New Deal: The Urban Experience" (Ph.D. dissertation, New York University, 1973).

26. FDR quoted from "Informal Extemporaneous Remarks of the President on the occasion of the Visit to the White House of 36 State Superintendents of Education, December 11, 1935," in Appell, "Roosevelt and Education," p. 136.

27. Educator quoted in Roscoe Pulliam, "The Influence of the Federal

Government on Education," *School and Society* 47 (January 15, 1938): 71. Two insightful brief overviews of New Deal policies in education are: Diane Ravitch, "Education and Economic Depression," *New York University Education Quarterly* 7 (Winter 1976): 9–15, and Paula Fass, "The New Deal: Anticipating a Federal Education Policy," Institute for Research on Educational Finance and Governance, Stanford University, 1981.

28. Zeitlin, "Federal Relations in Education," p. 285, note 76; H. E. Buchholz, "Pedagogues Leap to Save Us," *American Mercury* 26 (July 1932); Buchholz, "Pedagogues at Armageddon," *American Mercury* 29 (June 1933); Appell, "Roosevelt and Education," p. 52; George P. Rawick, "The New Deal and Youth: The Civilian Conservation Corps, the National Youth Administration, and the American Youth Congress," Ph. D. dissertation, University of Wisconsin, 1957—a study that we found consistently insightful and useful.

29. Quotation from Zeitlin, "Federal Relations in American Education," pp. 289–290, 293–295; "The Economic and Educational Crisis," *School and Society* 37 (February 25, 1933): 259–260; letter of Sidney B. Hall to President Roosevelt, September 13, 1933, in Zeitlin, "Federal Relations in Education," p. 292; Frederick Redefer to the president, April 16, 1936, in Appell, "Roosevelt and Education," pp. 239–240. Not even a speech given by the president to the NEA and an honorary membership graciously accepted by Eleanor Roosevelt in 1938 quite healed the breach. See NEA, *Addresses and Proceedings, 1938,* p. 122.

30. U.S. Office of Education figures from *U.S. Budget, 1932–1941* (Washington, D.C.: GPO, 1932–41).

31. Rawick, "New Deal and Youth," pp. 184, 181–182, chap. 7.

32. Relief administrator quoted from "The Significance of the Emergency Education Program," from FERA files, in Zeitlin, "Federal Relations in Education," p. 164; on mutual dislike of Williams and Studebaker, see John Salmond, *A Southern Rebel: The Life and Times of Aubrey Williams, 1890–1965* (Chapel Hill: University of North Carolina Press, 1983), pp. 68, 83, 128, 144–146.

33. "Editorial," *Clearing House* 10 (November 1935): 132; Arthur J. Jones, "The Need for a Permanent National Youth Service," *School and Society* 43 (May 23, 1936): 707. For positive views of the CCC in education journals, see Frank E. Hill, "Laboratory for Adult Education," *Phi Delta Kappan* 19 (May 1937): 302–303, and Kenneth Holland, "Education in CCC and European Camps," *Phi Delta Kappan* 19 (May 1937): 317–322.

34. John T. Wahlquist, "An Evaluation of the New Deal in Education," *School and Society* 42 (December 21, 1935): 859–863.

35. Givens, "New Deal a Raw Deal," p. 198.

36. *Phi Delta Kappan* 20 (October 1937): 75–76; Williams quoted in Rawick, "The New Deal and Youth," p. 227.

37. The disenchantment of New Dealers and social reconstructionists was mutual. Rexford Tugwell said this about Counts's desire to use schools to build

a new social order: "In this I disagree with Mr. Counts as fundmentally as it is possible to disagree with anyone on anything"—quoted in Arthur M. Schlesinger, Jr., *The Crisis of the Old Order, 1919–1933* (Boston: Houghton Mifflin, 1957), p. 197.

38. Baldwin as quoted in Studs Terkel, *Hard Times: An Oral History of the Great Depression* (New York: Pocket Books, 1978), p. 299.

39. Floyd Reeves, "What Has the WPA Been Doing?" *School and Society* 51 (May 4, 1940): 570.

40. Engineer as quoted in Schlesinger, *Coming of the New Deal*, p. 271.

41. Melvin R. Maskin, "Black Education and the New Deal: The Urban Experience" (Ph.D. dissertation, New York University, 1973), chap. 1.

42. William Stott, *Documentary Expression and Thirties America* (New York: Oxford University Press, 1973), chap. 6.

43. Roy E. Stryker and Nancy Wood, *In This Proud Land: America 1935–43 as Seen in the FSA Photographs* (Greenwich, Conn.: New York Graphic Society, 1973), pp. 8–9; Botkin quoted in Ann Banks, *First-Person America* (New York: Vintage Books, 1981), p. 29.

44. Schlesinger, *Coming of the New Deal*, p. 558.

45. Floyd W. Reeves, "Education in the Tennessee Valley Authority," *NEA Proceedings, 1935*, pp. 329–336.

46. Harold Rugg, "Creative America: Can She Begin Again?" *Frontiers of Democracy* 6 (October 1939): 10; Reeves, "Education in the Tennessee Valley Authority," pp. 329–336; Schlesinger, *Politics of Upheaval*, pp. 431–432.

47. Schlesinger, *Coming of the New Deal*, pp. 337–339; Zeitlin, "Federal Relations in Education," p. 73.

48. Civilian Conservation Corps, *Camp Life Reader and Workbook*, Language Usage Series Number 3, selections from books 1–3 (Washington, D.C.: U.S. Office of Education, n.d.), book 1, pp. 38, 42, 46, 50; book 2, pp. 22, 30, 98–99; book 3, pp. 34, 46, 102, 106–107. We are indebted to the lively and insightful paper of Victor Henningsen, " 'I Thought that you mite helpt me some'—The Educative Potential of the CCC Appraised" (seminar paper, Stanford University, 1980).

49. As quoted in Henningsen, "Educative Potential of the CCC," pp. 8, 9–10; L. John Uttall, Jr., "Possible Influences in the Public Schools of the CCC Educational Program," *School Review* 43 (September 1935): 508; *A Handbook for Educational Advisers in the CCC Camps* (Washington, D.C.: GPO, 1934), p. 3.

50. Fred E. Lukens, "The CCC and the Schools," *Education* 61 (October 1940): 85; Rawick, "New Deal and Youth," p. 136; Kenneth Holland and Frank E. Hill, *Youth in the CCC* (Washington, D.C.: American Council on Education, 1942), p. 223; Studebaker as quoted in Zeitlin, "Federal Relations in Education," pp. 97, 96.

51. Critic as quoted in Zeitlin, "Federal Relations in Education," p. 78;

pp. 88–89, 106; officer as quoted in Henningsen, "Educational Potential of CCC," p. 7.

52. Rawick, "New Deal and Youth," pp. 128, 127; Lukens, "CCC and the Schools," p. 83.

53. Nuttall, "Influences on the Public Schools of the CCC," pp. 509–510; Kirkland Sloper, "Guidance Possibilities of the CCC," *Education* 61 (October 1940): 88–90; Lukens, "CCC and the Schools," p. 85.

54. Zeitlin, "Federal Relations in Education," pp. 88, 90–95; Calvin W. Gower, "The Civilian Conservation Corps and American Education: Threat to Local Control?" *History of Education Quarterly* 7 (Spring 1967): 61, 62; Howard W. Oxley, "Educational Activities in the CCC Camps," *Clearing House* 10 (November 1935): 139–144.

55. C. S. Marsh, "Problems of Youth as Seen in the Civilian Conservation Corps," NEA, *Addresses and Proceedings, 1935*, pp. 99–102; John W. Studebaker, "An Overview of the Civilian Conservation Corps," *Clearing House* 10 (November 1935): 134–138.

56. Charles Judd, "Educational Programs of the CCC," *Phi Delta Kappan* 17 (December 1934): 49–50; "Banned from the CCC Camps," *Social Frontier* 1 (February 1935): 39; Henningsen, "Educational Potential of CCC," pp. 17–20.

57. Rawick, "New Deal and Youth," chap. 6; Arthur J. Todd, "Social Implications of the CCC," *Clearing House* 10 (November 1935): 157.

58. Roosevelt as quoted in Rawick, "New Deal and Youth," pp. 124–125; Appell, "Roosevelt," pp. 167–169, 185–186; Zeitlin, "Federal Relations in Education," p. 110; Howard W. Oxley, "The CCC and the Defense of the Nation," *Education* 61 (October 1940): 74–77.

59. Salmond, *Southern Rebel;* Rawick, "New Deal and Youth," chap. 6.

60. Williams as quoted in Rawick, "New Deal and Youth," p. 197; as quoted in Zeitlin, "Federal Relations in American Education," pp. 202–203; Aubrey W. Williams, *Work, Wages, and Education* (Cambridge, Mass.: Harvard University Press, 1940), pp. 35, 42–48; Williams, "The Role of the Schools," in Thatcher Winslow and F. P. Davidson, eds., *American Youth: An Enforced Reconnaissance* (Cambridge, Mass.: Harvard University Press, 1940), chap. 4.

61. Lindley and Lindley, *New Deal for Youth*, pp. 77, 196, 193; we thank Mary Ellen James for suggesting the notion that the NYA actually assisted educators by providing programs for alienated youth.

62. Rawick, "New Deal and Youth," pp. 26–28, 176–179, 194–197; Lindley and Lindley, *New Deal for Youth*, pp. 6–7, and Foreword by Charles Taussig; Harvard Sitkoff, *A New Deal for Blacks: The Emergence of Civil Rights as a National Issue* (New York: Oxford University Press, 1978), pp. 72–73.

63. Lindley and Lindley, *New Deal for Youth*, pp. 14, x, xiii; U.S. Congress, Senate, Committee on Education and Labor, *Hearings on Termination of CCC and NYA: S. 2295*, 88th Cong., 2nd sess., March 24, 1942, pp. 61–62; for some complaints about delays in getting projects approved, see "What Progress in

the National Youth Administration?" *School Review* 44 (March 1936): 161–164; Rawick, "New Deal and Youth," chap. 10.

64. Zeitlin, "Federal Relations in Education," pp. 210–213; Sitkoff, *New Deal for Blacks,* p. 75.

65. Hopkins quoted in Zeitlin, "Federal Relations in Education," p. 349; also 214, 210.

66. Ibid., p. 219.

67. Lindley and Lindley, *New Deal for Youth,* pictures and text between pp. 4 and 5.

68. John E. Bryan, "Youth Learn Manual Skills: Alabama NYA Out-of-School Work Program," *Education* 61 (October 1940): 78–79.

69. Ibid., pp. 80–81.

70. Secretary of the Treasury, *Annual Report* (Washington, D.C.: GPO, 1941); Lindley and Lindley, *New Deal for Youth,* p. xiii; evaluation of Johnson quoted in Zeitlin, "Federal Relations in Education," p. 229.

71. Works Progress Administration, *Employment on Projects in March, 1936* (Washington, D.C.: GPO, 1936), p. 10.

72. Works Progress Administration, *Inventory: An Appraisal of the Results of the Works Progress Administration* (Washington, D.C.: GPO, 1938), p. 40; Zeitlin, "Federal Relations in Education," pp. 131–136.

73. Zeitlin, "Federal Relations in Education," pp. 136, 153–155, 137; WPA, *Inventory,* pp. 39–40.

74. Hilda W. Smith, "Workers' Education and the Federal Government," *Progressive Education* 11 (April–May 1934): 239–245; WPA, *Inventory*; WPA, *Government Aid during the Depression to Professional, Technical, and Other Service Workers* (Washington, D.C.: GPO, 1936), p. 12.

75. Ravitch, "Education and Economic Depression," p. 14; "What Has the WPA Been Doing?" *School and Society* 51 (May 4, 1940): 569–570; WPA, *Inventory,* pp. 23–24, 43–44; Zeitlin, "Federal Relations in Education," p. 148.

76. Zeitlin, "Federal Relations in Education," pp. 153–162.

77. Mort, *Federal Support for Public Education,* p. vii.

78. Zeitlin, "Federal Relations in Education."

79. Smith, *Limits,* pp. 34–36, 65–70, 75–77, 83; Appell, "Roosevelt."

80. Glenn Frank, "The Double Crisis of the Schools," NEA, *Addresses and Proceedings, 1935,* p. 517.

81. Educational Policies Commission, *The Civilian Conservation Corps, the National Youth Administration, and the Public Schools* (Washington, D.C.: NEA, 1941), pp. 3, 60, 46, 72–78, 56; John Sexson, "The Educational Policies Commission," NEA, *Addresses and Proceedings, 1936,* p. 465. "Youth studies" was a growth industry in the 1930s—see Louise A. Menefee and M. M. Chambers, *American Youth: An Annotated Bibliography* (Washington, D.C.: American Council on Education, 1938).

82. Charles H. Judd, "The Real Youth Problem," *School and Society,* 55

(January 10, 1942): 31, 32, 30; see also Charles H. Judd, "The Federal Government and Youth," *Education* 61 (October 1940): 70–74.

83. Williams, "Role of the Schools," pp. 63–69; Franklin J. Keller, "Youth Challenges Society: How Much Responsibility Should Government Take?" *Clearing House* 10 (May 1936): 546.

84. American Youth Commission, *Youth and the Future* (Washington, D.C.: American Council on Education, 1942).

4. Behind the Schoolhouse Door

1. Interview with Professor Arthur Phelps, University of Nevada-Reno, January 30, 1983. A survey of New York high schools at the same time suggests that the conservative curriculum of the Buffalo high school was fairly typical of the state at that time: Francis T. Spaulding, *High School and Life* (New York: McGraw-Hill, 1938), pp. 125–173.

2. L. S. Tireman and Mary Watson, *Community School in a Spanish-Speaking Village* (Albuquerque: University of New Mexico Press, 1948), p. 35, chap. 1.

3. Ibid., chap. 4.

4. Charles S. Johnson, *Growing Up in the Black Belt: Negro Youth in the Rural South* (1941; reprint ed., New York: Schocken Books, 1967), p. 105.

5. Ibid., pp. 105–106.

6. For "progressive" trends in the 1930s—a period that Lawrence A. Cremin calls the "high-water mark" of reform—see Cremin, *The Transformation of the School: Progressivism in American Education, 1876–1957* (New York: Vintage Books, 1964), p. 324, chap. 8.

7. U.S. Bureau of the Census, *Historical Statistics of the United States: Colonial Times to 1970* (Washington, D.C.: GPO, 1975), I, 368, 379, 373–374; figures 1–5 are taken from that source.

8. Abbott L. Ferriss, *Indicators of Trends in American Education* (New York: Russell Sage Foundation, 1969), pp. 23–44.

9. Ibid., pp. 27–35; Glen Elder, *Children of the Great Depression: Social Change in Life Experiences* (Chicago: University of Chicago Press, 1974), p. 66.

10. Patricia Albjerg Graham, *Progressive Education: From Arcady to Academe—A History of the Progressive Education Association, 1919–1955* (New York: Teachers College Press, 1967), pp. 62, 85; Richard Hofstadter, *Anti-Intellectualism in American Life* (New York: Alfred Knopf, 1963), p. 340.

11. Graham, *Progressive Education,* chaps. 4–5.

12. J. Wayne Wrightstone, *Appraisal of Newer Elementary School Practices* (New York: Teachers College Press, 1938), pp. 12–26; Cremin, *Transformation.*

13. Max McConn, "Freeing the Secondary School for Experimentation," *Progressive Education* 10 (November 1933): 367.

14. Ibid., pp. 368–369, 370–371.

15. Edward A. Krug, *The Shaping of the American High School, 1920–*

1941 (Madison: University of Wisconsin Press, 1972), pp. 255–265; Robert D. Leigh, "Twenty-seven Senior High School Plans," *Progressive Education* 10 (November 1933): 377–380; Wilfred D. Aiken, *The Story of the Eight-Year Study* (New York: McGraw-Hill, 1942).

16. Aiken, *Eight-Year Study*, p. 25, chaps. 2–3.

17. Cremin, *Transformation*, pp. 257, 256, note 6; Krug, *Shaping the High School*, pp. 263–266.

18. Harry J. Otto, *Changes in Classroom Teaching Made during 1937–39 in One-Room Schools in the Area of the Michigan Community Health Project* (mimeographed; Battle Creek, Mich.: W. K. Kellogg Foundation, 1940), pp. 1, 3, 4, 7–8, 9, 13, 176–178, passim. For other accounts of rural schools, see Julia Weber, *My Country School Diary: An Adventure in Creative Teaching* (New York: Harper Brothers, 1946); Ella Enslow, *Schoolhouse in the Foothills* (New York: Simon and Schuster, 1935). For a "progressive" approach to Latin, see C. B. Hicks, "Latin as a New Course," *Texas Outlook* 17 (July 1933): 9.

19. Irving H. Hendrick, "California's Response to the 'New Education' in the 1930s," *California Historical Quarterly* 53 (Spring 1976): 27, 29–30.

20. Ibid., principals quoted on pp. 34, 35; for a similar waiving of requirements in Los Angeles, see "Liberalizing the Curriculum," *Phi Delta Kappan* 17 (September 1935): 36.

21. Hendrick, "California's Response to 'New Education,' " p. 35.

22. Robert S. Lynd and Helen Merrill Lynd, *Middletown in Transition: A Study in Cultural Conflict* (New York: Harcourt, Brace, and World, 1937, p. 204.

23. Ibid., pp. 204, 220–228.

24. Arthur Zilversmit, "Education—Ideology and Practice: Case Studies in Progressive Education" (paper delivered at the meeting of the American Studies Association, San Antonio, Texas, November 6–8, 1975), pp. 1–15.

25. Ibid., p. 14.

26. Ibid., pp. 10–12.

27. Ibid.; Ronald D. Cohen and Raymond A. Mohl, *The Paradox of Progressive Education: The Gary Plan and Urban Schooling* (Port Washington, N.Y.: Kennikat Press, 1979), chap. 7.

28. W. S. Deffenbaugh, *Effects of the Depression upon Public Elementary and Secondary Schools and upon Colleges and Universities,* U.S. Office of Education, Bulletin No. 2, 1937 (Washington, D.C.: GPO, 1938), p. 29.

29. Michael W. Sedlak and Robert L. Church, "A History of Social Services Delivered to Youth, 1880–1977," Final Report to the National Institute of Education, Contract No. 400-79-0017, 1982, pp. 40, 56–57; Francis T. Spaulding, *High School and Life* (New York: McGraw-Hill, 1938), pp. 124–125; John F. Latimer, *What's Happening to Our High Schools?* (Washington, D.C.: Public Affairs Press, 1958), p. 30; *Historical Statistics,* I, 377.

30. Spaulding, *High School,* pp. 169, 173; Howard M. Bell, *Youth Tell Their Story* (Washington, D.C.: American Council on Education, 1938), p. 74;

O. Williams, D. S. Bryant, and A. E. Jones, *Youth: California's Future* (Sacramento, Calif.: State Relief Administration, 1940), p. 33; Lynd and Lynd, *Middletown in Transition,* p. 223.

31. National League of Compulsory Education Officials, *Addresses and Proceedings, 1937,* p. 18; David Tyack and Michael Berkowitz, "The Man Nobody Liked: Toward a Social History of the Truant Officer, 1840–1940," *American Quarterly* 29 (Spring 1977): 31–54.

32. Teacher as quoted in Frances Donovan, *The Schoolma'am* (New York: Frederick A. Stokes, 1938), p. 191; Larry Cuban, "Teacher as Leader and Captive: Continuity and Change in American Classrooms, 1890–1980," Report to National Institute of Education, Grant No. NIE-G-81-0024, 1982; Arthur Zilversmit, "The Failure of Progressive Education, 1920–1940," in Lawrence Stone, ed., *Schooling and Society: Studies in the History of Education* (Baltimore: Johns Hopkins University Press, 1976), pp. 256–258.

33. Zilversmit, "Failure of Progressive Education," p. 258; Howard E. Wilson, *Education for Citizenship* (New York: McGraw-Hill, 1938), pp. 166–167.

34. Cuban, "Teacher," pp. 145–146.

35. Ibid., pp. 162–167.

36. Superintendent as quoted in Cuban, "Teacher," p. 63; Zilversmit, "Failure of Progressive Education," p. 256.

37. Donovan, *Schoolma'am,* pp. 1, 156–157; Willard W. Waller, *The Sociology of Teaching* (1932; reprint ed., New York: John Wiley and Sons, 1967), p. 10, chaps. 4–5.

38. Howard K. Beale, *Are American Teachers Free? An Analysis of Restraints upon the Freedom of Teaching in American Schools* (New York: Charles Scribner's Sons, 1936); Robert L. Church and Michael W. Sedlak, *Education in the United States: An Interpretive History* (New York: Free Press, 1976), p. 370; "Can the School-Strike Nuisance Be Eliminated?" *American School Board Journal* 97 (March 1938): 54.

39. Lynd and Lynd, *Middletown in Transition,* pp. 231–241.

40. August Hollingshead, *Elmtown's Youth: The Impact of Social Classes on Adolescents* (New York: John Wiley, 1949), chaps. 6, 8.

41. Ibid., pp. 187–192.

42. Ibid., pp. 202, 204.

43. "What People Think about Youth and Education," *NEA Research Bulletin* 18 (November 1940): 215, 196, 203; W. Lloyd Warner, Robert J. Havighurst, and Martin B. Loeb, *Who Shall Be Educated? The Challenge of Unequal Opportunities* (New York: Harper and Brothers, 1944); W. Lloyd Warner and Paul S. Lunt, *Social Life of a Modern Community* (New Haven: Yale University Press, 1945), pp. 359–365.

44. Williams as quoted in American Association of School Administrators, *Youth Education Today,* Sixteenth Yearbook (Washington, D.C.: AASA, 1938), p. 35—the yearbook commented that poverty was a problem, but their chief

complaint seemed to be that the poor had low IQs and too many children, thereby lowering the national IQ average; *Historical Statistics,* I, 299–301.

45. Educational Policies Commission, *The Civilian Conservation Corps, The National Youth Administration, and the Public Schools* (Washington, D.C.: National Education Association, 1941), pp. 48–49; the many writings on "democracy" in the 1930s stressed this norm of fairness.

46. Waller, *Sociology of Teaching,* chaps. 4–5, and passim; Samuel Bowles and Herbert Gintis, *Schooling in Capitalist America: Education and the Contradictions of Economic Life* (New York: Basic Books, 1976).

47. Spaulding, *High School,* pp. 35, 36–37; Harvey Kantor and David Tyack, eds., *Work, Youth, and Schooling: Historical Perspectives on Vocationalism in American Education* (Stanford, Calif.: Stanford University Press, 1982).

48. Spaulding, *High School,* pp. 61, 63.

49. Bell, *Youth,* p. 85.

50. Detroit Public School Staff, *Frank Cody: A Realist in Education* (New York: MacMillan, 1943), p. 315.

51. AASA, *Youth Education;* AASA, *Schools in Small Communities,* Seventeenth Yearbook (Washington, D.C.: AASA, 1939).

52. Horace Mann Bond, "Horace Mann in New Orleans: A Note on the Decline of Humanitarianism in American Education, 1837–1937," *School and Society* 45 (May 1, 1937): 607; Belmont Farley, "The Superintendents at New Orleans," *School and Society* 45 (March 13, 1937): 45.

53. Thompson as quoted in *Phi Delta Kappan* 19 (May 1937): 386–387; "The White Clause," *Phi Delta Kappan* 14 (December 1931): 99; *Phi Delta Kappan* 14 (February 1932): 285, and 20 (September 1937): 19, and 21 (February 1939): 285.

54. Ronald K. Goodenow's essays on educators in the 1930s are the following: "The Progressive Educator on Race, Ethnicity, Creativity, and Planning: Harold Rugg in the 1930s," *Review Journal of Philosophy and Social Science* 1 (Winter 1977): 105–128; "The Southern Progressive Educator on Race and Pluralism: The Case of William Heard Kilpatrick," *History of Education Quarterly* 211 (Summer, 1981): 147–170; "The Progressive Educator as Radical or Conservative: George S. Counts and Race," *History of Education Quarterly* 17 (Winter 1977): 45–57; "Racial and Ethnic Tolerance in John Dewey's Educational and Social Thought: The Depression Years," *Educational Theory* 26 (Winter 1977): 48–64.

55. Ronald K. Goodenow, "Paradox in Progressive Educational Reform: The South and the Education of Blacks in the Depression Years," *Phylon* 39 (March 1938): 49–65.

56. Horace Mann Bond, "The Curriculum and the Negro Child," *Journal of Negro Education* 4 (April 1935): 168.

57. Johnson, *Growing Up in the Black Belt;* Johnson, *Shadow of the Plantation* (Chicago: University of Chicago Press, 1934); E. Franklin Frazier, *Negro Youth at the Crossways: Their Personality Development in the Middle States*

(Washington, D.C.: American Council on Education, 1940); Horace Mann Bond, *The Education of the Negro in the American Social Order* (New York: Prentice-Hall, 1934); Bond, *Negro Education in Alabama* (Washington, D.C.: Associated Publishers, 1939); Allison Davis and John Dollard, *Children of Bondage: The Personality Develoment of Negro Youth in the Urban South* (Washington, D.C.: American Council on Education, 1940); Wilkerson, *Special Problems of Negro Education.*

58. Bond, *Education of the Negro,* pp. 171, 169.

59. Wilkerson, *Special Problems of Negro Education,* pp. 15, 19, 29, 36, 49, 99.

60. U.S. National Advisory Committee on Education, *Federal Relations to Education,* part 1, *Committee Findings and Recommendations* (Washington, D.C.: GPO, 1931), pp. 25–26; U.S. Advisory Committee on Education, *Report of the Committee* (Washington, D.C.: GPO, 1938), pp. 85–86; Bond, *Education of the Negro,* p. 447.

61. Ambrose Caliver, "Certain Significant Developments in the Education of Negroes during the Past Generation," *Journal of Negro History* 35 (April 1950): 113–116.

62. Walter G. Daniels, "The Aims of Secondary Education and the Adequacy of the Curriculum of the Negro Secondary School," *Journal of Negro Education* 9 (July 1940): 467–468. See also D. A. Wilkerson, "A Determination of the Peculiar Problems of Negroes in Contemporary American Society," *Journal of Negro Education* 5 (July 1936): 324–350; Wilkerson, "Educating Negro Youth for Occupational Efficiency," *National Educational Outlook among Negroes* 1 (October 1937): 7–10, and 1 (December 1937): 6–9; Charles S. Johnson, "On the Need of Realism in Negro Education," *Journal of Negro Education* 5 (July 1936): 375–382; W. E. B. DuBois, "Education and Work," *Journal of Negro Education* 1 (April 1932): 60–74; Clark Foreman, *Environmental Factors in Negro Elementary Education* (New York: W. W. Norton, 1932); Harvard Sitkoff, *A New Deal for Blacks: The Emergence of Civil Rights as a National Issue* (New York: Oxford University Press, 1978), pp. 72–73, 75, 239–240.

63. Charles H. Houston, "How to Fight for Better Schools," *Crisis* 43 (February 1936); Doxey A. Wilkerson, "The Negro in American Education: A Research Memorandum for the Carnegie-Myrdal Study, 'The Negro in America' " (typescript in Schomburg Library, New York City); articles on segregation in *Crisis* during the 1930s; Eve Thurston, "Ethiopia Unshackled: A Brief History of the Education of Negro Children in New York City," *Bulletin of the New York Public Library* 69 (April 1965): 227–228; Provisional Committee for Better Schools in Harlem, *Call to a Conference for Better Schools in Harlem* (New York: Committee for Better Schools, 1936); Melvin R. Maskin, "Black Education and the New Deal: The Urban Experience" (Ph.D. dissertation, New York University, 1973), chaps. 5, 7, 9; Vincent P. Franklin, *The Education of Black Philadelphia: The Social and Educational History of a Minority Community, 1900–1950* (Philadelphia: University of Pennsylvania Press, 1979), pp.

135–150; Judy Jolley Mohraz, *The Separate Problem: Case Studies and Black Education in the North, 1900–1930* (Westport, Conn.: Greenwood Press, 1979).

64. Myles A. Page, "The School System of Harlem," *Education* 2 (April 1936): 2, 7 (magazine published by the Negro Needs Society); Maskin, "Black Education," chap. 5.

65. The description of the Harlem school is by Edith M. Stern, "Jim Crow Goes to School in New York," *Crisis* 44 (July 1937): 201–202; Cuban, "Teacher," pp. 57–82.

66. *Phi Delta Kappan* 19 (April 1937): 291.

67. Geraldine Joncich Clifford, " 'Marry, Stitch, Die, or Do Worse': Educating Women for Work," in Kantor and Tyack, eds., *Work, Youth, and Schooling,* pp. 223–268; American Youth Commission, *Youth and the Future* (Washington, D.C.: American Council on Education, 1942), p. 110; George P. Rawick, "The New Deal and Youth: The Civilian Conservation Corps, the National Youth Administration, and the American Youth Congress" (Ph.D. dissertation, University of Wisconsin, 1957), p. 21; Albert Westefeld, *Getting Started: Urban Youth in the Labor Market* (Washington, D.C.: GPO, 1943), pp. 50, 110–111, 124.

68. An exception to the general lack of awareness of gender issues in public education was the widespread protest against the firing of women teachers in the depression years, as illustrated in these articles and studies: Naomi J. White, "Let Them Eat Cake! A Plea for Married Women Teachers," *Clearing House* 13 (September 1938): 138, 135–139; E. D. Johnson, "For the Rights of Married Women," *Texas Outlook* 17 (December 1933): 2; "Married Women the Best Teachers," *Texas Outlook* 18 (October 1934): 19; "The Competence of Married Women as Teachers," *School and Society* 52 (October 5, 1940): 294–295; Dennis A. Cooke and Clinton O. McKee, "Pupils Prefer Married Teachers," *School Executive* 59 (April 1940): 22–23; Louise D. Blades, "Tenure and Marriage Discrimination," *Texas Outlook* 24 (September 1940): 44; Charles E. Reeves, "Should the Married Woman Teacher Be Disqualified?" *Nation's Schools* 2 (October 1938): 13–18. There was, at the time, a conscious campaign to persuade more men to enter teaching (they did) and a replacement of women administrators by men—see, for example, the following: "Teaching: A Man's Job," *Phi Delta Kappan* 20 (March 1938): 215; Elisabeth Hansot and David Tyack, "The Dream Deferred: A Golden Age for Women School Administrators" (Stanford, Calif.: Institute for Research on Educational Finance and Governance, 1981).

5. Then and Now in Public Education

1. Teachers' attitudes reported in *Phi Delta Kappan* 62 (May 1982): 579; Michael W. Kirst and Walter I. Garms, "The Political Environment of School Finance Policy in the 1980s," in *School Finance Policies and Practice: The 1980s:*

A Decade of Conflict, James W. Guthrie, ed. (Cambridge, Mass.: Ballinger, 1980), pp. 47–75.

2. Nelson B. Henry, "What the Depression Has Done to the Schools," *Public Management* 16 (June 1934): 204–208.

3. Erick L. Lindman, "Are Teacher Salaries Improving?" *Phi Delta Kappan* (April 1970): 420; Gallup Poll results reported in *What People Think about Youth and Education,* NEA Research Bulletin, No. 5, November 1940 (Washington, D.C.: NEA, 1940), p. 195; John K. Norton, "Report of the Joint Committee on the Emergency in Education," DS, *Official Report, 1933,* pp. 292–293.

4. David Tyack and Elisabeth Hansot, *Managers of Virtue: Public School Leadership in America, 1820–1980* (New York: Basic Books, 1982), part 3.

5. *What People Think about Youth and Education,* p. 201.

6. Charles R. Foster, *Editorial Treatment of Education in the American Press,* Harvard Bulletins in Education, No. 21 (Cambridge, Mass.: Harvard University Press, 1938), chaps. 8, 12.

7. Robert S. Lynd and Helen Merrill Lynd, *Middletown in Transition: A Study in Cultural Conflict* (New York: Harcourt, Brace and World, 1937), p. 204.

8. Ellwood P. Cubberley, "Independence in School Government a Necessity," *School and Society* 37 (March 4, 1933): 266, 269.

9. The New York teacher quoted was Isidore Starr—letter to Robert Lowe, March 7, 1983; Benjamin W. Frazier, "Minimum Certification Requirements for Teachers," *School Life* 26 (October 1940): 27–28; Edward S. Evendon, Guy C. Gamble, and Harold G. Blue, *National Survey of the Education of Teachers,* Vol. 12, U.S. Office of Education, Bulletin No. 10 (Washington, D.C.: GPO, 1935), p. 43; L. A. Pittenger, "Raising Certification Requirements," NEA, *Addresses and Proceedings, 1931,* pp. 897–899; Spencer Stoker, "Progress in Certification Standards," *Journal of Educational Research* 33 (January 1940): 351–356.

10. On the blurring of lines between teachers and administrators, see Tyack and Hansot, *Managers of Virtue,* pp. 192–193.

11. "Wants All Classes Represented," *Texas Outlook* 17 (July 1933): 2; Vera Strong, "Democracy for Teachers," *Texas Outlook* 18 (July 1934): 20–21; "Frederick Houk Law Urges Teachers to Help Form School Policies," *Texas Outlook* 18 (December 1934): 38–39; *New Republic* 76 (October 25, 1933): 309; Ronald D. Cohen, "The Fate of Progressive Schooling: William A. Wirt and the Gary Schools in the 1930s" (paper delivered at the meeting of the American Studies Association, San Antonio, Texas, November 6–8, 1975); *Social Frontier* 3 (November 1936): 36; *Social Frontier* 3 (October 1936): 4; Gertrude Diamont, "The Teachers' Union," *American Mercury* 33 (September 1934): 108–113. For a cogent discussion of teacher militance, which sees the 1930s as more of a watershed, see Jeffrey Mirel, "Out of the Cloister of the Classroom: Political

Activity and the Teachers of Detroit, 1929–39, *Journal of the Midwest History of Education Society* (Summer 1983).

12. David Tyack and Elisabeth Hansot, "Conflict and Consensus in American Public Education," *Daedalus* 110 (Summer 1982): 1–26; Paul Saettier, *A History of Instructional Technology* (New York: McGraw-Hill, 1968), pp. 302–303.

13. James S. Coleman, "The Struggle for Control of Education," ERIC Resume ED 015 158, October 7, 1967, pp. 5–6.

14. John K. Folger and Charles B. Nam, *Education of the American Population* (Washington, D.C.: GPO, 1967), p. 66; Susan Abramovitz and Stuart Rosenfeld, eds., *Declining Enrollment: The Challenge of the Coming Decade* (Washington, D.C.: GPO, 1978), pp. 3–5.

15. Mark Rodekohr, "Adjustments of Colorado School Districts to Declining Enrollments," Nebraska Curriculum Development Center, University of Nebraska, 1975, p. 37; Daniel E. Griffiths, "The Crisis in American Education," *New York University Education Quarterly* 14 (Fall 1982): 3; National School Public Relations Association, *Declining Enrollment: Current Trends in School Policies and Programs* (Arlington, Va.: National School Public Relations Association, 1976).

16. National Center for Education Statistics, *The Condition of Education, 1982* (Washington, D.C.: GPO, 1982), p. 48; Kirst and Garms, "Environment"; Abramovitz and Rosenfeld, eds., *Declining Enrollment*, introduction.

17. Melvin Bins and Alvin Townsel, "Changing/Declining Enrollments in Large City School Systems," in Abramovitz and Rosenfeld, eds., Declining Enrollment, p. 133; Allen Odden and Phillip E. Vincent, "The Fiscal Impact of Declining Enrollments: A Study of Declining Enrollments in Four States—Michigan, Missouri, South Dakota, and Washington," ibid., pp. 218–226; W. F. Keough, Jr., "Ways of Dealing with Enrollment Decline," *Phi Delta Kappan* 60 (September 1978): 20–25.

18. Ross Zerchykov, *A Review of the Literature and an Annotated Bibliography on Managing Decline in School Systems* (Boston: Institute for Responsive Education, 1982), pp. 108–109; Keough, "Dealing," p. 21.

19. Michael J. Bakalis, "American Education and the Meaning of Scarcity," *Phi Delta Kappan* 63 (September 1982): 10; Diane Divoky, "Burden of the Seventies: The Management of Decline," *Phi Delta Kappan* 61 (October 1979): 87–91.

20. Larry Cuban, "Shrinking Enrollment and Consolidation: Political and Organizational Impacts in Arlington, Virginia," *Education and Urban Society* 11 (May 1979): 367–395; for a general study of resource scarcity in urban public finance, see the special issue of *Public Administration Review* 41 (January 1981).

21. National Center for Education Statistics (NCES), *Digest of Education Statistics, 1980* (Washington, D.C.: GPO, 1980), p. 60; David Tyack, *The One Best System: A History of American Urban Education* (Cambridge, Mass.: Harvard University Press, 1974), pp. 21–27.

22. William Lowe Boyd, "School Governance in an Era of Retrenchment," N.I.E. Report on Grant No. NIE-G-78-0086, Pennsylvania State University, 1982, pp. v–xix; Zerchykov, *Review,* ix–xv. An example of the 1930s prescriptive literature is William J. Cooper, *Economy in Education* (Stanford, Calif.: Stanford University Press, 1933).

23. NCES, *Condition of Education, 1982,* pp. 62, 86–87, 102.

24. Abramovitz and Rosenfeld, eds., *Declining Enrollment,* p. 8; Stanley Elam, ed., *The Gallup Polls of Attitudes toward Education, 1969–1973* (Bloomington, Ind.: Phi Delta Kappa, 1973).

25. Baker as quoted in Richard A. Eribes and John S. Hall, "Revolt of the Affluent: Fiscal Controls in Three States," *Public Administration Review* 41 (January 1981): 111; Gary Hoban, "The Untold Golden Gate Story: Aftermath of Proposition 13," *Phi Delta Kappan* 61 (September 1979): 18–21; James Catterall and Thomas Thresher, "Proposition 13: The Campaign, the Vote, and the Immediate Aftereffects for California Schools" (Stanford, Calif.: Institute for Research on Educational Finance and Governance, 1979); Michael W. Kirst, "The New Politics of State Education Finance," *Phi Delta Kappan* 60 (February 1979): 427–432.

26. Economist as quoted in Richard L. Lucier, "Gauging the Strength and Meaning of the 1978 Tax Revolt," in Charles H. Levine, ed., *Managing Fiscal Stress: The Crisis in the Public Sector* (Chatham, N.J.: Chatham House Publishers, 1980), pp. 123–136; Catterall and Thresher, "Proposition 13."

27. Chris Pipho, "Rich States, Poor States," *Phi Delta Kappan* 62 (June 1981): 722–723; Eribes and Hall, "Revolt of the Affluent"; Lucier, "Strength and Meaning."

28. Quotes from Hoban, "Golden Gate Story," p. 19.

29. "Effects on the Districts Vary," *California School Boards* 37 (July-August 1978): 14; Bill Anderson, "Don't Tell This Little California System that Proposition 13 Hasn't Hurt," *American School Board Journal* 167 (April 1980): 40–41, 46.

30. Michael W. Kirst, "Short and Long-Range Consequences," *California School Boards* 37 (July-August 1978): 27–30; see also issues of *Tax Revolt Digest,* December 1978 and October 1979; *Nevada State Journal,* February 22, 1983, p. 1A.

31. Katherine Bradbury and Helen F. Ladd, "Proposition 2½: Initial Impacts" (Stanford, Calif.: Institute for Research on Educational Finance and Governance, 1982); *Public Administration Times,* November 1982, p. 2.

32. John Collins and Jeffrey S. Lucove, "Proposition 2½: Lessons for Massachusetts," *Educational Leadership* 39 (January 1982): 248.

33. Richard A. Bumstead, "One Massachusetts School System Adapts to Proposition 2½," *Phi Delta Kappan* 62 (June 1981): 721–725.

34. Dan Levin, "Robert Sperber: Grimly, He's Dismantling the Lighthouse He Toiled to Build," *Executive Educator* 4 (February 1982): 21–23.

35. *Reno Gazette-Journal,* February 16, 1983, p. 14A; Michael Harrington, *Decade of Decision: The Crisis of the American System* (New York: Simon and Schuster, 1980).

36. "Hard Times Threaten Public Schools in Michigan," *Education Week* (March 17, 1982): 1, 15; the NEA has identified the following states as ones in which there have been severe cutbacks: Alabama, California, Idaho, Massachusetts, Michigan, Ohio, Oklahoma, Oregon, Nevada, and Washington (*Nevada State Journal,* February 23, 1983, p. 5A).

37. George H. Gallup, *The Gallup Poll: Public Opinion, 1935–1971* (New York: Random House, 1972), I, 597, 598, 366; "The 13th Annual Gallup Poll of the Public's Attitude toward the Public Schools," *Phi Delta Kappan* 63 (September 1981): 37; Stanley Elam, ed., *The Gallup Polls of Attitudes toward Education, 1969–1973* (Bloomington, Ind.: Phi Delta Kappa, 1973), pp. 34, 169.

38. Hans N. Weiler, "Education, Public Confidence and the Legitimacy of the Modern State: Do We Have a Crisis?" *Phi Delta Kappan* 64 (September 1982): 10.

39. Jerry Duea, "School Officials and the Public Hold Disparate Views on Education," *Phi Delta Kappan* 63 (March 1982): 479.

40. NCES, *Condition of Education, 1982,* pp. 104–105; George H. Gallup, "Gallup Poll of the Public's Attitudes toward the Public Schools," *Phi Delta Kappan* 64 (September 1982): 46; J. Myron Atkin, "Who Will Teach in High School?" *Daedalus* 100 (Summer 1981): 91–103; Victor S. Vance and Phillip C. Schlechty, "The Distribution of Academic Talent in the Teaching Force: Policy Implications," *Phi Delta Kappan* 64 (September 1982): 28–32; "Teachers Are Better Educated, More Experienced, But Less Satisfied Than in the Past: NEA Survey," *Phi Delta Kappan* 62 (May 1982): 579.

41. Barbara Lerner, "American Education: How Are We Doing?" *Public Interest* 69 (Fall 1982): 59–82.

42. Edith K. Mosher, Anne H. Hastings, and Jennings L. Wagoner, *Pursuing Equal Educational Opportunity: School Politics and the New Experts* (New York: ERIC Clearinghouse on Urban Education, 1979); Michael W. Kirst, "Loss of Support for Public Secondary Schools: Some Causes and Solutions," *Daedalus* 110 (Summer 1982): 45–68.

43. David Tyack, Michael W. Kirst, and Elisabeth Hansot, "Educational Reform: Retrospect and Prospect," *Teachers College Record* 81 (Fall 1980): 253–269.

44. Christopher Jencks, *Inequality: A Reassessment of the Effect of Family and Schooling in America* (New York: Basic Books, 1972); Donald M. Levine and Mary Jo Bane, *The "Inequality" Controversy: Schooling and Distributive Justice* (New York: Basic Books, 1975); Samuel Bowles and Herbert Gintis, *Schooling in Capitalist America: Educational Reform and the Contradictions of Economic Life* (New York: Basic Books, 1976); Diane Ravitch, *The Revisionists Revised: A Critique of the Radical Attack on the Schools* (New York: Basic

Books, 1977); Robert B. Everhart, ed., *The Public School Monopoly: A Critical Analysis of Education and the State in American Society* (Cambridge, Mass.: Ballinger, 1982).

45. National Institute of Education, *Violent Schools, Safe Schools* (Washington, D.C.: GPO, 1978).

46. Tyack and Hansot, *Managers of Virtue*, part 3.

47. Larry Cuban, "Teacher as Leader and Captive: Continuity and Change in American Classrooms, 1890–1980," N.I.E. Report for Grant No. NIE-G-81-0024, Stanford University, 1982; Willard W. Waller, *The Sociology of Teaching* (New York: John Wiley and Sons, 1932).

48. Wiley quoted in Royce S. Pitkin, *Public School Support in the United States During Periods of Economic Depression* (Brattleboro, Vt.: Stephen Daye Press, 1933), p. 52, and passim for data on schools in depressions; businessman: Charles Francis Adams, *The New Departure in the Common Schools of Quincy* (Boston: Estes and Lauriat, 1881), p. 51; David Tyack, "Education and Social Unrest," *Harvard Educational Review* 31 (Summer 1961): 194–212.

49. Charles A. Beard and William G. Carr, "The Schools Weathering a Storm," *NEA Journal* 24 (May 1935): 149–152.

50. James S. Coleman et al., *Youth: Transition to Adulthood* (Chicago: University of Chicago Press, 1974); Bruce Fuller, "Educational Evaluation and Shifting Youth Policy," *Evaluation Review* 5 (April 1981: 167–188; Carnegie Council on Policy Studies in Higher Education, *Giving Youth a Better Chance* (San Francisco: Jossey-Bass, 1979).

51. NCES, *Condition of Education, 1980*, p. 38; NCES, *Condition of Education, 1982*, p. 46; Daniel L. Duke, Jon S. Cohen, and Roslyn Herman, "Running Faster to Stay in Place: Retrenchment in the New York City Schools," *Phi Delta Kappan* 63 (September 1981): 13–17; Daniel L. Duke and Adrienne M. Meckel, "The Slow Death of a Public High School," *Phi Delta Kappan* 62 (June 1980): 674–677; *Education Daily*, November 3, 1982, p. 12.

52. Weiler, "Legitimacy"; Griffith, "Crisis."

53. Gallup, "Poll of Attitudes, 1982," p. 46; on students' views on economic success and schooling, also see Theodore C. Wagenaar, "High School Students' View of Themselves and Their Schools: A Trend Analysis," *Phi Delta Kappan* 63 (September 1981): 31.

54. David K. Cohen and Barbara Neufeld, "The Failure of High Schools and the Progress of Education," *Daedalus* 110 (Summer 1982): 69.

55. Ibid., pp. 70–71.

56. David Kirp, *Just Schools: The Idea of Racial Equality in American Education* (Berkeley: University of California Press, 1982).

57. Lorraine M. McDonald and Milbrey W. McLaughlin, *Education Policy and the Role of the States* (Santa Monica, Calif.: Rand Corporation, 1982). We are indebted to McLaughlin for useful conversations on this topic.

58. NCES, *Condition of Education, 1978*, p. 79; NCES, *Condition of Ed-*

ucation, 1982, p. 58; James G. Cibulka, "Enrollment Loss and Financial Decline in Urban School Systems" (paper delivered at conference, Managing Enrollment Decline, Nashville, Tenn., February 26–27, 1982).

59. NCES, *Condition of Education, 1980,* pp. 278–291.

60. Richard F. Elmore and Milbrey W. McLaughlin, *Reform and Retrenchment: The Politics of California School Finance Reform* (Cambridge, Mass.: Ballinger, 1982), chap. 2.

61. Ibid.; Kirst, "New Politics."

62. NCES, *Condition of Education, 1980,* pp. 292–295; Stephen J. Carroll, *The Search for Equality in School Finance: Summary and Conclusions* (Santa Monica, Calif.: Rand Corporation, 1979).

63. McDonald and McLaughlin, *Role of the States,* pp. v–xii.

64. Charles E. Bidwell, "The Political Economy of the Schools" (paper presented to the National Academy of Education, May 1982).

Index

Please remember that this is a library book,
and that it belongs only temporarily to each
person who uses it. Be considerate. Do
not write in this, or any, library book.

DATE DUE
